Memory, Trauma and World Poli

Memory, Trauma and World Politics

Reflections on the Relationship between Past and Present

Edited by

Duncan Bell
Lecturer in International Relations
University of Cambridge

First published in 2006
First published in paperback 2010 by
PALGRAVE MACMILLAN

Palgrave Macmillan in the UK is an imprint of Macmillan Publishers Limited,
registered in England, company number 785998, of Houndmills, Basingstoke,
Hampshire RG21 6XS.

Palgrave Macmillan in the US is a division of St Martin's Press LLC,
175 Fifth Avenue, New York, NY 10010.

Palgrave Macmillan is the global academic imprint of the above companies
and has companies and representatives throughout the world.

Palgrave® and Macmillan® are registered trademarks in the United States,
the United Kingdom, Europe and other countries

ISBN: 978–0–230–00656–0 hardback
ISBN: 978–0–230–24745–1 paperback

This book is printed on paper suitable for recycling and made from fully
managed and sustained forest sources. Logging, pulping and manufacturing
processes are expected to conform to the environmental regulations of the
country of origin.

A catalogue record for this book is available from the British Library.

A catalog record for this book is available from the Library of Congress.

Printed and bound in Great Britain by
CPI Antony Rowe, Chippenham and Eastbourne

The choice that we have is not between remembering and forgetting; because forgetting can't be done by an act of will, it is not something we can chose to do. The choice is between different ways of remembering ... Memories do not always bear fruit and may even lead us astray. If we treat the past as holy, we exclude it from the world of meaning and prevent it teaching lessons that might apply to other times and places, to other agents of history. But we do just as much damage through the opposite approach: making the past trivial by likening present events to past ones too easily, trawling it for facile solutions to current issues, betrays history, distorts the present, and opens the door to injustice.

Tzvetan Todorov, *Hope and Memory:*
Lessons from the Twentieth Century (2003)

Contents

Acknowledgements

There are various people and institutions that I would like to thank for supporting this project. Tobie Whitman organized the excellent workshop on 'The Memory of Genocide in World Politics' in Cambridge (2003), out of which the idea for the book emerged. Casper Sylvest, Lynn Meskell and Jeff Olick offered sage advice on planning the book. Jeff, Casper, Richard Ned Lebow, Andrea Sangiovanni and Sarah Fine all offered incisive comments on the introduction. I am very grateful to the Master and Fellows of Christ's College, Cambridge, for electing me to a research fellowship – the college has provided a beautiful and stimulating environment in which to work. The Centre of International Studies, University of Cambridge, has likewise provided excellent practical and moral support. Above all, I would like to thank the contributors to this book for their interest in the project and their patience during its completion.

Notes on Contributors

Jens Bartelson is Professor of International Relations in the Department of Political Science, University of Copenhagen. He received his doctorate from the University of Stockholm in 1993, and has been a fellow of the Swedish Collegium for Advanced Study in the Social Sciences (SCASSS). He has written mainly about the concept of the sovereign state, and about the philosophical foundations of modern international relations. He is the author of *A Genealogy of Sovereignty* (Cambridge University Press, 1995), *The Critique of the State* (Cambridge University Press, 2001), as well as of articles in journals such as *International Studies Quarterly, Political Theory, Review of International Studies, European Journal of International Relations* and *International Sociology*.

Duncan Bell is a University Lecturer in International Relations at the University of Cambridge, and a Fellow of Christ's College. His research interests lie primarily in contemporary international political theory and the history of political thought. He is the author of *The Idea of Greater Britain: Empire and the Future of World Order, 1860–1900* (Princeton University Press, 2007), and the editor of two other volumes: *Victorian Visions of Global Order: Empire and International Relations in Nineteenth-Century British Political Thought* (Cambridge University Press, 2007); and *Pessimism, Power, and Global Ethics: Variations on a Realist Theme* (Oxford University Press, 2007).

Roland Bleiker is Reader in Political Theory and International Relations at the University of Queensland in Australia. From 1986 to 1988 he was Chief of Office of the Swiss Delegation to the Neutral Nations Supervisory Commission in Panmunjom. He has since frequently returned to Korea, including for a year as visiting professor to Pusan National University. Bleiker is the author of *Popular Dissent, Human Agency and Global Politics* (Cambridge University Press, 2000); *Divided Korea: Toward a Culture of Reconciliation* (University of Minnesota Press, 2005) and essays on political theory, social movements, aesthetics, international relations and Asian politics. He is currently pursuing a research project that engages key dilemmas in global security through a range of neglected aesthetic sources, such as literature, visual art, architecture and music.

Chares Demetriou is an Assistant Professor of Political Science at Ohio University, Ohio. His research pertains to processes that connect social and cognitive spheres. This includes the epistemological investigation of the socio-cognitive space between social memory and 'in time' intelligibility. He also studies the emergence, as a socio-cognitive phenomenon, of the legitimation of political violence, for example in the context of the anti-colonial insurgency in Cyprus in the late 1950s. He is also interested in the question of the formation and long-term transformation of public identity, focusing in particular on the Greek-speaking population of Cyprus.

Jenny Edkins is Professor of International Politics at the University of Wales, Aberystwyth, where she teaches postcolonial and post-structural politics and modules on famine and genocide. She is author of *Trauma and the Memory of Politics* (Cambridge University Press, 2003), *Whose Hunger? Concepts of Famine, Practices of Aid* (Minnesota University Press, 2000) and *Poststructuralism and International Relations: Bringing the Political Back In* (Lynne Reinner, 1999) and editor, with Véronique Pin-Fat and Michael J Shapiro, of *Sovereign Lives: Power in Global Politics* (Routledge, 2004) and with Nalini Persram and Véronique Pin-Fat of *Sovereignty and Subjectivity* (Lynne Reinner, 1999). She is currently working on an examination of the face and faciality in politics that looks at the way in which images of the face are used and abused and explores why the face seems to move us so powerfully and what this might tell us about subjectivity and political community.

Stephan Feuchtwang is a professorial research associate of the Department of Anthropology, London School of Economics. He has published books on Chinese popular religion, Feng-shui, and (with Wang Mingming) on grassroots charisma in southern Fujian and northern Taiwan. His research interests are on the relations between politics and religion and on the anthropology of history, which he is currently pursuing by an enquiry into the transmission of grievous loss, in Taiwan, the Mainland, and Germany.

K. M. Fierke is a Professor of International Relations at the University of St. Andrews. She has previously held positions at Queen's University, Belfast, Nuffield College, Oxford University, and the Amsterdam School for Social Science Research, University of Amsterdam. She is author of *Critical Approaches to International Security* (Polity, 2007), *Diplomatic Interventions: Conflict and Change in a Globalizing World* (Palgrave, 2005), and *Changing Games, Changing Strategies: Critical Investigations in Security*

(Manchester, 1998). She has published articles in, among others, *International Studies Quarterly*, the *European Journal of International Relations, Millennium*, and the *Review of International Studies*. She is the co-editor of *Constructing International Relations: The Next Generation* (M. E. Sharpe, 2001).

Young-Ju Hoang is a lecturer of International Relations, School of International Studies at the Pusan University of Foreign Studies, South Korea. He has a Ph.D. from the University of Hull. His research focuses on questions of identity, gender and nationalism in Korea. Together with Roland Bleiker he held a joint-fellowship from the Carnegie Council on Ethics and International Affairs in New York, where he was involved in a research project that examined the linkages between history teaching and reconciliation in Korea. He has published numerous essays in Korean and English on questions of culture, identity and conflict.

Lynn Meskell is Professor of Cultural and Social Anthropology at Stanford University. She is founding editor of the *Journal of Social Archaeology* and some of her recent books include *Object Worlds in Ancient Egypt* (Berg, 2004) and two edited collections *Embedding Ethics* (Berg, 2005, with P. Pels) and *Archaeologies of Materiality* (Blackwell, 2005). Her current research examines the constructs of natural and cultural heritage and the related discourses of empowerment around the Kruger National Park, ten years after democracy in South Africa.

Jeffrey K. Olick is an Associate Professor of Sociology at the University of Virginia. He is the author of *In the House of the Hangman: The Agonies of German Defeat, 1943–1949* (University of Chicago Press, 2005) and *The Sins of the Fathers: Governing Memory in the Federal Republic of Germany* (University of Chicago Press, forthcoming), and the editor of *States of Memory: Conflicts, Continuities, and Transformations in National Retrospection* (Duke University Press, 2003).

Larry Ray is Professor of Sociology at the University of Kent, where he has worked since 1998. Prior to that he was at Lancaster University. His research and publications range across sociological theory, globalization, memory, ethnicity and violence. During 1998–2001 he had an ESRC/Probation Service funded project with David Smith (Lancaster University) on racially motivated violence in Greater Manchester and its relationship to community dislocation. This has developed into research on 'hate crime' legislation and interventions and their effectiveness in tackling racist violence in a European context. He has published *Theorizing Classical Sociology* (Open University Press, 1999) and with Anthony Elliot he co-edited *Key Contemporary Social Theorists* (Blackwell, 2002). In 2005 he published (with William Outhwaite) *Social Theory and Postcommunism* (Blackwell). He is currently completing a book, *Globalization and Everyday Life* (Routledge) and developing a project on memory and the re-emergence of Jewish identities in postcommunist Europe.

Jay Winter is Charles J. Stille Professor of History at Yale. From 1979 to 2001, he was Reader in Modern History, University of Cambridge, and a Fellow of Pembroke College. He is the author of *Sites of Memory, Sites of Mourning: The Great War in European Cultural History* (Cambridge University Press, 1995), and co-author, with Antoine Prost of *The Great War in History: Debates and Controversies, 1914 to the Present* (Cambridge University Press, 2005). In 2006, he published *Remembering War: The Great War between History and Memory in the Twentieth Century* and *Dreams of Peace and Freedom: Utopian Moments in the Twentieth Century* (Yale University Press). In 1997, he received an Emmy award as co-producer of 'The Great War and the Shaping of the Twentieth Century', an eight-hour series broadcast on PBS and the BBC, and shown subsequently in 28 countries. He was one of the founders of the *Historial de la grande guerre*, in Péronne, Somme, France.

Maja Zehfuss is Reader in International Politics at the University of Manchester. Her recent research examines memory, war and the politics of ethics. She is the author of *Constructivism in International Relations: The Politics of Reality* (Cambridge University Press, 2002) and *Wounds of Memory: The Politics of War in Germany* (Cambridge University Press, 2007).

1
Introduction
Memory, Trauma and World Politics
Duncan Bell

> Language clearly shows that memory is not an instrument for exploring the past but its theatre. It is the medium of past experiences, as the ground is the medium in which dead cities lie interred.[1]

> ... Alice remarked, 'I can't remember things before they happen'. 'It's a poor sort of memory that only works backwards', the Queen remarked.[2]

I. Introduction

Memory seems impossible to escape. During the closing decades of the twentieth century it emerged as 'a cultural obsession of monumental proportions across the globe', a trend that looks set to continue for the foreseeable future.[3] Questions of historical memory have played a pivotal role in the rise of identity politics, most notably in the United States, and in fuelling the tragic proliferation of civil and ethnic conflicts around the world. They have been at the forefront of debates over transitional justice, post-conflict reconstruction, the legitimacy of political violence, the legacy of the Holocaust and a plethora of other processes and practices. These social and political trends have been mirrored in academia where the study of memory has swept a number of disciplines, especially history, sociology, anthropology and cultural studies. Indeed the 'boom' has echoed so widely that memory has emerged as a key 'organising principle of scholarly [and] artistic work'.[4] Yet the analysis of memory has not played a substantial role in the academic study of international relations.[5] The aim of this book is, as a consequence, to examine some of the theoretical approaches essential for elucidating and interrogating the multifarious roles played by the 'memory' of traumatic events

1

(broadly defined) in shaping the contours of contemporary global politics. It does so by drawing on various traditions of social and political thought, utilizing these to shed light on diverse examples from around the world, and highlighting patterns of continuity and change across cultures and polities.

At a very general level memory refers to the process or faculty whereby events or impressions from the past are recollected and preserved. Collective memory – or one of its many cognate terms, including social and cultural memory – refers, again in a general sense, to widely shared perceptions of the past. It shapes the story that groups of people tell about themselves, linking past, present and future in a simplified narrative. It is what keeps the past – or at least a highly selective image of it – alive in the present. This does not, of course, have to be an accurate and verifiable account: 'Memory ... is *knowledge from the past*. It is not necessarily *knowledge about the past*'.[6] The literature on memory subsumes several different practices that are analytically separable, although they frequently combine. The most common, and most controversial, concerns the constitution of personal and collective identity, the way in which self and society are formed and reproduced. Other modes include the use of historical analogical reasoning and the rhetorical employment of historical images and tropes in structuring arguments and motivating action.[7] But even the last of these, which on the face of it appears to be a merely instrumental deployment of history, presupposes as its condition of success the recognition and resonant impact of such usage in the target group. Like many of the ways in which the past is marshalled in the name of the present, it articulates a claim about the nature of political identities, for otherwise it would be largely unintelligible, irrelevant to contemporary concerns and lacking in motivational power. The following chapters interrogate a variety of these approaches to representing the past.

Although memory is related integrally to history, most contributors to the debates over memory (and most, although not all, of the contributors to this book) stress that it is also in some sense separable from it, even if the exact boundaries between the two are elusive. According to Jan Assman, for example, 'mnemohistory', the history of collective memory, is 'unlike history proper' for it is 'concerned not with the past as such, but only with the past as it is remembered'.[8] And it is memory, whereby the past is made present, rather than history, that which simply happened before, which is central to the construction of individual and collective identity, to the process of 'self-designation'.[9] Much that is historical has no impact on the present; much that has impact is not historical. And interpretations of the relationship between past and present not only shape contemporary identities, for in so doing they help to frame the horizon of the future.[10]

In this introduction I do not seek to offer precise definitions of memory or trauma. Not only would such an endeavour require a further book, it would foreclose much of the debate over the various meanings and uses of the terms in the chapters that follow. Instead, I sketch an intellectual matrix within which to locate the individual contributions. As Jeffrey Olick has observed, the study of memory forms a 'nonparadigmatic, transdisciplinary, centerless enterprise, and work in different historical, geographical, and disciplinary contexts proceeds largely independently of work in other such contexts'.[11] The contributors to *Memory, Trauma and World Politics* both reflect this diversity and seek to challenge the lack of disciplinary cross-fertilization. Indeed one of the main ambitions of the book is to showcase the plurality of approaches available for the analysis of world politics. The authors focus on theoretical aspects of the relationship between memory, identity and political action, drawing on intellectual traditions in social and political theory, history, social psychology, psychoanalysis, anthropology and philosophy. What unites the chapters and what provides the volume with its centre of gravity, is the focus on the manifold ways in which representations and echoes of the traumatic past influence contemporary political attitudes and iden-tifications, and how these dynamic processes shape prominent aspects of world politics.

Most of the literature on memory and politics focuses on the construction, reproduction and contestation of national identities.[12] This is a vitally important topic, and one explored in a number of the following chapters. It is not the only aspect of the multifaceted relation-ship between memory and politics, however, and this orientation has led to a relative lack of concern with the transnational and global features of memory practices (or, alternatively, the impact that communal memories play in shaping world politics). It also means that normative questions, so central to mnemonic and traumatic politics, are often side-lined. *Memory, Trauma and World Politics* seeks to engage these issues from a variety of angles and in a number of different registers. Part I views issues of memory and trauma through a wide-angle lens, explor-ing the origins and evolution of particular ways of conceiving the past. Jens Bartelson argues that memory (and forgetting) played a central role in the very foundation and subsequent stabilization of the modern spatially differentiated international system, and that only through understanding the manner in which this occurred can we attempt to forge a more cosmopolitan world. Jay Winter charts the way in which memory has been both a vital source of inspiration and an important category of social analysis for much of the twentieth century, and he stresses the importance of war – especially the two world wars and Vietnam – in generating interest in traumatic memory, as well as the particular forms that this interest has assumed. Memory and trauma, then, have always been intertwined with global politics. Jeffrey Olick and Chares Demetriou then explore some of the historical origins of our contemporary fascination with trauma, suggesting that it, along with *ressentiment*, are the twin results of the contradiction between certainty and randomness in modern life, 'aspects of a single discursive universe'. They serve as our substitutes for traditional theodicies. We should be less willing to condemn *ressentiment*, they argue, for it is perhaps the only appropriate response to the post-Holocaust condition. 'Trauma ... is not only an unfortunate by-product of modernity, but a central feature of it'.[13] In light of this, they offer a defence of the claims for reparations and resitutive justice that are so central to many contemporary facets of politics, domestic and international.

In the remaining chapters the nexus of memory, trauma and identity is probed through explorations of various dimensions of contemporary political life, including the construction of foreign policy perceptions, the shaping of national identities, ideas about transitional justice and visions of post-conflict reconciliation. Part II is comprised of essays – by Jenny Edkins, K. M. Fierke and Larry Ray – that discuss the theoretical relationship between memory, trauma and identity, although they all also employ a range of cases, including practices of ethnic mobilization in the former Yugoslavia and in post–communist states in general, and the functions of trauma in post–9/11 America and the Middle East. The essays in Part III also seek to provide theoretically innovative accounts of the relationship between past and present, but their empirical focus is narrower and they provide more detailed country-specific analyses. Lynn Meskell explores how apartheid and racial subjugation in South Africa are being remembered and forgotten, and the dangers that this portends; Maja Zehfuss reflects on the debates over 'humanitarian intervention' in Germany during the 1990s; Stephan Feuchtwang investigates how memories of conflict in Taiwan persist in shaping political understanding; and Roland Bleiker and Hoang Young-ju examine the ways in which memories of the Korean War continue to haunt relations between the North and South. Most of the chapters deal explicitly with the ethical issues arising from memory practices, confronting the question of whether there is an obligation to remember aspects of the past, and if so in what ways and for what purposes. In sum, the book provides a multi-disciplinary perspective on a series of essential yet often overlooked aspects of world politics.

II. Memory, trauma and the politics of identity

The connections between memory, trauma and identity have been drawn in various and often-conflicting ways. It is a fairly common assumption, however, that certain harrowing events, including genocide, war, terrorism, civil and ethnic strife and radical regime transitions, generate serious and often catastrophic challenges to communal self-understandings, and that the 'memory' of such 'traumas' play a significant and sometimes elemental role in shaping subsequent political perceptions, affiliations and action. In this section I sketch some of the ways in which scholars have traced these connections, exploring how trauma and identity can be related to one another and to understandings of the past.

Identity is one of the *ur*-concepts of the contemporary social sciences and humanities. It is usually understood in a constructivist manner to refer to the relatively stable – though not essentialist – sense of 'self' that either an individual or a group (or both) maintain over time. Identities are, to varying degrees, malleable, negotiable and open to challenge, although the extent of their fluidity and the mechanisms that shape and transform them differ according to the theoretical position adopted.[14] Despite these differences, memory plays a central role in virtually all conceptions of identity.[15] It is, according to Allan Young, 'the proof as well as the record of the self's existence, and the struggle over memory is the struggle over the self's most valued possessions'.[16] This insight is generalized by those concerned with exploring the dynamics of human communities, and it is commonly argued that group identities require a relatively widely shared understanding of history and its meaning, the construction of a narrative tracing the linkages between past and present, locating self and society in time.[17] It is this understanding that helps to generate affective bonds, a sense of belonging, and which engenders obligations and loyalty to the 'imagined community'.[18] As Anthony Smith argues: 'one might almost say: no memory, no identity; no identity, no nation'.[19] Communal memories act as subtle yet powerful mechanisms for generating and sustaining social solidarity. While such memories can act as a social adhesive they are always contestable, and it is in this realm of conflict, and the complex power relations that underpin and structure it, that the politics of memory is enacted.

Questions of identity have been central to debates over social memory since the turn of the twentieth century. The first 'memory boom', stretching from the *fin de siècle* into the 1920s, focused on the creation of largely homogeneous national identities. During the second 'boom', which gathered pace in the 1970s and continues to this day, attention switched more to the fragmentation of identities: 'Memory has become in recent years a way of casting about in the ruins of earlier identities and finding elements of what has been called a "usable past" '.[20] History has been shaped and mobilized in order to justify current political projects, whether in the name of political or ethnic self-determination, in the demand for justice, or to ground claims for the legitimacy of new regimes. Today memory, or the struggle over and for memory, constitutes 'a larger and larger component of politics'.[21] In order to understand many aspects of world politics, from the dynamics of ethnic wars to the calls for justice in newly democratic regimes, an appreciation of the multiple functions of historical memory is essential.

Allan Megill argues that 'memory is valorized' when identity is threatened. Memory may well be central to the construction and reproduction of political identities over time, but in moments of crisis people hark back to the past with amplified intensity.[22] As identities are challenged, undermined and possibly shattered, so memories are drawn on and reshaped to defend unity and coherence, to shore up a sense of self and community. Although this claim is unlikely to hold in all cases, and while it implies an unrealistic degree of voluntarism, it is nevertheless a useful frame for analysing the fluid interface between memory and political identity. We will see its main intuition recur throughout the following chapters. Challenges to identity emanate from a variety of sources. Diagnosing the problem of the modern self, Charles Taylor argues that it has been stripped from its original moral-theological roots and left suspended in an alienated, instrumentalized and atomized condition.[23] On a more pressing level, the economic and cultural forces of 'globalization' have led as much to fragmentation as to harmony, and the resurgence of ethnic and identity-based conflicts, where memory is invoked repeatedly, are (at least partly) a sign of anxiety in the face of uncertainty. The disruptive, destructive dynamics of national and ethnic conflict have challenged, destabilized and sometimes threatened the very existence, of numerous communities around the world.[24] The wars in the former Yugoslavia during the 1990s are only the most prominent recent example of the insidious power of belief in national destiny, and it should come as little surprise that questions of historical memory were prominent in the origins and course of the fighting;[25] nor also, as we shall see, that they played an important role in the responses of the wider world.

It is in the characterization of such moments of extremity and their impact that the language of trauma is employed. Like both 'identity' and 'memory', the term is open to multiple interpretations. In pathology, it is used to designate 'a wound, or external bodily injury in general'.[26] In psychology, trauma is understood as an emotional or psychic injury, and in psychoanalysis it is argued that such injuries are often repressed, remaining unhealed and leading to various forms of 'acting out'. It is the languages of social psychology and psychoanalysis that have been invoked most frequently in discussions of social memory, although there is a considerable difference between the arguments of those who utilize them purely metaphorically and those who insist that the mechanisms of trauma operate in a homologous fashion for both societies and individuals. Whilst there are undoubtedly dangers in translating from the individual to the collective, and also in stretching the idea too far, the notion of trauma can be helpful in encapsulating the impact of horrific events on the formation of communal identities, for if we accept the claim that communities 'constantly tell and retell their constitutive narratives' then 'there can be genuinely collective traumas insofar as historical events cannot easily be integrated into coherent and constructive narratives'.[27] As such, trauma is inherently also a challenge to identity. Other scholars make bolder claims. Cathy Caruth, for example, argues that while trauma cannot be adequately represented, escaping the bounds of intelligibility, it is nevertheless transmissible through society, as if it were an infectious disease. It is capable of being passed on not only between people, but also across generations and cultures.[28]

Some scholars, notably Jeffrey Alexander, have sough to re-interpret the category of trauma in non-psychological terms. Alexander claims that both psychological and psychoanalytical accounts, whilst occasionally illuminating, fall prey to the 'naturalistic fallacy' as they stipulate a direct connection between a specific kind or quality of experience and the effects that it produces. In other words, some extreme events are regarded as naturally traumatizing. For Alexander, on the other hand, trauma is entirely a social construct: 'Events are not in themselves inherently traumatic.' 'Traumas occur', he argues, 'when individuals and groups *feel* they have been subjected to a horrendous event that leaves indelible marks upon their consciousness, will mark their memories forever, and will change their future in fundamental and irrevocable ways'.[29] In this account trauma is 'attributed to real or imagined phenomena, not because of their actual harmfulness or their objective abruptness, but because these phenomena *are believed* to have abruptly, and harmfully, affected collective identity'. He uses this approach to model the 'trauma process', the way in which people come to accept that they have experienced trauma, in order to outline the emergence of Holocaust discourse in the post-war era. In particular, he highlights the complex interaction of various groups and practices across a range of national and institutional spaces in the construction of affective narratives and the moral power they exert.[30] But the Holocaust is far from the only event that can be conceived in this manner. One of his collaborators, Neil Smelser, characterizes 9/11 as the 'quintessential cultural trauma', an event 'experienced as an incredible violation' and afterwards endowed with a sacred character. It was also, he contends, a 'fully ambiguous' trauma, 'simultaneously shocking and fascinating, depressing and exhilarating, grotesque and beautiful, sullying and cleansing – and leaving the country feeling both bad and good about itself'.[31]

Trauma implies a breakdown of both meaning and trust – in a world that has been shattered, overturned. It encompasses 'rapid, sudden, and radical' impacts on the 'body social'. Trauma occurs, then, 'when there is a break, a displacement, or disorganization in the orderly, taken-for-granted universe'.[32] Exemplifying this process on a micro-level, Jean Améry wrote that 'Every morning when I get up I can read the Auschwitz number on my forearm ... Every day anew I lose my trust in the world'.[33] The world can no longer be accommodated to previous, and relatively stable, understandings. W. G. Sebald, in a wonderful essay·on Améry, writes that the 'experience of terror ... dislocates time, that most abstract of all humanity's homes'.[34] It is the absence of temporal distance, the failure to regard the past as past, as something that can be left behind, that has such a profound effect on identity, and which can make the study of trauma (however understood) illuminating when exploring the contours of politics. Indeed, according to Olick and Demetriou trauma and *ressentiment* may well be an inescapable part of post–Auschwitz consciousness, the only response left in a universe in which the meliorative power of theodicy is no longer available.

A number of serious challenges have been levelled at the use of trauma as a category of social and political analysis. Recent scientific research has called into question the adequacy of psychoanalytic accounts of repression.[35] And even if psychoanalysis can provide a satisfactory account of individual behaviour, it is often not clear how useful it is as a concept for analysing collectives. Though 'specific visions of the past might originate in traumatic experiences', Wulf Kansteiner contends, 'they do not retain that quality if they become successful collective memories. The concept of trauma, as well as the concept of repression, neither captures nor illuminates the forces that contribute to the making and unmaking of collective memories'.[36] The problem lies partly in the indeterminacy of the concept. The idea of trauma remains highly contested, even within psychology, where there is little agreement on its nature, effects or how best to treat it. Ruth Leys argues that the history of the concept is split between two main interpretations, the 'mimetic' and 'antimimetic'. Mimetic theories suggest that traumatic events cannot be absorbed or represented, and as such the victim is fated to repeat or act it out in various ways. 'The idea is that the traumatic experience in its sheer extremity, its affront to common norms and expectations, shatters or disables the victim's cognitive and perceptual capacities so that the experience never becomes part of the ordinary memory system.' Antimimetic theories also stress the imitative aspects of traumatic experience, but push this insight in a different direction. Here the subject, rather then being perpetually immersed in the original experience, is instead disassociated from it, 'in the sense that she remains a spectator of the traumatic scene, which she can therefore see and represent to herself and others'. Despite the psychological (let alone physical) damage that has been caused, there is in principle no problem with either representation or recall. Leys argues that throughout the twentieth century approaches to trauma have oscillated between these two antithetical understandings, often combining elements of each, and that this explains the lack of conceptual clarity in contemporary psychiatric usage. The problem with the notion of trauma, she argues, is the combination of its 'absolute indispensability' in characterizing acts of extremity and their consequences and its 'debased currency' in an age in which it is used to describe the simply unpleasant or uncomfortable.[37]

The historian Joanna Bourke, meanwhile, has argued that the widespread use of trauma discourse in western societies has led to an abdication of individual and political responsibility and the emergence of an undifferentiated 'victim' culture. It has had a politically neutering effect. Perhaps most damagingly, the language of trauma has been 'co-opted by the perpetrators of violence'. Bourke points firstly to the creation of 'post-traumatic stress disorder' in the 1980s, arguing that this came to mask, even to absolve, the cruel violence inflicted by US soldiers in Vietnam. It had the effect of turning killers and rapists into victims equally deserving of compassion and pity. And she further suggests that this dynamic is repeating itself in Iraq, where 'trauma' is being used to explain and justify obscene brutality. But it is not only soldiers who are complicit. The 'witness', the civilian exposed daily to the imagery of conflict, torture and death, is also coded as a victim of trauma, a further victim of war: 'In the end, torture is about us.' But perhaps the most damaging function of trauma discourse is the removal of individual agency – which lies, of course, at the root of responsibility. 'One effect of the trauma trope has been to create a universal suffering subject outside of history. Individuals are reduced to bodies-in-pain. Yet pain is always local. To universalise it is to remove the specifics of an individual's history; it is to situate torture in the realm of moral edification.'[38]

A number of contributors to this volume confront the challenges of employing trauma as a pivotal category for analysing contemporary political life. Jenny Edkins stresses the indeterminacy of the political implications of traumatic memory, its potential to both threaten and reinforce state power and the sovereign political order. Traumatic violence betrays what she labels (following lines traced by Derrida and Lacan) as 'relationality', the 'radical interconnectedness' of human beings. Such moments – and she here concentrates on 9/11 and its aftermath – usually generate state responses, manifested in the attempt to link the trauma and the memory of it to narratives of sovereign authority. 'After a traumatic event what we call the state moves quickly to close down any openings produced by putting in place as fast as possible a linear narrative of origins.'[39] This is attempted primarily through practices of memorialization and commemoration. But such traumatic violence can also disclose possible lines of opposition, creating 'specific openings for resistance to centralized political power'. For if political trauma is defined as a moment that through its catastrophic impact ruptures settled narratives and frames of meaning, and for which (following Caruth) there can exist no adequate language, discourses of state authority and legitimacy are called into question, exposed as social 'fantasies', and a window for re-inscribing new understandings of the world emerges, albeit briefly. The 'openness' and 'indistinction' generated by 'trauma time', seen in such a revelatory mode, are thus key markers of 'the political'. K. M. Fierke, meanwhile, argues than a Wittgensteinian account of memory should supplant a Freudian (or broadly psychoanalytic) one. 'Political trauma', she contends, 'can be understood as a state in which fear and hypervigilance become habitual'. And arguably, she continues, it

> ... is less censorship or repression, in and of itself, whether by self or others, than the *assimilation* of a past context of trauma such that it comes to structure identity within a linguistic world of action and interaction vis-à-vis others. It is less the existence of a repressed memory than the habitual acting out of the life world of the past

in the present, mirroring a past experience of humiliation and destruction.[40]

Using the examples of contemporary Israeli society and post–9/11 America, she argues that this 'habitual acting out' of past trauma helps explain important aspects of world politics.

Mainstream political science remains wary of employing the concepts of memory and (even more so) trauma. For many political scientists, they are simply too vague to be incorporated into parsimonious social scientific models. It should therefore come as little surprise that the IR scholars who have focused on questions of memory tend to be those employing non-mainstream approaches, and especially those influenced by post-structuralism.[41] The study of global politics, however, does not only occur in departments of Political Science or IR; indeed much of the most interesting work on a plethora of topics central to the study of modern political life emerges from a variety of other disciplines, ranging from anthropology to history. The study of memory – an essentially multi-disciplinary exercise, requiring constant shuttling between various fields and interpretative methodologies – promises to throw new light on old questions, and to help open up the study of international relations to a variety of different intellectual traditions.

III. Memory and trauma in the study of world politics

There are multiple pathways along which to trace the relationship between memory, trauma and world politics. In this section I outline three ways in which various dimensions of this question have been charted: the characterization of national identity; the possible globalization of memory; and finally, ethical questions that arise from mnemonic practices.

Shaping the nation: identity and interests

The belief that the way in which groups of people perceive the past shapes the nature of political communities is far from novel. In his *Considerations on Representative Government* (1861) John Stuart Mill talked of the necessity of a 'community of recollections' as a perquisite for the development of a strong sense of 'nationality', while Alexis de Tocqueville, in his critical analysis of *L'Ancien Regime* (1856), lamented the proclivity of the French to 'put an abyss between what they had been and what they wished to become', between, that is, the worlds before and after 1789.[42] The French historian Ernest Renan, in his classic lecture 'Qu'est-ce qu'une nation?' (1882), emphasized the importance of forgetting the often recent and violent origins of the nation in order to provide a sense of longevity and continuity.[43] In so doing he was unconsciously echoing a point made a century earlier by Edmund Burke.[44] Such insights have been at the centre of much of the recent academic work on the construction of national identities and the multitude of challenges to them.

Whilst the majority of these studies have been undertaken by historians and sociologists, an increasing number of constructivist IR scholars have investigated the formation of collective identities in order to explain the configuration of national interests, the development of foreign policy positions, and the evolution of international norms and institutions.[45] In so doing they challenge the conception of interests as exogenous that predominates in mainstream rationalist IR. Consuelo Cruz has argued that collective identity 'is a robust declarative statement that a group makes, under the pressure of collective memory and contextual forces, to itself and to others about its normative constitution and its practical competence when facing the world'.[46] As such, it is essential to understand both the elements of collective identities and the way in which these have evolved and are reproduced over time. Constructivists also argue persuasively that it is impossible to comprehend the content and structure of national 'interests' without understanding first the way in which these are grounded in and shaped by the values and norms of societies. As a result, the 'neo-positivist' scholars who dominate American political science can only ever provide an inadequate account of the nature of contemporary international relations.[47]

In discussions of memory, two geographical zones in particular have been the focus of scholarly attention: Europe and the United States. Most of the literature on Europe focuses on the developmental trajectories of individual countries, although there has recently been an upsurge of interest in exploring these processes in a comparative framework. As these studies have demonstrated, the ways in which national elites and wider political cultures have conceived of their history – and the conflicts over those conceptions – have had a profound effect on perceptions of their role in the world. For example the United Kingdom, with its memories of imperial power, has been keen to 'punch above its weight' on the international stage, and this has shaped attitudes to Europe as well as the direction of its foreign policy.[48] It has likewise shaped policies towards the post-imperial members of the 'commonwealth'.[49]

The most obvious case, though, is Germany. *Vergangenheitsbewältigung* ('coming to terms with the past'), and the often-acrimonious debates over what this entails and how far it should proceed, have moulded German public culture and identities since the end of the Second World War. They continue to do so to this day. The bifurcated post-war political development of Germany – mirrored in significant differences towards the immediate past in East and West[50] – was shaped and haunted by (often very selective) memories of the Nazi period.[51] Much was conveniently suppressed in the name of moving forward, including initially the Holocaust itself. As Jeffrey Herf writes of the early post-war years, 'On the whole, the most common public attitude towards the crimes of the Nazi past was silence, avoidance, premature amnesty, and delayed and denied justice.' It was only during the 1960s that things began to change, when a 'minority tradition of memory' led mainly by leftwing and liberal intellectuals forced a reconsideration of national history.[52] But this led to other aspects of the past remaining sidelined. The complicity of the Wehrmacht in war crimes, the catastrophic destruction of German cities by allied aerial bombing, the forced expulsion of millions of German citizens from Central and Eastern Europe, and the mass rape of German women by Soviet soldiers in 1945, were all subject to historical amnesia, and only recently have they been exposed to widespread scrutiny.[53] Now, in a united country, the past continues to structure the present. Perhaps the most obvious manifestation of this, at least in terms of global politics, concerns German attitudes to war. 'Guilty remembrance of terrible hardship conjoins with an unevenly-grounded recognition of social responsibility to produce the present breadth of German aversion against war.'[54] Memory of the war, and in particular of the Holocaust, seems impossible to escape. Indeed the 'memory of memory', the 'recursive commentary' on the way in which the past has been remembered, has been a preoccupation in recent decades.[55] The dynamic between remembering and forgetting was illustrated by the fraught debates over the potential employment of German military force in the Balkans in the 1990s, a topic examined in Maja Zehfuss's chapter.[56]

Given the power and global reach of the United States, an adequate understanding of American political identities is of overriding importance. The way in which American elites (as well as the powerful mnemonic vectors of popular culture) view and represent the position of America in the world, the elaboration of strategic doctrines, and the understandings of American interests and 'destiny', have all been marked deeply by specific and often widely shared interpretations of the past. Analysts of US foreign relations, a leading historian argues, will 'gain a greater understanding when they study the continuing conversation betwen past and present and the role that memories play in determining how people conduct their affairs'.[57] Perhaps most obviously the impact of the war in Vietnam on military strategy, foreign policy, political identity and popular culture has been pronounced.[58] In post 9/11 public life memories of both Vietnam and the attack on Pearl Harbour have been invoked repeatedly and for multiple and often contradictory reasons.[59] Revealingly, George W. Bush has made evocative references to the purported lessons of the past – drawing in particular on the memory of the 'greatest generation' – a central element of his strategy for legitimating the actions of his administration.

> Like the Second World War, our present conflict began with a ruthless, surprise attack on the United States. We will not forget that treachery, and we will accept nothing less than victory over the enemy. Like the murderous ideologies of the 20th century, the ideology of terrorism reaches across borders, and seeks recruits in every country. So we're fighting these enemies wherever they hide across the earth.[60]

As well as highlighting the saliency of mnemonic practices in contemporary political life, the (most recent) war on Iraq also highlights the dangers of falling prey to the illusions and distortions of social memory. As Niall Ferguson has pointed out, policy-makers and pundits often lack detailed historical knowledge of the events from which they claim to have learnt. In this case, rather than looking to the disastrous British experience in attempting to 'liberate' and then pacify Iraq in the wake of the First World War, Americans have frequently looked instead, and inappropriately, to the Second World War or Vietnam for guidance[61] – although if Ferguson adopted a rather less selective view of British imperial history, his support for much recent US foreign policy would also need to be seriously rethought.[62] With the post-war descent into chaos and with the emergence of a bloody insurgency, Bush has been ever-keener to draw the connection between the 'good war' and 'Operation Iraqi Freedom', to paint the present in the glorious light of the past.[63]

But it is not only in times of war that memory can be seen at work. Cruz has argued in relation to the conflicting cases of Costa Rica and Nicaragua that the success of economic and political development depends to a large degree on the modulations of national identity, itself reliant on the types of collective memory drawn upon in constituting the horizons of political understanding.[64] And, as she rightly insists, the manner in which societies 'remember' their past is central in determining how they plot their futures, for it serves to both enable and constrain practical action and the imagining of political possibilities. Post-colonial analyses likewise stress the memory of empire as a key determinant in both the continuing imperial designs of the West and in the political-economic trajectories of post-colonial states.[65]

It is vital to remember that memory practices are not only the preserve of the state, of manipulative elites, and that neither communal identities nor social memories are homogeneous.[66] They are always contingent, indeterminate and contestable. Memory is capable of being yoked to state power, in the name of nationalism, or employed in opposition, as a challenge to the dominant narratives. The aftermath of 9/11 serves as a case in point. In the following days and months various mnemonic practices were discernable, and they impacted on politics in different ways. The Bush administration engaged in a 'rush to memory' – a rush to commemorate the victims, to code them as sacrificed heroes (drawing, notably, on the narrative of Pearl Harbour), and to use this memory in defending subsequent military strategy.[67] The State Department sponsored a travelling photographic exhibition in order to generate international sympathy and support for American policy.[68] Memory and 'memorialization' were thus tied intimately to justifying and perhaps even shaping American foreign policy decisions.[69] Simultaneously, and also in the name of the memory of the dead, assorted victim groups offered a sustained and vocal, though ultimately unsuccessful, challenge to the administration. The memory of the victims, in other words, became a 'site of contestation and struggle'.[70] The politics of memory was articulated on multiple scales, from local remembrance ceremonies and protest up to the tectonic forces of global geo-politics.

The globalization of memory?

It is clear, then, that deeply ingrained perceptions of the past play a powerful role in shaping communal identities, and that this helps mould political perceptions and policy choices. But is it possible to talk of transnational, or even global memories?

This question has several aspects. Firstly, it is possible to relate memory, especially of the Second World War, to the general institutional structure and norms of international politics. Many of the post-war institutions, including international legal regimes, the United Nations, the European Union, as well as the constitutional postures of both Germany and Japan, are anchored in memories of the harrowing triptych of 'total war, totalitarianism, and the Holocaust'.[71] In an age following catastrophe, political thought and institutions were fashioned by perceptions of the immediate traumatic past. The injunction to 'never forget' has been heard repeatedly – if ignored equally as often – in defence of all sorts of policies and practices, and much of Western Cold War political discourse was at least partly rooted in memories of the mid-century fight against totalitarianism. It is heard today in the calls to avoid the strategic mistakes and moral failure of 'appeasement'. In particular, the invocation of memories of the war has figured repeatedly in debates about the necessity of humanitarian intervention, and it will no doubt continue to do so well into the future. The way in which potential enemies – most recently Saddam Hussein – are compared to Hitler only serves to remind us of the presence, as well as the rhetorical force, of the past in the present.

Second, is it possible to talk of regional memories, of conceptions of the past linking otherwise separate but proximate political communities? Once again, Europe, and in particular the experiences of the Second World War, has been the focus of considerable research.[72] One possible line of argument concerning the existence of or potential for a pan-European identity follows from a claim about the 'Europeanization' of the memory of the Holocaust. Daniel Levy and Natan Sznaider argue, for example, that in the post-Cold War period the Holocaust has become a foundation stone in the attempt to forge a new European identity.[73] Klaus Eder, meanwhile, suggests that the formation of a strong European collective identity, grounded in a pan-continental collective memory, is both possible and likely. The mechanisms for the creation of such a memory-identity complex follow from the very process of integration itself. 'The more Europeans are integrated into a common market and follow the same directives, the more they experience a performative paradox: due to their communication, they can no longer escape the emergence of one's own collective past and the collective past of others.' They are consequently 'forced into communicating their past' and the 'reciprocal presentation of the collective self in public communication sets off the reconstruction of the collective memories of the Europeans'.[74]

Such claims seem rather premature. While certain historical moments figure prominently in all the diverse national memories of Europe – and indeed in many other countries around the world – it is far from clear that this can be forged into an integrated and harmonized memory, especially as the ways in which the events are represented (and the meanings attached to such representations) differ so significantly from place to place. As Tony Judt observes, the 'new Europe is being built upon historical sands at least as shifting in nature as those upon which the post-war edifice was mounted'. And this, he reminds us, should come as little surprise given the extent to which collective identities 'are always complex compositions of myth, memory, and political convenience'. This is not enough to forge unity, however, for the 'frontiers of memory remain solidly in place'.[75] Conflict rather than harmony seems likely to determine the contours of future mnemonic politics. The pressing issue will be to channel such conflict away from violence into more peacable forms of human interaction, something that has all too frequently proved impossible to achieve.

Third, there is a question as to whether in an 'age of globalization' we can now discern truly global memories. In a discussion of David Held's vision of cosmopolitan democracy, Alexander Wendt argues that through the mechanisms of an 'internationalized' education policy and the creation of 'transnational memories' it might be possible to produce the communal feelings necessary to 'build a constituency for cosmopolitan democracy'.[76] Indeed, if Bartelson's account of the way in which conceptions of memory and the self were woven into the origins and evolution of the modern state system is correct, then there is at least a chance of future transformation: once we apprehend the historical contingency of this constellation of political forces, then one of the key conceptual preconditions for moving into a post-national world could be realized. Jeffrey Alexander, meanwhile, has argued that over the course of the last forty years the Holocaust has escaped its spatial and temporal particularism to emerge as a 'generalized symbol of human suffering and moral evil' which, through a complex and still developing process of symbolic extension and psychological identification, 'has created unprecedented opportunities for ethnic, racial, and religious justice, for mutual recognition and for global conflict to become regulated in a more civil way'. It has helped to create and regulate new moral codes. 'The project of renaming, dramatizing, reifying and ritualizing the Holocaust contributed to the moral remaking of the (post) modern (western) world.'[77] Levy and Sznaider, moreover, argue that the global spread of Holocaust discourse provides the foundations for a 'cosmopolitan memory', and as such they decouple the traditional link between the nation and memory. This 'symbol of transnational solidarity' has emerged as a major force following the collapse of the ideological blocs that dominated the preceding decades; it is something about which all (or at least most) people can agree, a 'global icon' of suffering. Such a global 'memoryscape', they argue, can provide the basis for an emergent universal human rights regime. This was demonstrated repeatedly in the debate over Kosovo ('Kosovocaust') and in the on-going acrimonious exchanges over the conflict in Israel/Palestine. The Holocaust has become 'a measure stick for international politics and a transnational value system'.[78]

Whilst the transnational dynamics of memory practices are indeed important, visions of global memory also seem rather premature.[79] Arguments about the 'globalization of memory' can be criticized for making the same mistake as many of the countless proponents of globalization itself. They exaggerate the extent and depth of the changes in the patterns of international politics. They also tend to conflate sections of the planet (usually 'the west') with the totality of world politics.[80] Globalization, after all, is not a truly global phenomenon. Memories are too closely bound to (and reproduced by the agents of) communities defined by 'thick' social relations – indeed they are partly constitutive of those relations. This is not to suggest that memories cannot escape the bounds of community, only that when they do so they not only lose their original forms, they also lose much of their potency. Anthony Smith claims that the processes that fall under the rubric of globalization are essentially 'memoryless' and as such will never generate strong emotional or political bonds. This partly explains, he suggests, the residual power of nationalism and other particularistic attachments in a world defined by increasing economic and technological interdependence. '[W]e can discern no global identity-in-the-making, nor aspirations for one, nor any collective amnesia to replace existing "deep" cultures with a cosmopolitan "flat" culture.'[81] Memory cannot easily escape the bounds of political community, whether conceived of as a nation, a state, or the fateful combination of the two so central to the contemporary political imagination. As Michael Walzer writes,

> Societies are necessarily particular because they have members and memories, members *with* memories not only of their own but also of their common life. Humanity, by contrast, has members but no memory, and so it has no history and no culture, no customary practices, no familiar life-ways, no festivals, no shared understanding of social goods.[82]

Nevertheless, it would be foolish to ignore the power of the global media (and of diaspora communities) in projecting and disseminating key mnemonic imaginaries and technologies into and through various national and regional spaces. Despite the exaggerations inherent in the claim that we can discern the lineaments of a globalized or cosmopolitan memory, it would be a mistake to simply confine memories to actually existing political communities or to rule out the possibility of future transformation. Whilst the extent and novelty of globalization can be overstated, it is also the case that social, political and cultural developments can be underplayed. The choice is not simply between radical transformation and the status quo. There may be no global memory on the horizon, but we can certainly discern the globalization of memories. The ways in which memory politics were mobilized in the disintegration of the former Yugoslavia by diaspora communities, both for raising funds and with the aim of generating support and legitimacy for their cause, is testament to the ability of certain mnemonic discourses to be disseminated and to generate political effects, globally.[83] Memories of Abu Ghraib will no doubt perform a similar function in years to come.

It is important, then, to study the transnational dissemination of memory, and the uses to which images of and stories about the past translate across national and regional contexts, as well as the role that these movements play in international relations. Bounded political communities are not the only sites of memory. In an age of global media the vectors of memory cross-cut the planet, diffused through multiple mediums and channels at the mere click of a switch. Their effects are as multifarious as their modes of transmission. Responses to the wars of the 1990s have highlighted the way in which the past continues to haunt the present, and for scholars to avoid or ignore this phenomenon is to miss one of the key factors in understanding the nature of modern political consciousness.

A duty to the past?

The vast majority of studies of collective memory (however conceived) focus on various modes of political explanation. They seek to elucidate the plethora of ways in which perceptions, political identities and policies are shaped by understandings of the past. But questions of memory are often, if not always, bound up with questions about morality. This is not a logical necessity; we can imagine an ethics of memory in a world in which reflection on the impact of the past on the present was avoided or was simply unimportant; and likewise, a purely explanatory approach to memory might eschew any explicit normative claims. In most cases, however, this is not the case. The main reason for this lies in the crucial linkage between memory and identity, which means that understandings of the past are integrally linked with values and beliefs. It is for this reason that the study of memory is rarely (or at least not usefully) reducible to formal models based on assumptions about individual utility maximization. 'Memory', Omer Bartov reminds us, 'is elusive and ambiguous'.[84] And it is in this ambiguity that both the difficulty and the importance, of memory reside.

The ethics of memory has several different facets. First, there is a significant link between political legitimacy and memory. Policies, after all, 'are legitimated through appeals to the collective or national memory for social consumption both at home and abroad'.[85] In particular, the politics of memory has proven central in transitions to democracy throughout the world: 'Seldom does history seem so urgently relevant or important as in moments of sudden political transition from one state form to another.'[86] Perceptions of the past are essential in both de-legitimating previous regimes – often through a process of excavating and confronting their crimes, or alternatively in attempting to airbrush them from the history books – and in grounding new claims to political legitimacy. Questions about how to design constitutional structures, decisions about inclusion and exclusion in the political process, methods of dealing with past injustices and with the individuals responsible for them, and the way in which competing narratives of past experiences will continue to shape conflictual identities, are all essential to understand.[87] A linked issue relates to reparations and their role in structuring identities. Focusing on the issue of claims for the reparation of lands confiscated in communist Europe, Christopher Kutz argues that 'a chief function of reparations movements is to create and hallow a particular set of memories. To restore to collective consciousness events otherwise obscured by official histories and "common sense" as defined by dominant groups'. Communal lands and property (though not individual property *per se*) are essential to the collective identity of groups, and there is both a moral and a prudential requirement for reparation. Also, and more ambiguously, the making of claims can help in the 'birth of an entirely new national consciousness', as in South Africa.[88]

The ethics of memory can refer to the ethical impulse to commemorate the dead, most often those killed in wars, and commemorative practices are now the subject of a huge literature.[89] It can refer also to the perceived duty of individuals and groups to remember past injustices. This is usually done in the hope of reconciliation, often between previously antagonistic communities, as is highlighted in a number of the following chapters. Stephan Feuchtwang examines this process in Taiwan, while Roland Bleiker and Hoang Young-ju consider the possibilities of reconciliation in Korea. In both, explorations of mnemonic practices are combined with analyses of the ethical preconditions required in order to move beyond the prison house of the past. For Bleiker and Hoang a possible answer lies in the adoption of a mode of dialogical ethics, 'an ethics of difference with the promotion of a tolerant historical consciousness'. Such tolerance, they argue, is 'possible only once each side accepts within its own political culture the possibility of multiple pasts, presents and futures'.[90] Focusing on the necessarily conflictual nature of historical interpretation provides the first step in creating a political environment in which different group identities can co-exist peacefully. Feuchtwang outlines the general conditions necessary for sustainable reconciliation, analyses the modes of apology required in order to recognize and transcend previous injustices. He argues that memorials to past injustice, and apologies for previous misdeeds, constitute 'a civic ritual of recognition' essential for reconciling the oppressors and the oppressed. He also stresses the international elements of this process, noting the way in which much of the discourse demanding recognition and justice is structured as an appeal to a putative global jury, and in the name of legal and moral principles encoded in institutions such as the UN. In this way, those demanding an apology in Taiwan are 'interpellating each one of us as world citizen'.

The route to mourning and remembrance is, nonetheless, strewn with danger. Drawing on the Freudian distinction between 'mourning' (as 'memory work' that facilitates reconciliation with loss) and 'melancholia' (where the loss is continually revisited) Larry Ray demonstrates the problems of dwelling on and in the past. Exploring the case of Kosovo, he argues that 'Commemoration ... may take the form of mourning in which subjects are able to confront and effect reconciliation with the past; alternatively it can take the form of melancholia in which grief and anger predominate'. Melancholia constitutes the social psychological basis for 'the desire for vengeful justice' and can trigger a process of 'dycivilization', the turning back of the gradual and ever fragile civilizing of modern societies. Like Bleiker and Hoang, Ray suggests that 'discursively examining' memories and constructions of the past, of having a reflexive and open attitude towards historical claims, is essential in order for a plurality of identities to co-exist without the resort to violence. Meskell, referring to the case of South Africa, concurs and calls for an open-textured 'assimilative' understanding of history.[91]

The ethics of memory also encompasses the ways in which the perpetrators of political crimes are brought to justice, especially those falling under the ambit of 'crimes against humanity'. Once again, this is done (at least partly) in the name of reconciliation – it is an attempt to draw a line under certain aspects of the past in the name of the future. Such trials assume different forms, from prosecuting junior officials for their role in the machinery of mass death to indicting those accused of ordering and organizing the killings and deportations. The origins of this mode of institutional mnemonic justice stretch back to the post-war trials of German and Japanese commanders, which were followed by the Eichmann case, various German trials, and the high-profile and much delayed prosecutions of assorted Vichy collaborators in France.[92] What originated as a legal mechanism for bringing to account some of the perpetrators of crimes committed (mostly in Europe) during the Second World War became during the 1990s a global concern, encompassing events in the former Yugoslavia, Rwanda and East Timor.[93] The decade has also seen the blossoming of Truth and Reconciliation Commissions, most famously in South Africa, but also across the Americas.[94] This is an example of the globalization of a particular mnemonic practice. Here the emphasis is less on bringing the guilty to justice than on establishing a confessional space in which both perpetrators and victims recount their roles, in the hope that this will be a step on the difficult but necessary path to reconciling different communities with one another.

It is in the law courts in particular that questions about the ethical role of academics, and especially historians, have come to the fore. The responses that they have proffered differ greatly. Richard Evans, who was instrumental in discrediting the Holocaust-denier David Irving, insists that historians can and should play an essential role through utilizing historical truth in the name of justice.[95] Henry Rousso, on the other hand, refused to testify as an expert witness in the trial of Maurice Papon, a high-ranking civil servant accused of organizing the wartime transportation of French Jews. For Rousso, there are simply too many dangers in the 'instrumentalization' of historical knowledge – like Evans, he insists on the strict separation between memory and history – and he argues that the historian should not judge the past or wield a 'moral cudgel'.[96] As more trials are instituted, and as academics are called on with increasing frequency to provide expert knowledge, the pertinence of such arguments is likely to be an increasingly important topic. And so is the necessity of attempting to identify criteria for delineating or at least distinguishing memory and history, in practice if it proves impossible in theory.

Historical memory is as much about the present and the future as it is about the past – a point well understood by Lewis Carroll's Queen. Any attempt to provide a final, uncontestable, account of the past, and moreover to extract some sort of definitive 'meaning' from it, is fraught with danger. The infamous German 'historians debate' of the 1980s – the *Historikerstreit* – centred on the attempt by a few conservative historians (and especially Ernst Nolte) to 'normalize' the Holocaust by situating it in relation to other twentieth century mass killings. This historiographical revision focused on the attempt to re-assert a proud German national identity, one not forever burdened by shame.[97] Jürgen Habermas was one of the most vociferous critics of this revisionism, arguing that it constituted a betrayal of the duty of German citizens to the victims of German history; the past – or at least this specific national past – needed always to be central to the imagining of present and future political practice.[98] For Renan, forgetting was as much a part of the rationale of national consciousness as was remembering. For Habermas, this is simply not good enough. To forget is to betray both the victims of injustice and to endanger the future. Writing in the highly charged context of post-war Germany, he has attempted to sketch a political theory that recognizes as legitimate certain expressions of communal identity while projecting a sense of obligation to universalistic principles embodied in historical constitutions. This position can be seen as a mode of 'performative purification' seeking to expel 'metonymic guilt' – moral shame generated by association with a specific past – through positive, redemptive action.[99] Disengaging national consciousness from citizenship can also be characterized as an effort to deal seriously with questions of historical memory in the name of progressive politics. Whether the tension between a constant injunction to remember and the desire to move forward is consistent is, however, a different matter.[100]

Memory can also be seen as central to the concept of justice itself. W. James Booth argues for the importance of 'memory-justice', the duty to remember the victims; to rescue their traces from the dark void of silence. This is not simply for the sake of dwelling in the past. The 'great fear' for memory-justice, the core of which is 'fidelity to the victim', is that 'the crime will be allowed to slip into oblivion, into the forgotten; that the passage of time will, like a natural solvent or a willed forgetting, free the perpetrators and weaken the already weak hold of justice in the world'.[101] Forgetting is not simply a violation of a duty to the dead, it also endangers the future. But this is not the only way of linking the concept of memory to justice. In one of the most ambitious recent accounts of the ethics of memory Avishai Margalit argues that we can discern obligations to remember important aspects of the communal past. His argument is premised on a distinction between ethics and morality. The former concerns the links between members of communities bound by 'thick' social relations; the latter applies to the 'thin' relations that govern connections between those belonging to different communities. Morality, he argues 'is long on memory and short on geography. Ethics is typically short on geography and long on memory'.[102] In a communitarian account reminiscent of Walzer, he argues that due to the constitutive function of memory in the creation and reproduction of the normative architecture of societies, and hence of the 'personality identities' of the individuals living within them, it is possible to identify a mnemonic duty. However, there is no 'morality of memory', no obligation to the pasts of those outside one's own community, except where 'crimes against humanity' have been committed.[103]

The problem with this sort of argument, important though it is, lies in its etiolated account of memory. The literature on memory politics remains to a large degree bifurcated. On one hand, there is a large amount of work dedicated to empirical explorations of the ways in which memory shapes political identities – and this is bolstered by an equally large theoretical literature analysing the mechanisms through which this occurs. Although these writers often illustrate the moral character of memory, as Winter rightly notes, they rarely engage in sustained philosophical analysis of the questions presented. On the other hand, the small but growing literature dealing explicitly with the ethical aspects of memory is often based on weak accounts of how memory actually works in concrete circumstances. The essays in this collection, by explicitly interweaving empirical and ethical questions, illustrate some of the ways in which a balance can be achieved. Future work on memory and politics would profit from a more serious dialogue between the two domains.

The ethics of memory includes within it an ethics of forgetting. Memory is not always beneficial; it can be counter-productive. It can obstruct the potential for moving forward, for envisaging alternative futures. This was a point made most famously by Nietzsche in the second of his *Untimely Meditations*, 'On the Uses and Disadvantages of History for Life'. To live life actively and creatively it was essential to be able to escape the chains of history: 'Forgetting is essential to action of any kind, just as not only light but darkness too is essential for the life of everything organic.'[104] If the past is not to become the 'gravedigger of the present' it is essential to try and forget as much as it is to remember, a point re-iterated by Paul Ricoeur.[105] This complex issue is explored in Zehfuss's chapter, where, in the context of German memories of the Second World War and the contemporary debates over the use of force, she stresses that to remember something is always to forget something else, and that this is an intrinsically political relation. It is vital to understand the mutual constitution of remembering and forgetting, and to chart its modulations and its silences, for many politicians and scholars 'seem unaware of the implications of memory as a practice': 'Political debate deploys memories but it does not engage the problem of memory.'[106] Elsewhere she has insisted on the need to 'Forget September 11'.[107] The dialectic of memory and forgetting, and the ethical questions raised by the dynamics of this process, look set to disturb us for the foreseeable future.

IV. The limits of memory

We are living, then, through a 'memory boom', a 'memory fest', all beholden to a 'cult of memory'.[108] Has this infatuation gone too far? Is it the case that, as Alon Confino has argued, the value of the term memory has been 'depreciated by surplus use'?[109]

It is important first to disaggregate two lines of attack on the fascination with memory, although they intersect at important junctures. First, it has been asserted by a number of critics that societies in the West (and increasingly in the non-West) have become obsessed with memory to an unhealthy degree; that in a sense, the turn to memory represents a pathological condition of contemporary political life. Second, the concept of collective memory has been criticized as useless, counter-productive and sometimes even as dangerous. The former is a mode of culture critique, the latter is more concerned with theoretical or methodological questions. I will explore each of these briefly in turn.

For many scholars, an obsession with the past has pernicious social and political consequences. The most evident is the role of social memory in ethnic conflicts. There are, however, other less obvious concerns. Todorov, for example, argues that European societies are dangerously 'obsessed by a cult of memory': 'Possessed by nostalgia for an age now irrevocably past, we revere its relics and indulge in magic rituals that are supposed to keep it alive.'[110] Charles Maier suggests that this leads to the danger of 'complacency and collective self-indulgence' and he warns that 'an addiction to memory can become neurasthenic and dis-abling'.[111] It highlights the end of dreams about the possibility of radical political change; rather than looking towards the future, and retaining a belief in the transformative potential of politics, it seeks solace in the past. Elsewhere he argues that as territoriality declines, so memory politics come to the fore: 'Insofar as territory loses its role as a resource for polit-ical action, it reappears as a sort of elegiac enclave, transmuted from the site of policy contention to a landscape of memory.'[112] As people and communities lose control of the bounded political-economic spaces that previously governed their lives and their imaginations, so they look increasingly to the past for sustenance, and for a substitute, 'the locations of history tug at our heartstrings and allow us to debate endlessly over museums and memorials while accepting – whether realistically or from exhaustion, depending on the perspective of the observer – the continuing limits on public-policy responses to social problems.'[113] The turn to memory is another variation, in other words, of the millennial obsession with endings. This vision of the de-politicizing effects (even if unintentional) of much of the cultural mnemonic discourse is echoed by Andreas Huyssen. The turn to memory is a sign of a rupture in the nature of contemporary politics, defined as it is, he suggests, by the transformation of temporal and spatial experience heralded by globalization.[114] As people become increasingly worried about their 'obsolescence' in a world defined by rapid change, so they seek an anchorage in some 'authentic' past, in memory. The latest mnemonic turn is a function of technological transformation and the discipline imposed by the global neo-liberal economic regime. For such critics it remains essential to escape the fetters of the past, at least to a degree, in order to imagine and move towards alternative futures.

A second line of criticism, in many ways grounded on the insights of the first, offers a barrage of theoretical challenges to the concept of collective memory. For some it is simply too vague to be of much use, conflating and confusing different phenomena, and subsuming historical complexity under an often all-embracing terminology. It is simply a fashionable label that has unnecessarily supplanted existing terms such as myth, consciousness, ideology, stereotype and so forth. The concept of collective memory, it has been claimed, can only ever be 'useless and even misleading' as an explanatory device.[115] For Samuel Hynes, the 'problem is with the term *memory* itself'. Rather than employing it loosely to encompass the multiple ways in which people conceive of the past, memory should instead be regarded as intrinsically personal: 'Memory is the mental faculty by which we preserve or recover our pasts, and also the events recovered. Without that link – *now* reaching back to *then* – you may have an image of the past in your mind, but it isn't memory but something else, a social construction, history.'[116] This is not to suggest that individual memories are unmediated by the social environment, but rather that memory is an individual psychological phenomenon separable from other modes of representing the past. Too much is lost in collapsing them.

Indeed, elsewhere I have provided an account of the limitations of 'collective memory' as it is employed in the analysis of nationalism.[117] In place of the overly promiscuous employment of the term memory, I argue that a clearer grammar of historical representation can be sketched when exploring the ways in which national consciousness is formed and reproduced by distinguishing (albeit in an ideal-typical form) between social memory, mythology and critical history. Although they interpenetrate and overlap at various points it is nevertheless essential to try and delineate them, even if this undertaking can never be achieved completely.[118] Collective memory is understood as the process whereby groups of individuals share and to some extent harmonize (autobiographical) memories of past experiences, and it is therefore limited spatially and temporally. Myths, meanwhile, can escape the bounds of experience – they are simplified, highly selective and widely shared narrations of an imagined past, the stories that people and groups tell about their location (and meaning) in time. History is the infinitely complex past out of which these mythological narratives are hewn, and critical history, whilst always aware of the dangers of nationalist glorification and accommodation, stresses the contingency, opacity and plurality of the past. Its mode is multifaceted and qualified, as opposed to the intrinsic simplicity, univocality and dogmatic certainty of mythology. As J. G. A. Pocock maintains, 'the historian's function is to insist that there are always exceptions'.[119] This can serve, at least in principle, to help imbue and fortify an ethos of political openness.

Other scholars are wary of what Megill has labelled the 'arrogance of authenticity', where memory, at least in some of its manifestations, is seen to be superior to history or other forms of knowledge. This problem is especially acute in wider public discourse, but it also impinges on some areas of academic deliberation. This is particularly the case where, as in the debates over the Holocaust, the status of historical knowledge has been called into question. Memory is seen to provide, in some sense, succour or comfort in troubled (intellectual) times. It is little surprise, the charge runs, that many of the scholars who fall back on the concept of memory have been influenced by psychoanalysis and/or poststructuralism, and have been associated with the challenge to many of the former certainties of intellectual life, including the possibility of access to some form of historical truth. In memory they have found a substitute for lost certainty, a 'therapeutic alternative to historical discourse'.[120] The danger is that memory comes to be seen by many as what Ian Hacking describes as a 'surrogate for the soul'.[121] A significant element of this line of criticism is that, whether deliberately or not, mnemonic discourse often exhibits a theological tenor. This is especially pertinent due to the centrality of the Holocaust, and the attempt to discern some sort of meaning in it, during the second memory boom. Gabrielle Spiegel, noting the sacral, liturgical elements of mnemonic discourse, argues that in the 'rush to valorize memory' we witness a return to the 'metaphysics of presence' and the re-sacralization of the past. Pointing to the different temporal structures of history and memory, she warns against the current trend, as she sees it, for collapsing them into each other. Stressing the importance of the Holocaust, she argues that for many survivors and for much of the discourse that has grown up around them, 'memory remains the bearer of meaning, the vehicle of identity, and the promise of transcendence'.[122] For Spiegel, following Michel de Certeau, the premise of modern historiography is to draw a line under the past, to treat it in a sense as dead, to represent rather than to resurrect – as memory attempts – what went before.[123] This is a point reinforced by Kerwin Lee Klein, who notes the vague connotations of spirituality and authenticity found in many of the most prominent accounts of memory, including those of Pierre Nora, Saul Friedlander and Dominick LaCapra. In their writings, he argues, memory is often presented in the form of a devout and 'murky negative theology'. This invocation of the ineffable, this genuflection before remnants of the traumatic past, serves to obscure and to block the potential of radical politics. 'The new memory work displaces the old hermeneutics of suspicion with a therapeutic discourse whose quasi-religious gestures link it with memory's deep [theological] semantic past.'[124]

There is much to be said for these lines of criticism, and they need to be taken seriously by those embarking on the analysis of memory and politics. It would be injudicious, however, to claim that each holds across all or even most of the work done by scholars of memory, for the simple reason that this is too wide-ranging, too fragmented and too complex to be reduced to a single line of criticism. For example, whilst it is the case that some work on memory, and certainly much of the wider cultural obsession with the past, can be seen as a potential bar to radical politics, indeed as profoundly de-politicizing, this is not always the case. Jenny Edkins and Alison Lansberg both point to ways in which memory and trauma can embolden radical politics. For Edkins, following Giorgio Agamben, traumatic moments peel the lid off normal politics to expose the inner logic of the political, the violence underpinning and supporting state power. Such moments, she suggests, open brief windows for resistance and potentially transformative political action.[125] For Landsberg, the potential lies in memory, and she argues that contemporary media technologies, and mass cultural forms such as television and cinema, contain radical possibilities as they allow for the transmission across society of empathy for the historical experience of others. The resulting 'prosthetic memory' can generate social solidarity, create alliances between various marginalized groups, and help people to understand past injustices.[126] With careful scholarship, and with clear-sighted theoretical analysis, notions of social memory can be powerful in diagnosing and dissecting a number of key features in contemporary political life. This is especially the case in a world in which memory is itself becoming an increasing passion amongst large sections of the population, and where the search for 'useable' pasts, and for the sources of particularistic communal identities, proliferates around us.

V. Conclusions

The study of memory, though a complex and often elusive project, is invaluable in attempting to account for the processes, identities and structures of the international system. As an increasingly large and cross-disciplinary literature has demonstrated, perceptions of the past – and especially of the traumatic past – play a pivotal role in shaping many different aspects of contemporary global politics. Above all, memory plays a major role in determining the dynamics of individual and collective identity formation, which in turn shape both perceptions and political action. These processes are central to the origins and reproduction of communal identities, as well as in explaining many of the challenges to, and transformations of, such identities. It is increasingly argued, moreover, that memory is beginning to escape the bounds of national political communities, diffusing across and helping to restructure regional self-understandings (especially in Europe) and even, in the most ambitious accounts, the globe. The ethical issues arising from the study of memory, including the notion of duties to the past, and the nature of transgenerational justice, are central to some of the most pressing questions facing political philosophers and political agents alike. Furthermore, the very fact that memory and trauma have assumed such prominent roles in contemporary culture is itself a topic of considerable significance: 'its resonance and near ubiquity suggests that it discloses a quest we simply cannot do without'.[127] To ignore this quest is to miss one of the most intriguing, intricate and important dimensions of world politics.

Part I

2

We Could Remember It for You Wholesale

Myths, Monuments and the Constitution of National Memories*

Jens Bartelson

I. Introduction

The world of international relations is in many ways a strange one. Within the discipline devoted to its study, we have long believed this world to be composed of nation states, to the point of taking their existence for granted. On those rare occasions when we feel compelled to inquire into the historical foundations of these nations and states, we are likely to discover that they are the outcome of prior processes of homogenization. Yet these processes of homogenization seem to presuppose some primordial differentiation of humanity into territorially bounded communities in order to be fully intelligible.[1] In this chapter, I will explore the prehistory of this differentiation. Doing this, I will discuss the historical connection between distinct forms of memory and the formation of nation states, with particular reference to the intellectual history of Portugal, Britain and France. My reason for undertaking this task is the lingering suspicion that the present differentiation of humanity into distinct peoples is about to fade, leaving us with the laborious task of reorganizing our memories (and ourselves) in order to meet the challenges of what promises to be a more cosmopolitan future. I will therefore describe how a mnemonic practice has evolved from imperial to national forms and conclude by raising some questions about the possibility of a genuinely global memory. And as every such transition has brought a sense of loss, we must also ask to what extent we are traumatized by those transitions, past or future.

I have deliberately chosen to focus on the category of memory in order to widen the inquiry outside the realm of historiography. My reason for this choice is that a narrow focus on historiography frequently presupposes that the process of identity construction primarily is a narrative one. This is to a large extent true, and the importance of the narrative dimension of sociopolitical identities cannot be underestimated.[2] Yet this focus on historiography and its constitutive functions usually presupposes that this process takes place within an already differentiated domain: different histories are written in support of particular communities which already are present in distinct portions of time and space. While this kind of account forms an indispensable part of any story of identity construction, it says very little of how the required *substratum* of modern national identities was created in the first place. If we want to know more about the emergence of this substratum, we need to pay more attention to the changes in the very conception of memory that arguably precedes the rhetorical uses of history in the narrative construction of specific communities.

How can we make these stateless parts of our past more accessible to analysis? In a remarkable essay published in 1986, James Clifford predicted that future historians of ideas may look back on the twentieth century noting that this was a time when Western intellectuals became preoccupied with culture and language.[3] What Clifford appears to be saying is not simply that things like national identities are social constructs by virtue of being constituted in and through language, but rather that the very notion of 'being constructed' might have a history of its own. In my effort to explore this latter possibility, I will treat the tendency to equate collective social memory with historical narratives as itself symptomatic of a connection between memory and identity that is specific to the modern age. In order to understand how his connection was forged, we must venture beyond the study of mere historiography into the realm of *myths* and *monuments*. Doing this makes it imperative to transcend the sterile dichotomies of the linguistic turn, by realizing that things are signs as much as signs are things. Thus, when studying myths and monuments, we have to take them and their inherent claims to verisimilitude at face value.[4]

II. Memory and identity

The argument in this chapter revolves around the claim that the intimate connection between memory and identity *itself* is contingent rather than necessary. To my knowledge, this connection was first forged within philosophy as a result of efforts to redefine the category of the person to suit the needs of the modern secular state. As John Locke explains in *An Essay Concerning Human Understanding* (1690), it is

> the same consciousness that makes a man be himself to himself, *personal identity* depends on that only, whether it be annexed only to the individual substance, or can be continued in a succession of several substances. For as far as any intelligent being can repeat the *idea* of any past action with the same consciousness it had of it at first, and with the same consciousness it has of any present action, so far it is the same *personal self*.[5]

To Locke, a memory that connects past and present within one uninterrupted sequence is a condition of a unitary consciousness, and a unitary consciousness is what makes an individual identical with himself throughout time and the corporeal changes the passing of time inevitably brings. Furthermore, when Locke described memory as constitutive of personal identity, he did so with the important proviso that it applied to sane men only, and argued that personal identity thus conceived was a necessary condition of autonomy and thus also of legal responsibility.[6] The concept of memory was thus crucial to the definition of man as a bearer of rights within the early-modern state. Supposedly, to Locke, each man is master of his own memory in the sense that recollection itself is a conscious act undertaken by the subject, who thereby is also assembling himself as it were. But how, then, can we possibly account for the identity of that subject *doing* the recollection without ending up in infinite regress by postulating an infinite series of consciousnesses? Who is fashioning selffashioning?

Attempts to answer this question paved the way for Humean skepticism. This skepticism extends beyond induction into the realm of subjectivity and identity. 'I may venture to affirm of the rest of mankind', writes Hume, 'that they are nothing but a bundle or collection of different perceptions, which succeed each other with an inconceivable rapidity, and are in perpetual flux and movement'. Out of this 'memory not only discovers the identity, but also contributes to its production, by producing the relation of resemblance among the perceptions'. Yet these relations are themselves of a fluid and transitory nature, so 'we have no just standard, by which we can decide any dispute concerning the time, when they acquire or lose a title to the name of identity'.[7] Mankind would thus be at loss in the absence of a memory that can break down the chaotic totality of perceptions into *individual* bundles and arrange these in patterns according to the principles of resemblance and causation. To Hume, therefore, memory is as indispensable to identity as it is arbitrary in character.

If we are to believe these accounts of personal memory, we are all very much in the same position as Douglas Quail, the unfortunate protagonist of Philip K. Dick's short story *We Can Remember It For You Wholesale* (1966). In this story, Quail finds himself increasingly confused and lost as the agents of an interplanetary totalitarian regime are not only bugging his thoughts, but are also inserting some memories into his brain, while deleting others in order to cover up their clandestine operations, including the one of having tinkered with his memory.[8] This is a powerful allegory of the implications of turning memory into the touchstone of personal identity. If memory is constitutive of personal identity, yet infinitely malleable due to its lack of extrinsic criteria of validity, then personal identity is pretty much what we or other people make of it through the stories we tell each other about ourselves and others. As such, it can be tampered with for a variety of purposes, thus changing the identity of the bearer in surreptitious ways by changing storylines. As long as the flow of consciousness is connected to a continuous timeline, the disruption of the former invites the subversion of the latter, with profound and disturbing implications for personal identity.[9]

Yet when precariously extended to the categories of *collective memory* and *collective identity*, the above equation looks more like an accurate description of their actual interrelationship. This, at least, was what Nietzsche thought when he concluded that 'there is a degree of sleeplessness, of rumination, of the historical sense, which is harmful and ultimately fatal to the living thing, whether this living thing be a man a people or a culture'.[10] And in a sense, he was right. When later incorporated into modern social theory, this symbiotic relationship between memory and identity itself becomes dependent on the *social context* of remembrance and forgetting. Thus, according to Maurice Halbwachs, 'it is in society that people normally acquire their memories. It is also in society that they recall, recognize and localize their memories ... and the groups of which I am part at any time give me the means to reconstruct them'.[11]

If we would take Halbwachs's account seriously, we would find ourselves in the same predicament as poor Quail even in the absence of a totalitarian regime. There is no need for any secret agent to distort our memory, since such distortion becomes utterly redundant in the presence of a social context that performs the same function whether we know it or not. Nor can we talk coherently about 'distortion' in this case, since we are obliged to remember that the content of our memories is arbitrary. Thus, it only takes an empiricist account of the nature of personal memory coupled with a holistic understanding of society in order to create a shortcircuit between the concepts of memory and identity that cuts across the distinction between individual and group, thus connecting all these concepts in one powerful recipe for communal belonging.[12] Following this recipe, we will be inclined to believe that collective identities are produced out of collective memories as much as individual memories and identities are dependent on each other. The relationship between collective memory and identity is always a two-way street: there is no community without a corresponding memory that records its trajectory in time, and no such trajectory without the active construction of a past order to support or debunk a given identity in the present. This, I shall argue, is where we have found ourselves for quite some time.

To my mind, this equation is symptomatic of a world beset by amnesia when it comes to the historicity of the very category of memory.[13] The idea that memory is a social construct is itself peculiar to the modern age. The art of memory, in its many manifestations from antiquity onwards, is not confined to this linear and constitutive function attributed to it by the moderns.[14] Neither is it confined to the sphere of consciousness, but could as well reside in inanimate objects.[15] Nor did earlier accounts of memory imply that memory was constitutive of personal or collective identity.[16] But one thing about memory seems to be fairly recurrent: its association with spaces and places, whether material or merely symbolic.[17] Thus, in order to understand the function of memory in the creation and reproduction of spatial differentiation, we have to pay attention to the history of the category of memory itself, and how profound changes in the way this category is conceived have conditioned the modern equation between memory and identity; the spaces and places of memory gradually become coextensive with the territory of the modern nation state.[18]

Being dependent on the past for our identity will continuously both reflect and reinforce the modern equation between memory and identity at both the personal and collective level. As we shall see below, this attribution of specific social functions to memory not only brings distinct strategies of remembrance, but also ways of forgetting that in turn can be used in order to repress those memories that cannot be tailored to fit the functional requirements. It is to these strategies of remembrance and forgetting we now must turn, in order to analyse how they have manifested themselves during three formative phases from the Renaissance to the birth of modern social theory.

III.   Memory and myth

When modern states and nations were created, they were not created out of nothing. Leaving aside the material processes of state formation here, it is reasonable to suspect that they were created by means of resources already present within the world in which they arose. This was the world of empire rather than the world of citystates – the world of Rome rather than that of Greece. As Patricia Springborg has remarked, 'empire lurked in the wings of the nation state from its very inception. As those small spaces carved out of the great garment of Christendom, the early modern European nation states not only emulated empires rather than city-states ... but they quickly went on to found empires'.[19] This imagined world of empire constituted the symbolic backdrop of much European state formation and the later expansion of the state system.[20] The uptake of symbols from this world of empire was highly selective, however. While this imaginary world was a world populated by people who knew very little of spatial differentiation, it supposedly also had a centre, embodied in the legal and political institutions of early Rome. Subjected to a constant tug-of-war during the high Middle Ages, the nature and necessity of such a centre had increasingly become contested during the late medieval period. Simply put, the world of empire which Renaissance authors so eagerly entered into was very much like the Roman Empire, but without an emperor to uphold its authority.

Those who wanted to make sense of emergent states and nations faced the formidable task of reinterpreting and recontextualizing the rich world of signs, symbols and metaphors that had been handed down to them from the ancients and which had been duly filtered through Italian Renaissance attempts to appropriate the same sources in support of the citystate. Certain things had to be remembered in order to bestow the emergent political order with intelligibility and legitimacy. Other things had to be forgotten and for much the same reasons. Thus, in this section, I shall argue that the modern order of states and nations was crafted out of a set of resources whose origin was such that it constantly threatened this creation, and that this origin therefore had to be carefully repressed within collective social memory. Most commonly, this was done in poetry and rhetoric by *nationalizing* crucial symbols and metaphors, thus making them appear exclusive inventions of particular communities when in fact they had been around long before and had constituted parts of a cultural heritage common to the entire civilization of the West. That such visions of empire appealed to the Habsburgs is perhaps less surprising, so in this section I shall focus more on the uptake of imperial symbols by those who sought to counterbalance the westward expansion of the Spanish by creating nations, states and later empires of their own: Portugal and Britain.

As I have argued elsewhere, similar moves had been undertaken during the Italian Renaissance, and then most notably in the political context of citystates and their quest for survival in an increasingly hostile environment. Thanks to the peculiarities of Renaissance modes of knowing and writing, ancient sources could be reappropriated and important political insights distilled from them by means of the use of the esoteric doctrines of resemblance and *exempla*. Provided that the underlying conception of time was cyclical, history was bound to repeat itself infinitely. Against the backdrop of such a political cosmology, it was fully possible and indeed reasonable to argue by means of examples derived from ancient sources when legitimating different forms of rule or different lines of action against one's opponents. What once applied in Athens or Sparta now apparently applied in *quattrocento* Milan or Firenze, without the slightest degree of anachronism being felt as long as certain rules had been obeyed in the selection of and sampling from classical texts. In other words, there was no firm divide separating past and present, simply because the concept of secular and linear time (*tempus*) could not claim to be the sole legitimate foundation of historiography.[21] Perhaps the best example of the resulting propensity for time travelling is found in Petrarch's letters in support of Cola di Rienzo's effort to re-establish the Roman Republic in 1344, in which Petrarch seems to assume that the past millennium was merely a blip on the screen, having done nothing to violate the unshakeable identity of the Roman people.[22]

By the beginning of the sixteenth century, such rhetorical strategies were being employed in order to make sense of and justify a kind of entity that had not yet been conceptualized in fully independent terms before. Whereas high-medieval legal thought had the Roman concept of *patria* to command loyalty in exceptional circumstances and while the term *natio* certainly was used to denote common birth and ancestry,[23] the late Renaissance saw the emergence of a new kind of memory designated to account for the *coincidence* between a people and a territory, actual or desired. This kind of memory was based on the assimilation of ancient myth and was most frequently expressed in poetical form.

Let us be careful. This is not to say that any fully modern conceptions of nations or national identity originated at this point in time. The categorical difference between the entities envisaged by Renaissance and modern authors can be described in the following way. During the fifteenth century, it was believed in parts of continental Europe that Englishmen were equipped with tails, testifying to their beastly nature – the pragmatics of this belief not being too hard to divine in the aftermath of the Hundred Years War. Yet what was lacking was a conception of Englishness underlying and possibly also explaining the possession of tails or any other trait that could be attributed to individual Englishmen. Today, when we carelessly attribute, say, gullibility to a Swede or jealousy to a Dane, we do so with a certain reluctant readiness to deliver an explanation of what in their respective cultures puts a premium on the cultivation of such traits, so that, by means of a little innocent logical leap, those traits can also be regarded as expressive of the national culture in question, and vice versa. As Herbert Mead states, '[e]very individual self within a given society or social community reflects in its organized structure the whole relational pattern of organized social behaviour which that society or community exhibits or is carrying on, and its organized structure is constituted by this pattern'.[24] Such a leap could not as easily be taken by Renaissance authors, however, since the necessary underlying particularistic conception of community was as unavailable to them as was *any* consistent notion of a particular whole. Rather, the problem of identity was formulated against the backdrop of more universalistic conceptions of human society, conceptions that could be translated into imperial ideologies with equal ease.

Not surprisingly, the first authors to tell stories that purported to explain the spatiotemporal trajectory and gradual triumph of distinct peoples were from that corner of Europe that had the strongest reasons to do so, given their recent political experiences of conquest and discovery. For this purpose, they vernacularized predominantly Latin sources and used those sources in order to create poetic defences of their achievements. Thus, when Luís Vaz de Camões wrote his poem *Os Lusíadas* (1572), it was in order not only to celebrate the discoveries of Vasco da Gama, but also to instill a sense of peoplehood to the ancient races of Lusitania by means of poetic assimilation and innovation based on Roman sources. Thus, in *Os Lusíadas*, the triumph of the Portuguese discoveries is intimately connected not only to the glory and bravery of those who achieved it, but also, and more importantly, to the formation of the Portuguese people, *their* independence from the Castilian Crown, *their* expulsion of the Moors and the dynastic legitimacy of *their* Crown.[25] Connecting all of the above in one single epic, Camões assimilates and compares the Portuguese experience to that of other glorious empires in the past. Skillfully manipulating the line between fact and fiction, the gods of those empires are now on the side of Portugal, the legitimate heir to their imperial greatness. Thus no one less than Jupiter sets the stage in *Canto One*:

> Eternal dwellers in the starry heavens, you will not have forgotten the great valour of that brave people of the Portuguese. You cannot therefore be unaware of that it is the fixed resolve of destiny that before their achievements those of Assyrians, Persians, Greeks and Romans shall fade into oblivion. Already with negligible forces ... they have expelled the Moslem ... while against the redoubtable Castilians the have invariably had heaven on their side.[26]

Camões succeeds in mobilizing a wide range of mythological sources in his rhetorical celebration of the Portuguese discoveries. Yet this might strike a more inquisitive reader as strange, since these glorious battles also include Viriato's guerilla-like war against the Romans. But why so daringly count on the support of Roman deities while taking a fair amount of pride in their victory *against* the Romans? Would not that most likely upset the same deities and tempt them to withdraw their support with reference to the obvious *hubris* of the Portuguese?

But *Os Lusíadas* is built on a strategy of textual assimilation. Everything that is foreign to the Portuguese in time and space is gradually swallowed up and digested in the course of their providential march to unity and grandeur, so that the memory traces of earlier empires and their gods are visible and intelligible only to the extent that they condition the prehistory of the Portuguese people and its achievements. Portugal and the Portuguese become comprehensible only to the extent that the Romans are forgotten other than as a distant yardstick of military valour and aristocratic virtue. But in order to institute this forgetfulness in a coherent and persuasive way, the Romans must be confronted and beaten on their mythological home ground, so to speak. This is done by the fearsome creature of *Adamastor*, who introduces himself in the following way in *Canto Five*:

> I am that mighty hidden cape, called by you Portuguese the Cape of Storms, that neither Ptolemy, Pomponius, Strabo, Pliny nor any other of past times ever had knowledge of. This promontory of mine, jutting out towards the South Pole, marks the southern extremity of

Africa. Until know it has remained unknown: your daring offends it deeply. Adamastor is my name. I was one of the giant sons of earth, brother of Enceladus, Briareus, and the others. With them I took part in the war against Jupiter, not indeed piling mountain upon mountain but as a sea-captain, disputing with Neptune's squadrons the command of the deep.[27]

It seems like Vasco da Gama finally has met somebody in the same trade from whom he has things to learn. The discovery of Adamastor by Vasco marks the final poetic victory over the Romans, since this bizarre innovation by Camões is a total but potent newcomer in the Western gallery of mythological creatures. His claim to fame is to have fought none but Jupiter himself, if only in order to be turned into a rock as a punishment. Yet as we might recall from Matthew, being a rock is not necessarily a bad thing, since both empires and churches can be built on them.[28] And through this double move, Vasco da Gama is now admitted to the same aristocratic hall of fame, closely followed by his men, 'since no trial, however great, has caused them to falter in that unshakable loyalty and obedience which is the crowning quality of the Portuguese'.[29] While bearded Adamastor lacked a trident, he certainly knew how to blow winds into the sails of Portuguese imperialism.

Thus, Camões succeeded in creating a veritable poetic vortex that soaked up what was of value in both Roman and Christian symbolic heritage, and twisted all those memory fragments into a poetic defence of Portuguese peoplehood. In a gesture that later would find its full justification in Vico's attempt to shed light on the 'deplorable obscurity' of the origin of nations, Camões established a mnemonic practice that could make sense of a desired future of a people in terms of a past which then could be made to look increasingly alien and easily forgotten.[30] Doing this, he could draw on an established tradition of rhetorical prophecy that stretched back into the early Renaissance, and which had earlier been used to boost dynastic claims against the Castilians.[31] Now this was in a sense the final victory of the Portuguese over the Romans, a victory which made it possible for Camões to find his place side by side with the other heroes of the discoveries.

But the same textual tactics of assimilation could be used in cultural comparisons as well. When the illustrious Fernão Mendes Pinto, 'who in twenty-one years was five times shipwrecked, thirteen times taken captive, and seventeen times sold as a slave',[32] posthumously had his work defended against popular disbelief by the Lisbon editors of his *Peregrinaçam* (1614), they did so by appealing to the impeccability of

Pinto's memory.[33] Whether impeccable or not, his book certainly exemplified a structure that would prove fruitful to subsequent colonial exploits by both the Portuguese and the British. Pinto carefully chronicles his experiences and impressions from Africa, India, China and Japan and compares the mores encountered in those places with those of Portugal and its nobility. Not surprisingly, Pinto frequently finds the virtues of the latter reflected in the demeanor of local princes and is often greeted with hospitality by them.[34]

Pinto's narrative is based on a chronological recall of events. Before it was published, the manuscript had been entrusted to the chronicler Francisco de Andrade who subdivided it into chapters. This subdivision was done according to the principles of Renaissance cartography, so that each chapter eventually came to narrate experiences specific to distinct places as the voyage proceeded. Although somewhat cumbersome, the resulting division makes the *Peregrinaçam* look akin to the index of an atlas or to a modern guidebook. Consequently, in the English translation of 1653, names of places are consistently italicized, as are orations. Much in the same vein, Damião de Góis – a friend of Erasmus – had published his *Urbis Olisiponis Descriptio* in 1554 that applied similar geographical principles when describing the features of Renaissance Lisbon and its surroundings, all while still subscribing to Strabo's view that the city had been founded by Ulysses.[35]

The works of Pinto and Góis reflect other Portuguese concerns at that time, those of navigation and cartography. In 1450, Henry the Navigator had established his Naval Observatory in Sagres, devoted to the systematic study of astronomy, navigation and cartography.[36] Consequently, the ocean 'previously seen as an impassable barrier, by the last third of the fifteenth century had … become an intercontinental highway for those impious ships'.[37] And finally, in Portugal and elsewhere, this geographical and cartographical knowledge became intertwined with the rise of the territorial state. Dreams of unlimited territorial power 'found the beginnings of its realization in the map or sphere that was dedicated to the monarch, framed by his arms and traversed by his ships, and that opened up to his dreams of empire a space of intervention stretching to the limits of the terraqueous globe'.[38]

It is in this context that Pinto's work should be read.[39] Before imperial sensibilities led to a lust to dominate that which was foreign, however, the common response to the unknown was largely one of marvel. Thus Pinto's narrative is not so much a tale of subjugation and conquest as it is a tale of hardship and friendship and of the practical problems involved in getting to know foreign people in foreign places. But first you have to get there: in his hands, the concept of *peregrination* locates this enterprise of knowing firmly in the spatial realm, so that cultural and spatial barriers appear to be more or less coextensive. In their vernacular use, the equivalents of the Latin term *peregrinatus* came to mean something akin to aimless wandering. As such, it was a way of travelling different from that of pilgrimage, which had been the dominant paradigm of medieval travelling, until it was discredited during the sixteenth century.[40] And this is exactly what Pinto says he does: he wanders as a foreigner from place to place, his own chosen status as a foreigner permitting him to discover sameness wherever he goes. The harder it is to get to a place, the harder it is to get to know it and its inhabitants, Pinto seems to say. Yet the harder this is, the bigger the eventual payoff in terms of recognition. Whereas the Muslims encountered along the established trade routes allow for few real surprises and appear to corroborate standard prejudices against the Moor, the Chinese and Japanese come close to being unreachable and are therefore less comprehensible but all the more fascinating. The deluge in Canton and the reaction of its inhabitants is a good example. Pinto takes their panic and hysteria to be indicative of their devotion to God.[41]

Japan marks the spatial horizon of early Portuguese colonial experience in the same way Rome constituted its temporal horizon in Camões. It is in the encounter with this extreme otherness that the Portuguese attained full subjectivity. When Pinto and his companion Father Belquior eventually arrive in Japan, having survived a series of disasters in China, Pinto sets out to the Fortress of Osquy in order to meet the 'king' only to discover that the king has gone fishing on the Isle of Xequa, 'entertaining himself in the catching of a great Fish, whereof the name was not known, and which has come thither from the bottom of the Sea, with a great number of other little fishes'. Pinto's curiosity is momentarily relieved by a sumptuous feast, whereupon he receives an invitation to go fishing with the king, 'for on thy coming, and on the death which I hope to give to this Fish, my perfect content depends'. This done – whale killed and all – Pinto explains this act of hospitality in terms of the esteem enjoyed by the Portuguese, 'for all the inhabitants held it for most certain, that the King of Portugal was indeed the only Prince, which might terme himself the Monarch of the world, as well as for the large extent of his territories, as for his power, and mighty treasure'.[42] The same enthusiasm was obviously shared by the king himself, since he, upon hearing about the military strength of Portugal, said 'I sware truly unto you, that I should desire nothing so much in the world, as to see the Monarchy of this great Country, whereof I have heard such wonderful things ...'.[43]

It was accounts like these that were responsible for Pinto's reputation as a liar, at home as well as abroad. To be sure, the *Peregrinaçam* is sprinkled with other fantastic events, yet it lacked those chapters on mermaids and tritons that were more or less mandatory in the chorography of the day.[44] Yet it was Pinto – rather than Camões or Góis – that came to be known as the epitome of a liar.[45] Pinto, by virtue of his very method of cultural assimilation, simply failed to make exotic places appear sufficiently strange to command the credence of his contemporaries: in modern Portuguese there is still the idiom *Fernão Mendes, minto* as a playful way to fend off absurdities. With this in mind, Pinto's *Peregrinaçam* could safely be shuffled into the recesses of libraries in Coimbra and Oxford as an entertaining example of Renaissance travelogue. His tale of colonial experience could be celebrated as a masterpiece of vernacular prose and compared with the poetry of Camões, but with little factual accuracy attributed to its content. Yet *Peregrinaçam* contains a recipe for remembrance that would continue to resonate throughout the coming centuries. As we have seen above, the new meaning attributed to the concept of peregrination brings a silent revolution in the art of travelling, permitting the traveller to assimilate different experiences by virtue of casting *himself* rather than the other as the foreigner: where those chroniclers who had gone to the Americas had found little but insurmountable otherness, Pinto is shaking hands with people all over the East.[46]

When a spatial grid was superimposed upon this story of hardship and friendship, the flow of memory is broken up and confined to episodes taking place at distinct places at distinct times, as if the act of remembering – true to the credo established at Sagres – itself was a matter of navigating the seas of past experience. So what *Peregrinaçam* did to the overwhelming wealth of recently discovered cultures is somewhat similar to what Netscape Navigator and Internet Explorer have done to the equally overwhelming manifold of websites, that is, compartmentalizing them in a virtual spatiality. As a result, we are all free to feel like Vasco da Gama at the flick of a switch. In the process, we are as enticed to believe that we actually travel through some kind of space as we are cautioned to disbelieve in what we happen to discover there. Thus, to assimilate within a framework of spatial differentiation means making difference relative to space, and then making similarity contingent on the ability to move across the geographical boundaries erected by the same practice of differentiation. Moving across these boundaries is tantamount to finding infinite points of similarity, while effectively repressing all difference that cannot be understood as being conditioned by spatial distance. As we have seen in the case of Pinto, this is accomplished through a peregrination that takes us across the surface of the planet while keeping the range of resources used for explaining these differences constant: Christian virtue and natural accident. To Pinto, other worlds exist only to the extent that they can be incorporated into the tale of Portuguese identity and its ultimate mastery of this spatial grid.

The Portuguese were not alone in their quest for mastery. Similar efforts to build a national tradition on the basis of imperial resources, and then to erect an empire on the basis of that tradition, were made in Britain during the early seventeenth century. This quest for a common identity was conditioned by the political concerns of the Tudor and Stuart periods, but was also motivated by an attempt to answer a question that had haunted historians for some time: what is British history the history of? In order to answer this question, authors like Davenant, Drayton and Hakluyt joined together elements of poetry and cartography with ancient myth.[47] While notably absent from the major works of Hobbes and Locke, references to the Roman Empire, its deities and poets abound in the works of Drayton and Davenant. As Springborg has observed, the 'resources of antiquity and modernity were jointly plundered to fabricate a particular identity'.[48] True to this ambition, Drayton warns against staying local in the quest for nationhood in his *Poly-Olbion* (1613). Those who remain content to do this are,

> [p]ossest with such stupidity and dulnesse, that rather then thou wilt take pains to search into ancient and noble things, choosest to remaine in the thicke fogges and mistes of ignorance, as neere the common Lay-stall of a Citie; refusing to walker forth into the Tempe and Feelds of the Muses[49]

In order to achieve the desired effect of actually manifesting the same identity that it so eloquently describes, this poetic tradition had to be cleverly disseminated to the populace in order to stir the right sentiments in them. Thus Davenant speculated about how to turn his own and others proto-nationalist poetry into popular entertainment. In his *Proposition for the Advancement of Moralities* (1651), this was to be done through a spectacle, '[i]n which shall be presented severall ingenious Arts, as Motion and transposition of Lights; to make a more naturall resemblance of the great and virtuous actions of such as are eminent in Story; and chiefly of those whose famous Battails and Land and Sea by which this Nation is renown'd'.[50] That the theatre was chosen as the preferred channel of dissemination is perhaps no coincidence, since the English theatre had evolved in tandem with the art of memory since the early Renaissance.[51] Ultimately, this reappropriation and assimilation of the Roman heritage was designated to boost not only a sense of common identity among the tailed, but also to wrap their Crown in mythical splendor. As Selden commented on Drayton's efforts: 'If in Prose and Religion it were justifiable, as in Poetry and Fiction, to invoke a *Locall Power* (for anciently both *Jewes*, *Gentiles* & *Christians* have supposed to every Countrey a singular *Genius*) I would therin joyne with the Author.'[52]

When we reach the mid-seventeenth century, the substratum indispensable to modern nationhood had been created, with or without the aid of singular geniuses. Collective memory had been *nationalized* by means of a consistent recourse to Roman sources by the Portuguese and the British. Proceeding by means of an assimilation of symbols, metaphors and tropes within emergent vernacular literary traditions, the deities and heroes of the Romans were recycled to boost claims to peoplehood, dynastic legitimacy and royal authority, while simultaneously furnishing an important rhetorical impetus behind early imperial pursuits. It was then left to *ius naturalists* like Hobbes and Locke to provide the theoretical justification of that which now largely had been accomplished in practice, and, by consistent omission, help readers *forget* the fact that the meaning and experience of empire had constituted the ultimate resource out of which the early-modern state had been crafted.

IV. Memory and monument

In the previous section, we saw how early modern identities were created and sustained through a distinct strategy of remembrance that could assimilate everything useful outside the spatiotemporal horizon of the present, while erasing the traces of this assimilation. Memory and identity are forged together in such a way that Locke's psychological account of personal identity comes to possess a certain factual verisimilitude in the light of these efforts. These strategies of remembrance operated by transferring valuable qualities from the world of empire to the world of states. What was deemed of value in the imperial past was dug up from ancient sources, reinterpreted and then attributed to the vanguards of early-modern order, the Crown, the nobility and the church. It was then a truly monumental task to disseminate this collective memory to the populace and make it stick in an age when literacy was a privilege of the few. Poetry presupposed a degree of literacy that made it impractical for this purpose if not staged into spectacles, a fact which confined much of the knowledge of 'national traditions' to the elites that had invented them. But the early-modern strategy *par excellence* had been to create spatial marks of identity that could be deciphered in terms of those virtues that had been appropriated from the ancients. Cathedrals, royal palaces, public buildings and monuments were built with remarkable stylistic uniformity throughout Europe during this period – the Baroque – drawing on family-resemblant principles of construction and decoration.

The French Revolution put an abrupt end to all this extravagance, and further tightened the connection between memory and identity. This tightening was done in response to the problems of legitimacy that the revolutionaries had created for themselves. With the old authorities thoroughly discredited, from where was the young republic to derive justification in the absence of a ready-made *demos*? The solution to this problem proposed by Emmanuel de Sieyès may seem evident to us who have been accustomed to take it for granted, but was not at all that obvious to his contemporaries. As he explained, '[t]he nation is prior to everything. It is the source of everything. Its will is always legal; indeed, it is the law itself.'[53] As I shall argue in this section, creating that kind of this particular whole required a forceful intervention into the realm of collective memory.

As Françoise Choay and Thordis Arrhenius have shown, the French Revolution led to a new focus on monuments and their historicity.[54] The Latin term itself, *monumentum*, derives from the verb *monere*, to recall: the restorative practices of the French revolution amplified this function while imposing a systematic forgetfulness on the original symbolic meaning of the monuments thus restored. As Arrhenius argues, '[s]patial operations participated not just in constituting the monument but also in changing its significance ... it is shown how the monument, through spatial intervention, is transformed from an instrument of power into an object of knowledge and finally into a site of sentiment'.[55] In the French context, this was a way of undoing the symbolic meaning vested in monuments by *l'ancien régime,* and to bestow them with new meanings more consonant with the aspirations of the revolutionaries. In this process, contexts were altered, and objects were moved and reclassified according to new criteria. Indeed, this entire drive towards the restoration of monuments could later be celebrated as one of the significant achievements of the Revolutionary Age.[56]

But before these buildings and other objects could be recontextualized, they had to be appropriated, and rendered together as one homogeneous class of monuments. A first step in this direction was taken when *L'Assemblée Nationale* in November 1789 decided to dispossess the Church of its property. What then ensued was the giant task of ordering the confiscated objects by preparing careful inventories of statues, paintings, books and manuscripts. Consequently, a *Commission des Monuments* was appointed in November 1790 to take care of the inventory. The outcome of these efforts was the notion of a *patrimoine* and it was subsequently debated among the revolutionaries how this enormous collection of objects should be handled. Whereas some were in favor of selling most of it in order to cancel the substantial national debt inherited from *l'ancien régime*, others advocated restriction with reference to the fact that many of these objects constituted *historical monuments*. Such objects should not be valued as religious artifacts or in terms of their mere material value, but should rather be inserted in a grand narrative of French history leading up to the events of the revolution itself. As Arrhenius has noted, 'the notion of *monuments historiques* would turn the historical monument into a site of reflection in which the success or failure of the present epoch could be mirrored.'[57]

Eventually, those parts of ecclesiastical property that were not sold, melted down and molded into canonballs, or used as quarries for limestone and marble, were reclassified and rearranged as symbolic pieces of a collective memory that could legitimize the revolution and its outcome. Practices of conservation and restoration become integral to this entire process of rebuilding the banks of collective memory to cater to a new political agenda, while effectively erasing traces of the former authority of monarchy, nobility and church.[58] Yet as Arrhenius points out, this left the revolutionaries with the difficulty of explaining how they could claim to support the arts while condemning its former protagonist, *l'ancien regime*. After all, the revolution posed as a child of the enlightenment.[59]

The invention of the *museum* became the solution to this dilemma, since within its walls, 'iconoclasm was achieved without destruction'.[60] As a member of the revolutionary *Commission des Arts*, Alexandre Lenoir transplanted sculptures from the recently deconsecrated royal tombs at the church of Saint–Denis to the *dépôt* of Petits–Augustins. In 1793, this depot was opened up to the public, only to be formally granted the status of *Musée des Monuments Français* in 1795, and then as a branch of the *Louvre*.[61] In order to delete memories of an absolutist past while recontextualizing its leftovers, the museum employed a series of techniques not unlike those proposed by Davenant for the popular dissemination of English nationalist poetry. The monuments thus recovered were grouped together in chronological order and put on display in rooms decorated to convey the ambience of different centuries. In the first room – illustrating the thirteenth century – the fragments collected from the tombs of Saint–Denis were on display in virtual darkness. As the visitor progressed through rooms and centuries, the amount of light gradually increased until it reached its peak in the Age of Enlightenment. The progress of history, so dear to that age, was thus reflected in the sequential ordering of rooms and in the way daylight was distributed between them. The revolutionary museum thus solved the conflict between conservation and destruction: '[e]victed from the re-generated space of the Revolutionary city, re-assembled and confined to the museum, the monuments of the *ancien régime* represented the tangible evidence of a new form of knowledge: the History of the Nation'.[62]

Thus, at the very same time as the concept of the nation made its first modern appearance in Sièyes, this invention was supplemented and sustained by a field of visibility generated by the didactic layout of the revolutionary museum. The reality of the French nation, in all its historicity, became hard to doubt against the backdrop of these monuments and fragments, neatly lined up in progressive order in front of the spectator. In the process, memories of the absolutist past and the identities that had corresponded to *its* ways of remembering were repressed, and later gradually forgotten. A new world of symbolic significance had been created and another seemingly irretrievably lost. At the level of tactics, this meant that the revolutionaries had successfully escaped the 'thicke fogges and mistes of ignorance' that previously had been associated with going local in the quest for identity. Indeed, these 'fogges and mistes' were now deviously sprayed back onto that past as the very means of escaping it.

Yet underlying this profound change at the level of monuments we find a disturbing continuity, since the *strategies* of remembrance had remained fairly intact during the revolutionary transition. The revolutionaries had succeeded in doing to the absolutist state, the church and the nobility more or less what these prior forces had done to the meaning and experience of empire that they had recovered and reappropriated. To be sure, new mnemonic techniques were developed and used by the revolutionaries, as well as new and more advanced methods for disseminating memories thus retrieved to the populace. But at the level of strategic imperatives, few things had changed. Indeed, the very connection between memory, identity and spatiality had been *reinforced* in this process, since collective memory was not only expressed in a spatial context – the museum – but also rendered instrumental in codifying a collective historical experience within a defined portion of space. Memory was thus coupled to a historical and collective subject – the nation – that was made congruent with the territory of a state. So again, the coincidence of state and nation that we normally take to be the very culmination of a successful process of state formation had virtually been *remembered* into existence.

V. Memory and history

As we have seen in the previous section, the firmly territorialized connection between memory and identity forged by the revolutionaries was the end of a cumulative series of strategic interventions in the field of memory, taking us from the realm of myths into the realm of monuments. With this in mind, it seems like Hume had caught the enlightenment spirit of remembrance very well, as he insisted on *both* its constitutive relation to identity *and* its arbitrary character. Memory and identity had indeed been rigorously connected in practice, but in a way that was highly philosophically arbitrary. In this section, I will say a few words on how myth and monument gradually were replaced by *history* as the dominant locus of collective memory.

First, when Kant and Hegel took it upon themselves to make sense of the complex achievements of enlightenment and the French Revolution, the historicizing gesture could not be avoided since it was inherent in the topic of investigation itself. The revolution was not only a historical event, but was itself based on a wholesale reconfiguration of past and present.[63] The meaningful experience of human community was now the prerogative of historical inquiry and states and nations could hardly be understood other than as outcomes of long historical processes. Each state or nation had its own temporal trajectory and the totality of human history was ultimately reducible to the gradual formation, transformation and possible transcendence of these forms of political life, '[f]or only through the solution and fulfillment of this task can nature accomplish its other intentions with our species'.[64] Or, as Hegel argued, '[t]he principles of the national spirits in their necessary progression are themselves only moments of the one universal spirit, which ascends to them in the course of history to its consummation in an all-embracing totality'.[65]

Second, the emerging academic discipline of history had to make empirical sense of what went on within the by now inescapable spatial grid into which the entire human species was about to be locked. To Ranke, '[t]he most intensely enjoyed moments of our existence are fused in our memory and make up its living content'. Hence, to him, the great achievement of the French Revolution and its aftermath was 'the fact that nationalities were rejuvenated, revived, and developed anew. They became part of the state, for it was realized that without them the state could not exist'.[66] Thus, to the extent that Kant and Hegel had rendered the meaning of the nation state exhaustive of the category of history, historians like Michelet and Ranke rendered the category of history equally exhaustive of the empirical experience of nation and state. The remarkable fusion of nation and state finalized by the revolution was thus supplemented with modes of historical writing that purported to account for this fact by positing state and nation on converging planes of historicity.

As I have argued elsewhere, the outcome of this was that subsequent efforts to theorize the social and political world took place within a *living museum*, containing a vibrant manifold of customs, institutions and practices that had now been sealed off in distinct spatiotemporal compartments, as if only awaiting discovery by the historian or the early political scientist. As we have seen, this domain of objectivity had been carefully crafted by the sequential superimposition of memories and identities upon each other, so that by all measures, the nation and the state looked as indispensable in the present as they seemed to have been from the beginning of time.[67] It was this living museum that provoked Nietzsche's scorn and lament in his *Untimely Meditations* (1874), since history had become the history of states and nations and very little else. According to him, history had itself become *monumental* in the process of erecting the temporal foundations of this new world, forfeiting many of its more noble functions in human life.[68]

VI.   Conclusion

As we entered the twentieth century, these political communities acquired the ability to remember the past for us wholesale, fully consonant with the first attempt to theorize collective memory taken by Halbwachs. Yet in the general ambience of disenchantment accompanying this shift, there was an awareness that something precious was about to be lost. In the light of this, the mnemonic overwhelming of the West, another disciple of Durkheim reflected upon the question of personal identity. 'Who knows', wrote Marcel Mauss, 'whether this [category of the person], which all of us believe to be well founded, will always be recognized as such? It is formulated only for us, among us. Even its moral strength – the sacred character of the human person – is questioned ... even in the countries where this principle was discovered'.[69]

What happened to Doug Quail has also happened to us, leaving us as traumatized by the experience of nationhood as we are by the expectations of its demise. As long as we rely on collective memories as a source of personal identity, we will inevitably face a certain loss of self whenever those collective memories are strategically rearranged to cater to new political concerns. The prospective loss of national identity looks scary indeed, yet our sense of personal identity will inevitably remain fragile as long as we seek to derive it from belonging in a community thus constituted. There is neither a past nor a future that can provide the anchor points for individual or collective identity anymore, since what has been fractured in the present is the very connection between memory and identity. To some, this will pave the way for a brave new world of individualized memories, which know little of the mechanisms described by Locke or Halbwachs.[70] If this is the case, we would then cease to be what we remember and start to remember who we are. We would then again be free to peregrinate around in what remains of the world of nations and states as we would be in any other theme park, the world being but one giant repository of myths, monuments and narratives that when carefully crafted together would testify to the boundless nature of an emergent global community. But, the skeptic might retort, rather than facing the dawn of a new era, we have perhaps come full circle, back to Rome: for what is this giant repository but an empire in disguise?

3

Notes on the Memory Boom
War, Remembrance and the Uses of the Past

Jay Winter

I. Introduction

Memory is in the ascendancy these days. In virtually every corner of intellectual life, there is evidence of a sea change in focus, a movement towards the analysis of memory as the organizing principle of scholarly or artistic work. Whereas race, gender and social class were foci of earlier waves of scholarship, now the emphasis is on a set of issues at the intersection of cultural history, literary studies, architecture, cognitive psychology, psychoanalysis and many other disciplines besides. What they have in common is a focus on memory.

The argument of this chapter is that one pivotal source of this ecumenical interest in memory has been a steadily increasing recognition of the need to acknowledge and account for the victims of war, living and dead. Starting in 1918, practices of remembrance have been first and foremost acts of mourning. In the interwar years, Europe was the centre of this activity, but since the Second World War, it has spread widely. The Holocaust is a focus of much memory work, and there are monuments to the victims in many parts of the world. In North and South America, in South Africa, in Australia, in the Middle East, in Africa and Asia, remembrance has become a subject of intense public debate. At times, these current discussions deal with fresh wounds, and victims of recent inhumanity, for instance in Rwanda, Cambodia and East Timor. In other cases, long-buried injuries are being addressed for the first time, as in post Civil War Spain, where after 60 years commemorative gestures are emerging.

The memory boom of the later twentieth century evokes earlier cultural movements. When we speak of memory as a focus of cultural life, we enter a space in which others have entered before us. We are not the first in line, and (whether we know it or not) we have inherited and are working through an earlier generation's fascination with, indeed obsession with, memory. What I would term the first generation of memory in the modern period spanned the years from the 1890s to the 1920s. Its focus was on memory as the key to the formation of identities, in particular national identities, although social and cultural identities were also in mind. The second 'memory boom', emerging in the 1970s and 1980s, has come to see in memory a way out of the confusion bred by the fragmentation of the very identities forged by and during the first 'memory boom'. Memory has become in recent years a way of casting about in the ruins of earlier identities and finding elements of what has been called a 'usable past',[1] or what the French historian Pierre Nora calls *lieux de mémoire*.[2] But today we do not seek the same past or set of sites that, for example, James Joyce sifted through in his *Portrait of the Artist as a Young Man* (1916). We are in another world. Who today would try to 'forge in the smithy of my soul the uncreated conscience of my race'?[3] The tortured history of Ireland – a fragmented identity if there ever was one – simply cannot be constituted in this way.

Instead, today we confront subjectivities, hybridities, multiple subject positions which we all occupy at different times and places in our lives. A century ago, the concept of memory was harnessed by a host of men and women as a means to constitute or fortify identities in an imperial age. That age has gone, and so have its unities and its certainties. In its place memory still stands, but as a source of fractured national, ideological and cultural forms, forms which are resistant to coherent reconstructions.

To be sure, memory defined history, ethics and art well before the late nineteenth century. The arts of memory were highly developed in the Renaissance,[4] and there is little we could add to ancient Egyptian commentaries on the plight of those 'without a yesterday', without memory understood as a sense of obligation and duty to those around us.[5] What modern commentators offer is less a set of new ideas than new configurations of old ones. Today those drawn to memory adopt widely varying styles and inflections in their work. For some the memory boom is nostalgic, a yearning for a vanished or rapidly vanishing world. For others it is a language of protest, seeking out solidarities based on common narratives and traditions to resist the pressures and seductions of globalization. For others still it is a means of moving away from politics, and of resacralizing the world, or of preserving the voice of victims of the multiple catastrophes of the last century.[6] And for some, it is a way of confronting the Holocaust at the very moment that the survivors are steadily passing away. To capture those voices, those faces, and through them, to establish a bridge to the world of European Jewry that the Nazis succeeded in destroying, is still another agenda fuelling the contemporary memory boom.

We are clearly dealing with a dissonant chorus of voices here, and the sheer variety of work on memory in contemporary culture precludes any easy analysis of its origin or quality. Above all, it is the overdetermined character of the memory boom that is its most striking characteristic. There are so many sources of it that it is hard to identify the marginal from the crucial, the transitory from the longlasting, and difficult somehow to put together the very disparate impulses symbolized by Oprah Winfrey and Primo Levi. The superficial and the profound coexist in our obsession with memory. In this highly charged and rapidly changing field, there is one certainty on which we can all agree: no two people invoking the term 'memory' use it in the same way. And yet, its resonance and near ubiquity suggests that it discloses a quest we simply cannot do without.

II.   Generations of memory

The first of the two generations of memory flourished, as the Victorians liked to say, between 1890 and 1925. That is to say, there is a cohort of men and women born between the 1860s and 1880s or so who came into academic, literary, professional or public prominence through their writings on or about memory. Most, though not all, of their work appeared in the period 1895–1914. Much is very familiar. Sigmund Freud, born in 1856, was at the older end of this cohort, alongside the French philosopher Henri Bergson, born in 1859, and author of *Matter and Memory* (1896).[7] A bit younger was the German art historian Aby Warburg, born in 1866, creator of a whole school of memory studies, embodied to this day by the Warburg Institute in London.[8] One of the most interesting figures in the transmission of ideas about memory was W.H.R. Rivers – physiologist, social anthropologist and psychiatrist at the Craiglockhart hospital where he treated shell shock victims of the Great War, including the poet Siegfried Sassoon. Rivers was born in 1864 and died in 1922.[9] In that year Marcel Proust, whose name is inextricably linked with the multiple pathways of memory, died at the age of 51.[10] Thomas Mann was born in 1875; a year later Maurice Halbwachs was born.[11] His path-breaking work *Les Cadres Sociaux de la Mémoire* was published in 1925, at the end of our period of interest.[12] Both Halbwachs and Proust were just a bit older than that master storyteller, James Joyce, born in Dublin in 1882, and whose *Portrait of the Artist* was published in 1916, in the midst of the stately appearance of Proust's masterpiece *A la Recherche du Temps Perdu*. Virginia Woolf was born in the same year as Joyce, and her representations of time appeared at the end of our period in many novels, among them *Mrs Dalloway* (1925) and *To the Lighthouse* (1927).

There is no documentation to indicate that these people wrote as part of a generation, but it is striking that their outlook and sensibilities all intersected with the subject of memory and that they did so at a very unusual time in European history. Here we can find affinities – rather than causal connections – between cultural history and political history. This was a period when the French Republic was just decades old, when the German state was in its infancy, and when British imperial power was both at its zenith and beginning to take on the distinctive aroma of an overripe fruit. It is little surprise that cultural explorations of memory intersected with political and social interrogations of the subject.

Both in the late nineteenth and in the late twentieth centuries there occurred a rush towards memory in which at least three vectors were of great importance. In a nutshell, they may be grouped under the headings of genesis, appropriation and circulation. Let me try to unpack these labels. The first vector was formed by independently generated work within the arts, science, the academy and the free professions. The memory work of Proust or Freud cannot be reduced to a set of quasi-Pavlovian responses to political or social stimuli; they lived very much in their social worlds, but their writing had its own internal dynamic and creative sources.

The second vector is one of the parallel development of cultural activity surrounding the construction of what Halbwachs came to call social memory – the memory of the people who form social groups, and whose recall gives those groups coherence and form. Halbwachs's position is a straightforward one. Collective memory, he argued, is constructed through the action of groups and individuals in the light of day. Passive memory – understood as the personal recollections of a silent individual – is not collective memory, though the way we talk about our own memories is sociallybounded. When people enter the public domain, and comment about or commemorate the past – their own personal past, their family past, their national past, and so on – they bring with them images and gestures derived from their broader social experience. As Halbwachs put it, their memory is 'socially framed'.[13] When people come together to remember, they enter a domain beyond that of individual memory.

That work of collective remembrance was everywhere in evidence in Europe between 1890 and 1920, and its multiple agendas were transparent.

And not only in Europe. South American Republics all had centenaries of their independence to celebrate in the early twentieth century. But in France, Germany, Italy and elsewhere, new political regimes had to invent or unearth an illustrious past to justify and stabilize their nascent political forms. Collective memory, performed in public and understood as an artefact, a construct, a kind of Potemkin village of the mind, constituted a significant part of that unifying force. It was expressed in many ways, from the celebration of days on the calendar, to what Maurice Agulhon calls '*statue-mania*',[14] to the highly visible veneration of newlyfound ancient traditions, to the constructions of historical narratives (some welldocumented, some mythical) written, published and recited in schools and other public venues. In Britain, there were parallels, though their origins were different. Imperial power under threat also cast a long shadow into a semi-fictional past, reconfigured in traditions invented for the purpose.[15] The cult of the British monarchy, David Cannadine has shown, was not based on practices observed time out of mind; this cult and the supposedly ancient ceremonial practice attached to it, were constructed in the years between 1870 and 1914. To some they reflected grandeur; to many others – Kipling among them – they reflected the beginning of the end of hegemony, the time when 'the captains and the kings depart'.[16]

Economic motives were evident in the first memory boom, but political agendas were probably of greater importance in our understanding of their genesis. The best-known contemporary formulation of this vision of memory as political glue was provided by Ernest Renan. In a series of lectures in Paris in 1882 – entitled 'What is a nation?' – he noted that

> A nation is a soul, a spiritual principle. Two things, which, in truth, are really one, constitute this soul, this spiritual principle. One is in the past, the other in the present. One is the possession in common of a rich legacy of memories; the other is the present-day consent, the desire to live together, the will to continue to value the undivided heritage one has received ... To have the glory of the past in common, a shared will in the present; to have done great deeds together, and want to do more of them, are the essential conditions for the constitution of a people ... One loves the house which one has built and passes on.[17]

Such ideas and images were commonplace in late nineteenth-century Europe. What was much newer were powerful means to disseminate them. Writers on memory reached a much wider audience than ever before. The expansion of the print trade, the art market, the leisure industry, and the mass circulation press, allied to developments first in photography and then in cinematography, created powerful conduits for the dissemination of texts, images and narratives of the past in every part of Europe and beyond.

Some of these means of capturing the past disclosed a degree of nostalgia about a vanished or vanishing world. In Britain and elsewhere, the use of photography to reach areas that were on the edge of absorption into the modern world was a late Victorian and Edwardian industry. The French banker Albert Kahn sent out scores of photographers to capture something about the entire world, and took especial interest in those areas like China or Equatorial Africa where what he took to be indigenous ways of life were being eroded by contact with the imperial gaze.[18] Photography could celebrate imperialism or expose its ravages.[19] Photography of the wilderness – in America or Mongolia – had a similar purpose: to reach the pristine before the philistines got there, or sometimes to record their arrival. Nostalgia was engraved onto nitrate plates, and whenever possible, onto the new practices of cinematography.

Warfare in this period moved the cult of memory onto the level of mass production and consumption. After the Franco–Prussian war, *Souvenir Français* emerged as an association within civil society to preserve the memory of the men who died in France's lost war of 1870–71. As Madeleine Rébérioux has shown, other lost causes were captured in stone too. The *Mur des Fédérées* in the Père Lachaise cemetery in Paris – more a secular shrine than a memorial – was preserved as the site where the last of the Communards – the diehards of the first communist revolution in history – were shot among the gravestones on 28 May 1871.[20] Less contested commemorative material proliferated in the new regimes of France, Italy and Germany after 1871. And especially in France, an army of Mariannes was sculpted and painted to symbolize the Roman origins of the new Third Republic on *mairies* and schools throughout the nation.[21] Bills of exchange, stamps, and coins all took on the imprint of national nobility expressed through historical or mythical notation.

This commemorative moment was powerful, but after 1914 it was eclipsed by the still more irresistible avalanches of images and words surrounding the dead of the Great War. And here the cult of memory became a universal phenomenon. War memorials were constructed in every French commune and in almost every British village. German, Austrian and Italian churches and village crossroads were littered with them too. Their message was to remember – the sacrifice, the suffering, the slaughter, the names of the fallen. And in a host of paintings and books and films, this cult of memory became a cult of mourning.[22] Thus the first generation of memory – Freud, Mann, Proust, Rivers, and Bergson among them – joined the memory boom of their generation in the collective work of burying the lost generation of the Great War.

III.   The second generation of memory

The second generation of memory emerged in the 1970s and 1980s, but many of its sources lay clearly in the Second World War. Mourning is also at its core, but its trajectory differed sharply from that of the first memory boom. For many reasons, the balance of creation, adaptation, and circulation was entirely different from the earlier case.

The first and most significant point about the second memory boom is that while the Second World War is central to it, there was a time lag before it emerged. Fully three decades had to pass before the new obsession with memory emerged fully. Why the delay? In the 1940s and 1950s, collective stories about the war focussed on heroic narratives of resistance to the Nazis and their allies. Even when such stories were true, they took on mythical proportions. The notion of a noble and ecumenical Resistance mixed accounts that were valid with claims that were not. The Resistance was not popular until late in the war; it did not shorten the war; and on balance, it did not liberate oppressed people from the night of Nazi rule. Why did this kind of idealising remembrance flourish? In part it appeared because intrepid chronicles of Resistance were more useful in the revival of the political culture of countries humiliated by occupation and collaboration.[23] But by the 1960s and 1970s, that narrative work had done its job; the transition to post-war political stability was complete. The European community was up and running.

The birth of the witness

There was now room for the victims of the concentration camps to come forward. And come forward they did. The memory boom of the late twentieth century took on momentum and cultural significance when the victims of the Holocaust came out of the shadows, and when a wide public was finally, belatedly prepared to see them, honour them, and hear what they had to say. When Primo Levi published his first book, *If This be a Man* (1947), its reception was polite but very restrained. It was only in the 1970s and 1980s that he became an international figure of the first order: *The Periodic table* (1975) and *The Drowned and the Saved* (1987) have become iconic accounts of the Holocaust and the astonishing power of one man to retain his quiet dignity and powers of sympathetic observation in its midst. What matters here is that they took 30 years to find an international audience and international acclaim.[24]

Collective remembrance is a matter of activity. Someone carries a message, a memory, and needs to find a way to transmit it to others. The second memory boom privileged a new group of people and their memories. No longer would one group or carriers of memory – the heroes and heroines of resistance – eclipse another group. Before the 1970s, as Annette Wieviorka has put it, Buchenwald (the camp for political prisoners) occluded Auschwitz (the camp for racial prisoners).[25] By the 1970s, new voices emerged with new memories. These were the new 'remembrancers', the new carriers of memory; they form a new singular collective that we term the witness.

Paralleling this shift in speakers and in audiences was a shift in the means of circulating their message. By the 1970s developments in audio and video-cassette recording meant that survivors could now testify before a camera, sometimes in private, one on one, sometimes for more general viewing. Both sets of image could be easily preserved. This was an event that seemed to validate their stories. 'For many of us', noted Levi, 'to be interviewed was a unique and memorable occasion, the event for which one had waited since liberation, and which even gave meaning to our liberation.'[26] In the 1940s and 1950s, many survivors feared that no one would ever believe what they had to say. Three decades later, their fears were laid to rest, and the interviews they gave are an enduring record for posterity. In other ways too filming the voices and faces of the survivors played a decisive role in the creation of the post-war memory boom. Here were preserved the testimony of those who struggled with the Nazis or who aided them outside the system of concentration and extermination camps. In 1969, Marcel Ophuls completed *The Sorrow and the Pity*, a four-hour documentary on French life in Nazi occupied Clermont–Ferrand.[27] The film obliterated the myth of heroic resistance, a myth symbolized, indeed completely embodied by de Gaulle, President of the French Republic from 1958 until April 1969.

De Gaulle's passing from the political scene was significant in a number of ways relevant to the post-war memory boom. The first was that with the departure of a figure totally identified with the romantic view of the Resistance as the nation in arms, the force of that myth began to fade. And when the myth evaporated, behind it emerged a nest of embarrassing issues pointing to the culpability of Frenchmen for crimes committed against Jewish French citizens. After the mid-1960s, French collaborators in mass murder were vulnerable to arrest and trial in France. This was an entirely unintentional effect of a change in the statute of limitations for war crimes in 1964, which was supposed to stop retired Germans who had committed crimes in the war from holidaying on the Riviera. What was aimed at Germans could be used against Frenchmen. And so it was in three famous trials. The first was against the Nazi officer Klaus Barbie, who had tortured to death the leader of the Resistance, Jean Moulin, and who had been deported to France from Bolivia in 1983. He was convicted and sentenced to life imprisonment four years later. Then came the trial of Paul Touvier, a French subordinate of Barbie in Lyons, who had executed seven Jews in 1944 as a reprisal for the assassination of a prominent collaborator. Touvier was convicted in 1994 and died in prison two years later. In 1998 it was the turn of the distinguished civil servant Maurice Papon, who had held many high posts in the Fourth and Fifth Republics, but who had efficiently administered the deportation of Jews from the Bordeaux region during the Vichy regime. He too was convicted of crimes against humanity, and after a brief period on the run, he was returned to prison to face a ten-year sentence for his complicity in murder.[28]

These trials brought out two critical features of the second memory boom. Firstly, they illustrated the way that discussions of the Second World War could not be separated from discussions of the Holocaust. And secondly, they brought out vividly the notion that memory was moral in character, and that the chief carriers of that message were the victims themselves. These points had emerged in part during the Nuremberg trials of 1946 and the Eichmann trial of 1961, but both had focused on the perpetrators. The memory boom of the 1970s and 1980s was based on a different optic: its gaze was increasingly turned to the victim.

Thus a new kind of performed act of remembrance was born, that of the witness, understood in both senses of the term. The witness was a survivor, a truth-teller, but he was also a visitor from another planet, as the Israeli poet Ka–Tchetnik put it during the Eichmann trial. These people spoke of things we could see only through a glass, darkly, but through their voices we might be able to reach out to those who did not return from the camps. Holocaust witnesses assumed therefore a liminal, mediating, semi-sacred role since the 1970s. They spoke of the dead, and for the dead, whose voices could somehow be retrieved in the telling of these terrifying stories. Their words, their acts of remembrance, gave them a quasi-religious tone, and listening to survivors appeared to be a kind of laying on of hands, an acceptance of the witness in the early Christian sense of the term, as a person who testifies to her faith, even while in danger of dying for it.

Commemorations of war and the holocaust

Once more we return to the linkage between memory and mourning. But in this contest, the problem which emerged in the 1970s, and which continues to bedevil commentators, witnesses and politicians alike, is how to link the new culture of the witness to commemorations of the Second World War. In the Soviet Union, which suffered by far the heaviest toll in terms of loss of life in the war, this issue hardly came up. Critical works like Vasily Grossman's *Life and Fate*, an account of Stalingrad and of anti-Semitism in wartime Russia, were suppressed, appearing only after the author's death.[29] But in the west, it became increasingly difficult to separate the war from the Holocaust.

Here is where official commemorations – publicly performed acts of remembrance defined by a politically-sanctioned script – became problematic. As in all forms of collective memory, the character of the event changed over time. V-E Day and V-J Day came to jostle with D-Day as moments of solemn recounting of the Second World War. In Israel Yom Hashoah comes a week before Independence Day, and is clearly intended to link the catastrophe of the Holocaust with the birth of the State of Israel. These commemorative moments were well established in the 1970s. Now they have been joined by 27 January, the day Auschwitz was liberated by the Red army. But this linkage of the commemoration of war and Holocaust brings us to another way in which the Holocaust has fuelled the memory boom and increased the tensions imbedded in it. The decision of the German government to build a Holocaust memorial near the Brandenburg gate in Berlin set off a massive argument. The monument, a stone's throw from the new Reichstag and from Hitler's bunker, is unavoidably part of the story of Germany reborn. Some believe the monument is an essential and properly placed part of the story; others opposed the location of a commemorative monument to victims of the Holocaust within such a narrative. Placing the monument in the heart of the national capital, geographically and metaphorically, and focussing on the national level of notation, locates the Holocaust within a political framework – that of Germany debased by the Nazis and Germany reborn today.

The difficulties were multiple, but among them was the use of a form of political culture developed in the first memory boom to mark a set of events of an entirely different political and moral order. In the first boom, commemorative projects had transparent political agendas, central to which was the stabilization of new or older nations and empires. The problem is that the Holocaust resists this kind of stable encapsulation, or in fact any encapsulation within a particular system of meaning. To paraphrase Primo Levi, a set of events about which one cannot in any recognizable manner pose the question of 'why?' is also an event about which it is impossible in any straightforward sense to pose the questions of historical context or meaning within twentieth-century history.[30] After the First World War, commemorative efforts aimed to offer a message that loss of life in the conflict had a meaning, that these sacrifices were redemptive, they prepared the ground for a better world, one in which such staggering loss of life would not recur. Two decades later those hopes were dashed. The problem of meaning only got worse after the emergence of the Holocaust witness in the 1970s. What did their testimony tell us about the question as to whether the Holocaust had any 'meaning'? Their voices, while poignant and indelible, did not offer any firm answers. Increasingly detached from the national trajectories of Israel or Germany, the Holocaust increasingly appeared to be an event without a meaning. It was a giant black hole in the midst of our universe of reason.

History, post-modernism and the new political order

If the Holocaust had no 'meaning' in any conventional sense of the term, was it possible that theories of Enlightenment or of progress were void of sense as well? Here was a point at which the memory boom and philosophical inquiry intersected. Through the works of the French scholars Jean François Lyotard and Emmanuel Levinas, and the Romanian born poet Paul Celan, amongst others, a radically subversive view of reason emerged in the post-war decades.[31] It is a perspective that offers a critique of earlier linear views of history and grand narratives of the progress of the human spirit. As Benjamin put it in his seventh thesis on the philosophy of history, etched on his gravestone in Port Bo, 'There is no document of civilization which is not at the same time a monument to barbarism.' To mediate on the dialectic between the two was a preoccupation of many of those who broke with the modernist project and its grand narratives, rooted in a belief in *Aufklärung*, in Enlightenment and reason.[32]

In parallel, a set of political changes seemed to prove these critics right. The grand narrative of nationbuilding, out of which the first memory boom had emerged, bore little resemblance to the political fault lines of the later twentieth century. Here too we turn from what I have termed 'construction' to the 'adaptation' of messages about memory in political and social discourse. And once more we can see how new technologies, in particular those associated with the computer, circulated these ideas in new and powerful ways.

The second memory boom coincided with what Charles Maier has called the 'end of territoriality'.[33] His point is that the process of state-building in Europe spanned the century between 1860 and 1960, after which different political forms and redrawn or more porous boundaries began to dominate international political life. The emergence of the European Union is one such development; the erosion and collapse of the Warsaw pact and the Soviet Union was another. The replacement of war between states by organized violence within states is a third. Globalization further perforated state borders constructed strenuously over the course of a century. With the demise of a certain kind of nationalism in Europe – symbolized by de Gaulle – and a certain kind of socialism – symbolized by Gorbachev – the pole stars of the political firmament in Europe and elsewhere began to fade from view. This led a number of observers to try to escape from their disorientation through a search for the elements of national identities that were now in question. This was the origin of Pierre Nora's inventory of the French *lieux de mémoire*. In seven learned tomes, he collected the work of over 100 leading scholars who catalogued the ways French men and women constructed their multiple identities. Now we have parallel ventures in Germany, Italy and Portugal, with more promised for the future.[34]

Identity politics and testimony

This interrogation of identities coincided with other facets of the memory boom rooted in what we now call identity politics. Here is a story with European origins but which must be distinguished from facets of the memory boom elsewhere, and in particular, in the United States. The distinction must be made because Nora's project rests on the assumption that identity politics is incompatible with the French definition of citizenship. In law, and in academic discourse, there are no Arab–Frenchmen or African–Frenchwomen. They are simply French men or women whose origins do not enter their political identity. Nora's exploration of *les lieux de mémoire* is not about ethnic or racial groups within France, but about Frenchness *tout court*.

Elsewhere, what Latin American scholars term 'living on the hyphen' is not only tolerated, but celebrated.[35] Ethnic identities are defined by narratives of the past, and in part by narratives of the suffering and survival of subordinate groups within a national polity. Here is yet another powerful source of the contemporary memory boom. State-bounded narratives increasingly compete with others of a regional or ethnic kind. On both sides of the Atlantic, in the developed 'north' and the developing 'south', many ethnic groups and disenfranchised minorities have demanded their own right to speak, to act, and to achieve liberation or self-determination. And those struggles almost always entail the construction of their own stories, their own usable past. Collective remembrance is a term that can no longer be collapsed into a set of stories formed by or about the state or about nations as a whole.

Each collective constructs its own collective memory. In North America, this phenomenon is at the heart of identity politics.[36] One clear example is the placement of the National Holocaust Memorial on the Mall in Washington. It is, in this sacred space, both a statement of universal truths, and an expression of Jewish–American pride. The museum speaks in a grammar living on the hyphen, the hyphen of ethnic identity. The framework cannot escape from its location. The redemptive elements in the story surround it on the Mall. They tell us of the wider struggle for tolerance, for freedom of religion, for freedom from persecution; they locate the Holocaust within the American narrative, itself configured as a universal.[37] Here we have arrived at the right-hand side of the hyphen 'Jewish–American'. The museum is the bridge between the two.

There have been many other instances of commemoration as an expression of the tragic history of persecuted minorities. The Aids quilt is one;[38] monuments to the struggle for African–American freedom raise the same point. Recent attempts to configure the imprisonment of Japanese–Americans during the Second World War express the same set of issues, both unique and universal. Again the hyphen of identity is strengthened by commemoration.[39] As I have already noted, in Latin America and elsewhere, identity politics takes on other forms, in particular, the cadences of persecuted minorities or political victims. Testimonial literature rescues histories trampled on by military dictatorships. The stories of cruelty and oppression once retold constitute acts of defiance; through the narrator, the voices of the dead and the mutilated can still be heard. The Truth and Reconciliation Commission in South Africa has been a focus for the release of imprisoned memory, in this case the stories of a majority imprisoned by a minority.

At times, the boundaries between truth and fiction become blurred in such storytelling, whether its setting is a public forum or an individual memoir. As Doris Sommer has put it, the boundaries between informing and performing are porous.[40] But even when the storyteller goes beyond what can be verified through other sources, or even when the witness distorts the past, her voice in Guatemala or Chile still stands for a generalized sense of oppression. Here is 'memory' understood as a set of narratives, a 'counterhistory that challenges the false generalizations in exclusionary "History" ', penned by those trapped in a Euro-centric and imperialist sense of what constitutes the past.[41] This dimension of the 'memory boom' has little purchase with respect to Holocaust testimonies, but it tells us much about other narratives of oppression.

IV.   Affluence and commemoration

I have tried to emphasize the multifaceted and eclectic nature of the 'memory boom'. There have been political, technological and philosophical impulses towards privileging the subject of memory in many discursive fields. In a moment, I will address what a demographer would call 'cohort analysis' – the tracing of generations and the stories they tell over time. There is a medical dimension to this story to which I shall also turn albeit briefly. The braiding together of these varied themes is a classic problem in overdetermination.

But there is yet another dimension to this story to which we must attend. It is more about audiences than about origins, and while not of fundamental significance, it still is part of the story of why so many people are talking about 'memory' today. In the west, one important precondition of the 'memory boom' has been affluence. In a nutshell, rising real incomes and increased expenditure on education since the Second World War have helped shift to the right the demand curve for cultural commodities. Higher education has played a central role. Since the 1960s there has been a rapid expansion in the population of university-trained people, whose education provided them with access to and a desire for cultural activities of varying kinds. In Britain, there were at least three times as many people studying in institutions of higher education in 1990 as there were in 1960. The same upward trend may be detected across Europe and in the United States. Part of the increase is demographic: the 'baby boom' generation was coming of age; but there was more at work here than the shadow of post-war fertility. Systems of higher education differ markedly, but even with a host of qualifications, the international trend is evident. There were eight times the number of students in higher education in Germany in 1990 compared to 1960; in France, six times more over the same period; in Italy, Belgium, Denmark, and the United States, 5 times more. Taken together, the 15 member states of the European Union had 12 million students in higher education in 1990; there were about 13.5 million such students in the United States. And the numbers continued to grow throughout the last decade of the twentieth century.

Changes in higher education had fundamental effects not only on the skill composition of the labour force, but also on the stock of cultural capital circulating in society as a whole.[42] By the 1990s there was a larger population of university-educated people than ever before. Their demand for cultural products of many different kinds was evident. What might be described as the industry of culture was in an ideal position for massive growth. The market was there; the target population for cultural products was there; and after two decades of retrenchment, state support for 'heritage' or *le patrimoine* was there, with greater or lesser degrees of generosity.[43]

Alan Milward has pointed to the material echoes of these two cultural bywords, 'heritage' and 'patrimony'. The 'memory boom', he rightly notes, has happened in part because both the public and the state have the disposable income to pay for it.

> The media are the hypermarket outlet for the consumption of memory. Stern moral and methodological rejection of earlier historical fashions does not alter the reality that this latest fashion, like the earlier ones, is driven by the all-too-positivist forces of the growth of wealth and incomes. The history of memory represents that stage of consumption in which the latest product, ego-history, is the image of the self not only marketed but also consumed by the self.[44]

There are differences among European countries, and I look forward to hearing more about the German story, which may not fit Milward's sardonic interpretation. But in the British and French cases, there is a symmetry between economic trends and cultural trends which we ignore at our peril.

Dwelling on memory is a matter of both disposable income and leisure time. Milward has a telling point: affluence has helped turn identity into a commodity, to be consumed by everyone during her (increasingly ample) leisure time. A 'common' identity is one sharing a set of narratives about the past. Many of these take the form of bricks and mortar – fixed cultural capital. Exploiting their attractiveness, as in Britain's National Trust stately homes and gardens, the patrimony or heritage trades became a profitable industry, with market niches and target consumers. The marketing of memory has paid off, in a huge consumer boom in images of the past – in films, books, articles, and more recently on the internet and television. There is an entire industry devoted to 'blockbuster exhibitions' in museums, whose visitors seem to respond more and more to spectacular shows. History sells, especially well as biography or as autobiography, or in Milward's (and Pierre Nora's phrase) egohistory.[45]

The British satirical writer Julian Barnes produced a marvelous *reductio ad absurdum* of this phenomenon in his futuristic spoof *England, England* (1998). Why should tourists have to travel to consume the icons of British history? Surely it makes more sense to bring or imitate the lot on the Isle of Wight? But whatever its potential for humour, the history business has never been more profitable. It would be important, though, to have more precise information about the choices cultural consumers make. I would guess that over the last two decades, the growth rate in attendance at the Imperial War Museum, the British Museum, and Madame Tussaud's in London, for instance, has been greater than the increase in attendance at sporting events or rock concerts.

Affluence has had another by now commonplace byproduct. One vector of the 'memory boom' may also be the exteriorization, or expression in public space, of the interior discourse of psychoanalysis. Just as Woody Allen has popularized therapy as an addictive way of life, so the nearly universal spread of therapy cultures have made memory a light consumer durable good for those – yet again – with the cash to afford it.

V.   History and family history: vectors of transmission

So far I have tried to sketch some of the political and economic preconditions for the contemporary 'memory boom'. But there is another level of significance in this story, one that is more demographic than political, more about families than about nations.

Historians should be grateful that history sells; one reason that it is such a popular and money-making trade is because it locates family stories in bigger, more universal, narratives. One way to understand the huge growth and financial viability of museums and fiction set in the wars of the twentieth century is to see them as places where family stories are located in a wider, at times universal context. Some grandparents knew the Blitz; now they can bring their grandchildren to the 'Blitz experience' of the Imperial War Museum in London. Such imaginings of war are attractive because they rest on the contemporary link between generations, and in particular between the old and the young, between grandparents and grandchildren, at times over the heads of the troublesome generation of parents in the middle. In the 1960s and 1970s, this link pointed back to the First World War; later on, to the Second.

Many best-selling novels set in the two world wars take family stories as their form. Examples abound: Jean Rouaud's *Champs d'Honneur* (1991), or Sebastian Faulks's powerful *Birdsong* (1993), or Pat Barker's fictional trilogy on the Great War.[46] Barker has written a sequel whose central figure is a 100-year old veteran and father of the narrator.[47] Faulks has placed within a later novel about the Second World War a story of the transmission of traumatic memory between father and daughter.[48] There are deep traces here of the history of several cohorts, moving through time, across this fictional landscape. Today's grandparents were children after the 1914–18 war, and their stories – family stories – are now imbedded in history, and fiction, and exhibitions, and museums, and pilgrimage, in all the stuff of ritual that deepen the 'memory boom'. The linkage between the young and the old – now extended substantially with the life span – is so central to the concept of memory that its significance may have simply passed us by.

VI.   Trauma and remembrance

When we encounter family stories about war in this century, we frequently confront another kind of storytelling, one we have come to call 'traumatic memory'. The recognition of the significance of this kind of memory is one of the salient features of the contemporary 'memory boom'. I take this term to signify an underground river of recollection, first discussed in the aftermath of the First World War, but a subject of increasing attention in the 1980s and 1990s, when post-traumatic stress disorder became the umbrella term for those (as it were) stuck in the past. The 'memory boom' of the later twentieth century arrived in part because of the belated but real acceptance that among us, within our families, there are men and women overwhelmed by traumatic recollection.

War veterans bore the scars of such memories even when they did not have a scratch on them. The imagery of the shell-shocked soldier became generalized after the Second World War.[49] In 1939–45, the new notation for psychological casualty was 'combat fatigue', an unavoidable wearing out of one of the components of the military machine. Holocaust victims had a very different story to tell, but the earlier vocabulary of trauma was there to be seized. And seized again. This was true in commemorative art as much as in medical care. It is no accident, in my view, that the notation of Maya Lin's Vietnam Veterans Memorial is that of Sir Edwin Lutyens's monument to the missing of the Battle of the Somme at Thiepval. The Great War created categories that have framed much of the language we use to describe the traumatic memories of victims of the Second World War, the Vietnam war and other conflicts.

This is also the case in the field of psychiatry, where the notion of post-traumatic stress disorder – previously termed 'shell shock' or 'combat fatigue' – was accepted as a recognized medical diagnostic classification only in 1980, a few years after the end of the Vietnam war. Once accepted as a syndrome, PTSD validated entitlements – to pensions, to medical care, to public sympathy. It also 'naturalized' the status of Vietnam veterans. The mental scars of Vietnam vets, once legitimated, could be treated alongside other victims of urban violence, or sexual or family trauma.[50] In all these cases, violence seemed to leave an imprint we now call 'traumatic memory'.

In this area, enormous progress has been made over the last 30 years in the field of neuroscience. The biochemistry of traumatic memory is now a field of active research, and various pathways have been identified which help us distinguish between different kinds of memory traces. There is now a biochemistry of traumatic memories, memories that are first buried and then involuntarily released when triggered by certain external stimuli. The world of neurology has had its own 'memory boom' which in turn has helped establish the scientific character and credentials of the notion of 'trauma'.[51]

Fiction and fictionalized memoirs have also been important vectors for the dissemination of notions of traumatic memory. This has been true since the Great War, and the appearance in print of the poems of Wilfred Owen, who did not survive the war, and Ivor Gurney, who did, but who spent the rest of his life in a lunatic asylum. Some veterans may have retreated into silence, but there were many storytellers among them, and among their contemporaries, who to this day continue to teach us much about what 'trauma' means. Virginia Woolf's *Mrs Dalloway* is one poignant example: the figure of Septimus Smith was drawn from her encounter with her brother-in-law and his condition. Two recent books, David Grossman's *See under Love* (1989) and Peter Balakian's *The Black Dog of Fate* (1998), are wonderful evocations of this mood of remembrance.

Here we confront a phenomenon of considerable interest to students of international politics. Jenny Edkins has spoken of 'trauma time' as that moment when through acts of remembrance, survivors of political violence refuse the 'normalizing' practice and narrative of the state.[52] The linearity of international politics since 1945 has been exploded by the fragmentation of warfare. Now it is no longer the case that organized violence is conducted primarily between states; war has 'degenerated' such that it is neither bounded by a state system nor by international law. Non-state actors attack states or other non-state actors, and in this kind of conflict, the Clausewitzian notion of war as politics by other means disintegrates. Violence tends to move rapidly out of the control of those initiating it, and since civilians both wage and suffer the consequences of this kind of war, the old rules of war, made manifest by the Geneva Conventions, no longer apply. It is hardly an accident that the United States has engaged in extra-legal treatment of detainees, and has used torture as a matter of course. The civil war within Islam has been disfigured by torture for decades. What has happened is that the cruelty and fanaticism of the Middle East has arrived in the centres of the international system, which created the conditions for this spiral of violence in the first place.

This ugly phase of international politics has produced witnesses by the thousands. Trauma time is today's time, and the voices of those whose lives have been scarred will be gathered and broadcast alongside the photographs of the atrocities they have suffered. Remembrance will entail nothing gentle; it will have no redemptive element to it, and a great deal of anger. No student of international politics will get very far without an understanding of this new set of memories, without a careful accounting of the multiple representations we see today about what happens to people in twenty first century warfare.

VII.   Conclusion

The over-determined character of the contemporary memory boom is its most striking characteristic. Each of the impulses to collective remembrance I have discussed in this chapter produced a set of commemorative practices; the fact that, for many reasons, so many people do this at one and the same time has turned a rivulet into a torrent.

Memory today has become a critical focus of cultural life. The turning point appears to have been in the 1970s, after decades of increasing affluence in the west, and when new forms of information technology emerged enabling many different groups to preserve and disseminate stories about their past and to locate them within what we have come to term identity politics. The notion of identity as a matter of construction and fragmentation was very familiar to those exposed to a kind of ecumenical psychoanalytic language. Such sensibilities may have found ways to express publicly emotions previously hidden or denied. Some have seen in these trends a shift in the boundaries between the public and the private, enabling men and women to grieve in public, and perhaps to escape from melancholia into a kind of mourning that could be circumscribed and transcended.

One of the challenges of the next decade or so is to try to draw together some of these disparate strands of interest and enthusiasm through a more rigorous and tightly-argued set of propositions about what exactly memory is, and what it has been in the past. The only fixed point at this moment is the near ubiquity of the term. No one should delude herself into thinking we all use it the same way. But just as we use words like love and hate without ever knowing their full or shared significance, so we are bound to go on using the term 'memory', the historical signature of several generations, including our own.

4

From Theodicy to *Ressentiment*

Trauma and the Ages of Compensation

Jeffrey K. Olick and Chares Demetriou

> History tells us that it is by no means a matter of course for the spectacle of misery to move men to pity; even during the long centuries when the Christian religion of mercy determined moral standards of Western civilization, compassion operated outside the political realm and frequently outside the established hierarchy of the Church ... Since then, the passion of compassion has haunted and driven the best men of all revolutions ... [1]

> Though non-Western history has had more than its own share of tragedy, of war, murder and devastation; though 1494 and 1789 may even be mere ripples on the surface of history if compared to the abject fate of the Aztecs, the American Indians or the unspeakable horrors that Mongol rule inflicted on Central Asia, it seems that only Western man was capable of a traumatic experience of history. [2]

> It is also true that risks are not an invention of modernity. Anyone who set out to discover new countries and continents – like Columbus – certainly accepted 'risks'. But these were personal risks, not global dangers like those that arise for all of humanity from nuclear fission or the storage of radioactive waste. In that earlier period, the word 'risk' had a note of bravery and adventure, not the threat of self-destruction of all life on Earth. [3]

I. Introduction

'Trauma' is of obvious interest to psychologists and human rights advocates, who are concerned, at the individual and aggregate levels respectively, with relieving and preventing suffering. Lately, it has become of great interest to historians as well. In their introduction to an important collection of essays, for instance, two leading historians of trauma have argued that 'the issue of trauma provides a useful entry into many complex historical questions and uniquely illuminates points of conjuncture in social, cultural, military, and medical history'.[4] Perhaps surprisingly given the emotional powers of the topic, key claims of this new historiography include at first glance quite dry comments, such as that '[t]here is an exact ratio between the level of the technology with which nature is controlled, and the degree of severity of its accidents' and that 'the industrialization process was [thus] reflected in accelerating accident rates and the new institutions such as liability laws and accident insurance policies which grew out of these'.[5] But the impression of dryness does not survive the first glance, for the historiography of trauma does indeed go to the very heart of the theory of modernity, establishing clear connections among industry, transportation, law, science, and social structure. As Wolfgang Schäffner has argued, the

> insurance-technical approach to trauma and accidents is part of a nonrepressive exercise of power, namely through stimulation and regulation. The normalization of nineteenth-century society that derives from extending police decrees and insurance regulations implies increased control of living conditions, a form of control that is an integral part of the social system.

As a result, Schäffner and others have pointed out, '[m]odern society, which the statistician Adolphe Quételet describes in 1848 ... as a probabilistic system, assumed canonical form in the system of accident insurance'.[6] Trauma, thus, is not only an unfortunate byproduct of modernity, but a central feature of it, and insurance, liability, and various forms of risk and compensation are remarkable prisms for theory.

Perhaps strange, then, that 'trauma' has not been nearly as central a topic for sociologists or scholars of international politics as it has been for historians, psychologists, or even literary critics, for whom it has been such a wellspring of innovative insights. Or perhaps not: in what follows, we argue that what 'trauma' does for cultural history, '*ressentiment*' does for social and political theory; that trauma and *ressentiement* are complimentary processes, the former an inner-directed, the latter an outer-directed manifestation of the same basic conditions; and that, taken together, 'trauma' and '*ressentiment*' map major transformations in how we understand history and our responsibility for it. In the first section of the essay, we review the theory of *ressentiment* through readings of its key figures – Friedrich Nietzsche, Max Weber, Max Scheler, and Hannah Arendt. Following this, we look at a number of theorists writing from the Second World War to the present under the influence of what they see as a new stage in the development of trauma and who, compellingly for our purposes, discuss whether this latest stage in trauma's biography – in which old remedies no longer give even the appearance of helping – has produced a new stage in the history of *ressentiment* as well.

One question that will emerge from this paired investigation is whether linking trauma to *ressentiment* brings our interest in trauma into disrepute, since *ressentiment* is generally considered an illegitimate reaction. Equally possible, however, is that linking them will *raise* the reputation of *ressentiment*, since suffering trauma generally evokes sympathy rather than the scorn one heaps on the person of resentment (indeed, *ressentiment* might even be a response, more or less legitimate, to the *ressentiment* of others). Given the widespread rise of reparations, restitution, and regret as coins of international politics in the face of epidemic trauma – and the possible association of these practices with a feeling of *ressentiment*, or the possibility that they may be a form of *ressentiment* politics – this kind of inquiry into *ressentiment's* origins, dynamics, and value is clearly a matter of some urgency. Are all demands for reparations and redress borne of *ressentiment*? And, if so, are they therefore illegitimate?

II. The theory of *ressentiment*

Nietzsche

The modern theory of *ressentiment* – and the widespread adoption of the term's francophone form[7] – obviously begins with Nietzsche. In brief, according to Nietzsche, originally the powerful generalized a distinction between good (themselves) and bad (others) into a moral distinction between good and evil. As Max Weber, to whose sociological development of *ressentiment* we will turn shortly, put it, '[w]hen a man who is happy compares his position with that of one who is unhappy, he is not content with the fact of his happiness, but desires something more, namely the right to his happiness, the consciousness that he has earned his good fortune, in contrast to the unfortunate one who must equally have earned his misfortune'.[8] What Nietzsche calls 'the slave revolt in morality' began when the Jews, a weak priestly caste, became jealous of the powerful and inverted the values being imposed on them. Just as the powerful seek legitimation of their privilege (by way of the dynamics identified by Weber), according to Nietzsche, 'every sufferer instinctively seeks a cause for his suffering'. The early Jewish solution, according to Nietzsche, then developed into the Christian doctrine that the meek shall inherit the earth: the implication is that privilege is attained only through guile and sin, and that suffering will be compensated. The weak thus revile the strong for their success and indict all their values: '... *ressentiment* defines such creatures who are denied genuine reaction, that of the deed, and who compensate for it through imaginary revenge'.[9]

At the heart of the matter is the problem of compensation. In the first place, Nietzsche points out, there is a close connection in German between the words for guilt (*Schuld*) and for debt (*Schulden*). The sense of guilt that slave morality foists upon the world – 'bad conscience' – developed in relation to the idea that every injury has its equivalent and that it can, in some way, be paid back, an idea which itself is rooted in the contractual, material relationship between creditor and debtor. Accordingly, an assumption developed whereby the injured, if not able to exercise immediate power over the perpetrator of his injury, gains a 'warrant for and title to cruelty'. While the desire for revenge is bad enough since the true noble 'Will' has no interest in others, this pro-duction of bad feelings in the perpetrators – and the demand for it when it does not come about automatically – is the fullest realization of slave morality, implicating master and slave alike. Both are caught in a per-petual torment that hinders true action and the liberating character of 'Will'. Memory of injury, in this regard, is the stumbling block to action, for both the noble soul, who is fettered by illegitimate claims, but especially for the victim, who cannot get past his injury: 'Willingness liberates; but what is it that puts even the liberator himself in fetters – "It was" – that is the name of the will's gnashing of teeth and most secret melancholy. Powerless against what has been done, he is an angry spec-tator of all that is past.' Making the connection between *ressentiment* and what we now know about trauma, Nietzsche concludes, 'He [the man of *ressentiment*] cannot break time and time's covetousness, that is the will's loneliest melancholy.'[10]

In present political circumstances, it thus seems that Nietzschean theory would classify all demands for reparation, redress, or regret as an expres-sion of *Ressentiment*, and hence consider them illegitimate.[11] Such demands seek a compensation that will never be adequate, and those who make politics out of pursuing such claims make themselves, and those they charge, slaves to what cannot be changed. Since that demand for compensation is morally charged, moreover, it is a poor imitation to revenge, which would be more noble because more honest. Reparation demands, as sublimated revenge from a position of weakness, are, we extrapolate from Nietzsche, the worst of all possible solutions. That it never satisfies is just further evidence against it.

Weber

If Nietzsche single-handedly invented the theory of *ressentiment*, it remained for others to develop and to sociologize it. Almost immediately, Max Weber began to do so, drawing out the important connection, to which we return later, to forms of theodicy, the explanation of evil and suffering. Theodicy, according to Weber, is part of every salvation religion that draws its members from disadvantaged classes. In Weber's analysis, *ressentiment* is a 'theodicy of disprivilege', an effort by ordinary people to come to terms with their position in a status and class hierarchy: '*Ressentiment* is a concomitant of that particular religious ethic of the disprivileged which, in the sense expounded by Nietzsche and in direct inversion of the ancient belief, teaches that the unequal distribution of mundane goods is caused by sinfulness and the illegality of the privileged, and that sooner or later God's wrath will overtake them.' As a result, Weber concludes, 'the moralistic quest serves as a device for compensating a conscious or unconscious desire for vengeance'. This compensation takes the form of a delayed reward:

> ... the sense of honor of disprivileged classes rests in some concealed promise for the future ... What they cannot claim to be, they replace by the worth of that which they will one day become, to which they will be called in some future life here or hereafter ... by their sense of what they signify and achieve in the world as seen from the point of view of providence.[12]

Disprivilege, then, is compensated by righteous indignation at oppressors, though tempered by confidence in redemption of suffering; worthiness of this redemption is thus demonstrated, as Nietzsche made clear in Book Three of *The Genealogy of Morals*, by asceticism, the intentional exacerbation of one's own suffering and hence the ultimate perversion of Will.

Nevertheless, Weber points out, it is clear that not every class has the same need for theodicy's compensations, nor will that need be constant over time. For instance, he claims, the urban middle classes, because of their distinctive pattern of economic practices, thought, and distance from nature, incline toward a rational religious understanding, as does, to a slightly lesser degree, the work ethic of the merchant and artisanal classes, who experience a more direct relationship between effort and reward than others.[13] The need for salvation, and for promises of it through theodicy, then, emerges largely among the disprivileged because the need for salvation grows out of some sort of distress; social and economic oppression are powerful sources of salvation beliefs. In contrast, the privileged require legitimation and self-confidence, while the need for salvation is more remote to them; again, injury and suffering (trauma) not only occur more frequently in the lower strata, but require the most complex compensations because their victims are without recourse other than theodicical; their only possibility for revenge is imaginary. We reserve for later the question of whether this social structure of theodicical need remains stable under the partially-democratizing influence of the railway accident, if industrial accidents and other sources of trauma, in contrast, are indeed *un*democratically distributed. One thinks here as well of Ulrich Beck's assertion, quoted at the top of this chapter, about the universalisation of risk in late modernity.

Scheler

While the theme of *ressentiment* was widespread in German social thought in the first decades of the twentieth century, the most significant development in the theory was that of Max Scheler – an apostate sociological disciple of the phenomenological philosopher Edmund Husserl – who published an extended essay entitled *Ressentiment* in 1912, and expanded it in 1914. As opposed to Weber's effort to connect *ressentiment* and theodicy in his sociology of religion, Scheler's approach was that of a sociologist of emotions concerned with the destructive effects of *ressentiment* on contemporary Man's psychic life. Scheler largely accepted and elaborated Nietzsche's ideas about *ressentiment* through his own socio-psychological observations, relating it to the concepts of revenge and envy. As a sociologist, however, and this time broadly in line with Weber, Scheler places the powerful emotions of revenge and envy, and their tendency to become *ressentiment*, in a social structural context, emphasizing the importance of social distance and mobility.

First, Scheler expostulates, the impulse for revenge leads to *ressentiment* the more it changes into actual vindictiveness, the more its direction shifts towards indeterminate groups of objects which need only share one common characteristic, and the less it is satisfied by vengeance taken on a specific object. Hence, the tendency of *ressentiment* is to become principled yet impersonal. In a later test of Scheler's theory, the Danish sociologist Svend Ranulf thus equated *ressentiment* with 'moral indignation' and with the 'disinterested disposition ... to assist in the punishment of criminals', which is embodied in law (such a disposition is far from universal; indeed, in many cultures it is incomprehensible why one who himself was not injured has any stake in the conflict).[14] Interestingly, when it is groups that hold *ressentiment*, what is decisive is the discrepancy between the political, constitutional or traditional status of the group and its factual power. Thus social *ressentiment* will be slight both in a democracy that features equality and in an extremely stratified yet legitimate system, such as India's caste system; conversely, social *ressentiment* is strongest in a system like ours, which proclaims but does not meet equal rights. Moreover, revenge tends to become *ressentiment* the more it is directed against lasting situations which are felt to be 'injurious' but beyond one's control. Thus Jewish *ressentiment* exemplifies both of the above points: on the one hand, there is a discrepancy between the pride of being the 'chosen people' and the experienced contempt and discrimination, while, on the other hand, the contempt and discrimination appear to be a lasting situation, a destiny.[15]

Second, according to Scheler, envy develops when a desire for an object that remains unfulfilled becomes hatred against the object's owner. Envy thus leads to '*ressentiment* when the coveted values are such as cannot be acquired and lie in the sphere in which we compare ourselves to others. The more powerless envy is also the most terrible. Therefore *existential envy*, which is directed against the other person's very *nature*, is the strongest source of *ressentiment*'.[16] There is, nevertheless, a psychological law that comes into play amidst the tension between desire and impotence and, up to a point, interferes with the development of *ressentiment*. It is the law, Scheler argues, that underpins the story of the fox and the sour grapes, that is a law of the release of tension through illusory valuation. Here, then, we do not have a falsification of values, but rather a new opinion about the qualities of the desired object; it is not that sweetness is bad, just that the grapes are sour. The values as such are acknowledged as before. Theodicy motives thus operate at the level of emotion as well as of politics, though they can be revolutionary or conservative.

Scheler's major point of dissent from Nietzsche, however, concerned the blame the latter assigned to Christian love, Nietzsche's identification of Christianity with humanitarianism (the doctrine of charity for the weak) and resultant condemnation of it as slave morality *par excellence*. A highly complex personality struggling with temptation and his own sense of sin, Scheler was a convert to Catholicism and thus believed that Nietzsche was wrong to implicate Christianity per se in *ressentiment*.

While Nietzsche is correct, Scheler argued, in his condemnation of humanitarianism, he was wrong to equate it with Christian love. Humanitarianism, Scheler followed Nietzsche in arguing, is the idea and movement of modern universal love of man, which means that its focus is on the sum total of human individuals – to such an extent, in fact, that it renders the love for any part of mankind, such as family or nation, an unjust deprivation to what we consider to belong to humanity. But nowhere in Christianity's vocabulary, Scheler inveighed, is the concept of mankind to be found; on the contrary, Christianity's primary concept, he claimed, is 'love your neighbor'. Besides having different objects of love, moreover, primitive Christian love and humanitarian love differ on the subjective side of the process of loving. 'Christian love', Scheler claimed, 'is primarily a spiritual *action* and *movement*, as independent of our body and senses as the acts and laws of thinking. Humanitarian love is a *feeling*, and a passive one, which arises primarily by means of psychical contagion when we perceive the outward expression of pain and joy'. Finally, the two differ also in the foundation of their valuation. Whereas what gives value to Christian love is the salvation of the lover's soul, the justification of humanitarian love is the advancement of 'general welfare'.[17] Despite Scheler's analysis, however, this disjunction between some originary Christian love and modern humanitarianism is fairly clearly elided in the present, where religious organizations are often at the forefront of humanitarian efforts.

Despite his imputed misreading of the two kinds of love, however, Nietzsche was right, Scheler believed, to argue that *ressentiment* was the root of the humanitarian idea. For the force in the development of this idea in modern times was not an affirmation of positive values, but a 'protest, a counterimpulse against ruling minorities that are known to possess positive values'. And along with that, humanitarianism is born out of *ressentiment* also *vis-à-vis* the idea of God: 'Bitterness against the idea of the highest lord, inability to bear the "all-seeing eye", impulses of revolt against "God" as the symbolic unity and concentration of all positive values and their rightful domination.' Moreover, humanitarian love was the 'manifestation of the inner protest and aversion against the immediate *circle* of the community and its inherent values – against the "community" which has physically and mentally formed a man'.[18] The latest form of this manifestation, Scheler argued, is the protest against patriotism and any organized political community, clearly a protest at the heart of contemporary tendencies to replace proximate identity forms (namely nations) with humanity in general. Humanitarianism – in this light the antithesis of sovereignty – is hostile to the very carriers of Will, to any genuinely creative impulse at all. Like a physician who gives up medicine for fear of malpractice claims or companies that stop making a product because of the liabilities involved, humanitarianism one might say drives the carriers of Will right out of business.

Arendt

Scheler's interpolation of Nietzsche has had a number of interesting afterlives. One of the most remarkable is in Hannah Arendt's essay *On Revolution* (1963), the writing of which obviously drew heavily on Scheler's book, though Arendt does not explicitly acknowledge it.[19] There Arendt reworked Scheler's critique of humanitarianism into a theory of revolution's violent worldview. In the first place, as demonstrated by the quote we placed at the top of this essay, though Arendt did not use the language of *ressentiment* she saw it as a uniquely modern principle that in turn underlay uniquely modern politics: 'The social question', she also wrote,

> began to play a revolutionary role only when, in the modern age and not before, men began to doubt that poverty is inherent in the human condition, to doubt that the distinction between the few, who through circumstances of strength or fraud had succeeded in liberating themselves from the shackles of poverty, and the laboring poverty-stricken multitudes, was inevitable and eternal.[20]

The central distinction she drew, then, was between the sense of compassion and that of pity – clearly related to Nietzsche's and Scheler's contrast between the noble morality which abjures reference to others and the slave morality caught in endless comparison. Compassion, for Arendt, is a genuine emotion that is specific and limited, inspired only by real individuals rather than expressed toward entire classes; its strength comes from the strength of emotion rather than from reason and thus remains ungeneralizable and unprincipled (being principled, in this context, would be a bad thing). Compassion, she concluded, is mute, or at least awkward with words. Because compassion abolishes distance, the public space in which politics matters, it remains without larger consequence or motive: 'if virtue will always be ready to assert that it is better to suffer than to do wrong, compassion will transcend this by stating in complete and even naïve sincerity that it is easier to suffer than to see others suffer'.[21]

In contrast to compassion, what Arendt calls 'pity' is loquacious, even eloquent. Pity, which she alternately claims has nothing whatsoever to do with compassion or is merely a perversion of it, works where compassion does not: 'Pity, because it is not stricken in the flesh and keeps its sentimental distance, can succeed where compassion will always fail; it can reach out to the multitude and therefore, like solidarity, enter the marketplace.' Nevertheless, this does not speak for pity's virtues: 'pity, in contrast to solidarity, does not look upon both fortune and misfortune ... and it therefore has just as much vested interest in the existence of the unhappy as thirst for power has a vested interest in the existence of the weak'.[22] For Arendt, the 'politics of pity', the desire to ameliorate, to use suffering as an excuse to seize power, underlies the revolutionary impulse as well as underwrites its violent, principled extremism. Where Nietzsche's revolt was against moral philosophy and he wrote that 'the sphere of legal obligations ... has really never quite lost a certain odor of blood and torture' and that 'the categorical imperative smells of cruelty', Arendt argues that '[p]ity, taken as the spring of virtue, has proved to possess a greater capacity for cruelty than cruelty itself'.[23]

III. Legacies of *ressentiment*

We take the politics of pity so much for granted today – we are all now humanitarians, are we not? – that it is easy to forget this powerful alternative tradition of critique. Arendt certainly appreciated the achievements of the French Revolution and valued the public discourse at which pity is so adept, but is not willingly content with the costs. Whether we call it the politics of pity, moral indignation, or *ressentiment*, it seems to motivate us to unimaginable horrors. From Nietzsche to Arendt, then, the central modern principle of legitimation – humanitarianism – seems ironically to be at the heart of our downfall; in the name of eliminating suffering and bettering ourselves, we have unleashed suffering on an unprecedented scale. Later, we will inquire into the difference implied here among the suffering inflicted in the name of revolution, the stochastic trauma of the railway accident, and the 'useless suffering' – to borrow a term from Emmanuel Levinas, whose contribution we will examine shortly – caused when revolutionary ideology combines with technology to reorder the world through industrial and scientific violence, and even threatens human self-abnegation.[24] Here it is enough to point out this strange inversion in the heart of our philosophical tradition, an inversion at odds with the dominant contemporary discourse of reparation and regret through which we seek to make up for the misdeeds of Will (pity).

Brown

It is interesting to note, then, that the kind of 'humanitarianism' in the dock here is not merely the extremism of the French revolutionary 'Terror', nor the total domination of National Socialism, but, some would argue, affects liberalism as well, even particularly. Humanitarianism, after all, sees itself as a liberal ideology, as liberalism sees itself as part of a humanitarian project. Indeed, this is the position of the American political theorist Wendy Brown, who is concerned that contemporary identity politics, with its emphasis on injustice and disadvantage, operates largely through accusation and the demand for redress. 'Identity politics', Brown thus writes, 'may be partly configured by a peculiarly shaped and peculiarly distinguished form of class resentment that is displaced onto discourses of injustice other than class, but a resentment, like all resentments, that retains the real or imagined holdings of its reviled subject as objects of desire.' The liberal solution to disenfranchisement, in other words, is inclusion in power. In order to achieve it, however, there must be a redistribution of power downwards, which means that the claim for equal freedom can be achieved only by violating the principle of freedom for the strong. The welfare state's progressive tax structure, some argue, penalizes the successful, thus not treating all equally; indeed, not only is this idea in some respects illiberal, but is often motivated by *ressentiment* against the powerful. Enfranchisement for the weak comes at the cost of freedom for the strong. The contradiction, thus, is not soluble within liberalism itself because, Brown argues, '[l]iberalism contains from its very inception a generalized incitement to what Nietzsche terms *ressentiment*, the moralizing vengeance of the powerless, "the triumph of the weak as weak" '.[25] Nietzschean thought, thus, does not only incline towards the right; in many ways, the theory of *ressentiment* raises much larger challenges to a theorist of the left, like Brown (though through all of these transformations, the left-right categorization is no longer so clear). Whether or not one agrees with Brown's diagnosis of liberalism or its strategies of compensation and redress, the combined weight of the tradition she brings to bear on the critique of liberalism should serve as a warning to our easy approval of redress as a strategy of humanitarian politics.[26] After all, it was not just Nietzsche, nor only guilty parties, who believe that too much memory can be the 'gravedigger of the present'. Even Paul Ricoeur, the suspicious hermeneutician, has recently asserted the value of forgetting.[27]

Améry

Brown also offers some intriguing sociological suggestions for explaining the rise of *ressentiment* in contemporary politics, to which we will return in our conclusion. Nevertheless, there remains one major moment in the literature on *ressentiment* of decisive importance, the argument of Jean Améry. Améry, who changed his name from Hans Maier when he felt his freedom of identity choice was being robbed by the Nuremberg racial laws, is important for two reasons. First, his essays make clear the connection between the socio- and psycho-dynamics of *ressentiment* and those of trauma, and second, and for our present purposes even more significant, because he makes a compelling case for the positive value of *ressentiment* in certain circumstances.

As a Holocaust survivor and torture victim, Améry makes the point that '[a]nyone who has been tortured remains tortured'. Indeed, this kind of removal from progressive temporality is the very heart of trauma. For Améry, it is the heart of *ressentiment* as well. In an intentionally provocative turn of phrase, he argues that *ressentiment* 'nails every one of us onto the cross of his ruined past. Absurdly, it demands that the irreversible be turned around, that the event be undone'. As a result, for Améry, 'Resentment blocks the exit to the genuine human condition, the future'. In this, then, he clearly agrees with Nietzsche's diagnosis, the burden of the 'it was'. In contrast to Nietzsche, Scheler, and Arendt, however, the connection between *ressentiment* and humanitarianism is perhaps not so clear in Améry:

> I know that the time-sense of the person trapped in resentment is twisted around, dis-ordered, if you wish, for it desires two impossible things: regression into the past and nullification of what happened ... For this reason the man of resentment cannot join in the unisonous peace chorus all around him, which cheerfully proposes: not backward let us look but forward, to a better, common future![28]

Humanitarianism, it seems, leans it two directions: too progressive, and too concerned with the past. Améry can abide neither.

Améry's putative *ressentiment*, and hence rejection of forward looking humanitarianism, thus has two sources: in the first place, it is the illegitimate ease with which the Germans, in whose midst he wanders, reject the obligations of their own past. His inability to move forward, he argues, is matched equally by his persecutors' excessive ease. Indeed, one can well imagine the sense Améry had, twenty years after his traumatic experience, that he was out of synch with the world around him and that the perpetrators were exacerbating his discomfort by moving more quickly, by relieving themselves of their burdens, more than they had a right to.

Second, however, Améry is also arguing with those fellow victims who claim they do not have the same resentments he does: not all of the desire to move forward came from perpetrators. In this regard, Améry was arguing particularly with Primo Levi, who believed more fully, perhaps, in the critique of *ressentiment*. Levi thus argued in his memoir of Améry that Améry's choice to fight against what he saw as premature forgetting 'led him to positions of such severity and intransigence as to make him incapable of finding joy in life, indeed of living'. In a classic condemnation of revenge and the *ressentiment* that motivates it, Levi wrote, '[t]hose who trade blows with the entire world achieve dignity but pay a very high price for it because they are sure to be defeated'.[29] Levi's attitude, one might say, is closer to the Sermon on the Mount – turn the other cheek – than it is to full blown *ressentiment*, a distinction possible only in Scheler rather than Nietzsche, though Levi does not express it in those terms. Nevertheless, as a result of this diagnosis, Levi claims, he was not at all surprised by Améry's suicide in 1978. By the same token, few commentators seemed surprised when Levi took his own life too.

What kind of *ressentiment*, then, did Améry suffer? Surely, in Nietzsche and Scheler's account, there is something similar to Marx's description of reification, the process whereby we suffer under systems of objective-seeming domination which nevertheless we ourselves created; in a way, it is possible that for *ressentiment* to have its full effect, one must remain unaware of it. And this Améry certainly was not. As such, he sought to take control of the idea, both theoretically and politically. 'My personal task', he thus wrote, 'is to justify a psychic condition that has been condemned by moralists and psychologists alike. The former regard it [*ressentiment*] as a taint, the latter as a kind of sickness. I must acknowledge it, bear the social taint, and first accept the sickness as an integrating part of my personality and then legitimize it.' Améry thus remains a 'vigilant' observer, and understands well why he wants what he wants: 'Self-confessed man of resentments that I am, I supposedly live in the bloody illusion that I can be compensated for my suffering through the freedom granted me by society to inflict injury'.[30] Despite an episode of having exchanged blows with a Polish guard in the concentration camp, and feeling empowered by this futile act of defiance, the blows Améry now exchanges are metaphorical, intellectual and institutional: 'The horsewhip lacerated me; for that reason, even I do not dare demand that the now defenseless thug be surrendered up to my own whip-swinging hand. [But] I want at least the vile satisfaction of knowing that my enemy is behind bars'. This is the only way, he believes, for his trauma to heal: 'Thereupon I would fancy that the contradiction of my madly twisted time-sense were resolved'.[31]

Améry's *ressentiment*, then, was a 'special kind ... of which neither Nietzsche nor Max Scheler was able to have any notion'.[32] In reaction, Améry argues that 'lazy' or 'cheap' forgiveness is a form of self-subjugation and amoral at its core. Subjugation to what? For previous theorists of *ressentiment*, and of trauma as well, the special nature of traumatic suffering is its disjuncture from natural time, which is 'actually rooted in the physiological process of wound-healing'. For Améry, submission to natural time under his special circumstances is immoral: 'Man has the right and privilege', Améry claims, meaning *he* has the right and privilege, 'to declare himself to be in disagreement with every natural occurrence, including the biological healing that time brings about. What happened, happened. This sentence is just as true as it is hostile to morality and intellect'. In these unusual circumstances, '[t]he moral person demands annulment of time – in the particular case under question, by nailing the criminal to his deed'.[33] The message here, it is important to note, is both therapeutic and political: this moral refusal to submit to time is essential for healing the victim's trauma; by the same token, Améry argues, this kind of refusal also performs 'a historical function'.

Levinas

Améry's is clearly a highly complex position, not necessarily consistent with the tradition of critique nor internally with itself. One might even doubt that it is *ressentiment* exactly that he is suffering, since his demand for justice is not disinterested. Or perhaps his case is so bad that he is unable to see it as clearly as he claims. The major difference between the conditions of Améry's theory and that of his predecessors, however, is the nature of his injury, not just the injuries to his body and soul, but to his ability to hope for a tolerable social existence. However horrible the French revolutionary terror or the anonymous death of the railway accident, something important has changed in the possible meaning of the suffering represented by the Holocaust. While 'uselessness' or 'senselessness' has always been a feature of suffering, the difference now is that there are no longer any compensations, even illusory, for useless suffering, which reached its apotheosis in the gas chamber. Perhaps this is why *ressentiment* is not just a syndrome or weakness for Améry, but his only recourse. This, at any rate, is the position implied by the theories of Emmanuel Levinas, a Lithuanian-born Jewish philosopher, also a student of Husserl and later of Martin Heidegger, who lost most of his family in the Holocaust.

Following Nietzsche, Levinas has argued that people want to believe evil has some intention and direction behind it, that injury is somehow connected to malice. But as Améry pointed out, '[t]he atrocity as atrocity has no objective character. Mass murder, torture, injury of every kind are objectively nothing but chains of physical events ... They are facts within a physical system, not deeds within a moral system'.[34] In Levinas' language, this means that our capacity to cope with suffering has been dramatically altered. According to Levinas, theodicy, the desire to save morality in the name of faith or to make suffering bearable, still existed 'in a watered down form at the core of atheist progressivism which was confident, nonetheless, in the efficacy of the Good which is immanent to being, called to visible triumph by the simple play of natural and historical laws of injustice, war, misery, and illness'.[35] Nevertheless, Levinas argues, '[p]erhaps the most revolutionary fact of our twentieth century consciousness ... is that of the destruction of all balance between explicit and implicit theodicy in Western thought and the forms suffering and its evil take in the very unfolding of this century'. If Nietzsche preferred to say God is dead, Levinas points out that we tried but failed to save him:

> This is the century that has known two world wars, the totalitarianisms of right and left, Hitlerism and Stalinism, Hiroshima, the Gulag, and the genocides of Auschwitz and Cambodia. This is the century which is drawing to a close in the haunting memory of the return of everything signified by these barbaric names: suffering and evil are deliberately imposed, yet no reason sets limits to the exasperation of a reason become political and detached from all ethics.

For Levinas, 'the disproportion between suffering and every theodicy was shown at Auschwitz with a glaring, obvious clarity'.[36] The fundamental philosophical problem for Levinas is thus whether there can be any morality and faith after this end of theodicy. Levinas' project, then, is to rescue theodicy from history and sociology – a difficult task indeed.

IV. 'Ressentiment' and the account of modernity

The conceptual history we have undertaken in the foregoing pages has been motivated by our sense that *ressentiment* and trauma are related aspects of a single discursive universe. This was particularly clear in Améry, though also in the other authors, who emphasized both the origins of *ressentiment* in suffering and the temporal disruptions that characterize its operation. Nevertheless, it is important to point out that the differences among the authors are not just disputes over how to define an ideal type but are also differences of history and context, which shape the conditions both for the operation and epidemiology of *ressentiment* as well as for theorizing about it (the same applies to trauma as well).

Is it really appropriate to parse the definitional peculiarities of Nietzsche versus Améry? Or is something more sociological and historical required? In conclusion, we explore some of the resources we have at our disposal to answer this question, and sketch an as yet highly speculative theoretical account as a first gesture to redeeming the promise identified by the historians of trauma we quoted at the beginning: the unique potential of the history of the concept of trauma – and by the implication we hope we redeemed, in the foregoing, of *ressentiment* as well – for the sociological account of modernity. Such an account, it must be added, fits squarely with the current Westphalian order and its unfolding contradictions. Is it not the case, after all, that legitimation in modern times oscillates irresolutely between humanist and nationalist claims, between recourse to the rights of man and to the rights of states? Modern world order has not yet provided a global system to appease collective national insecurities, despite some regional progress.

Indeed, some scholarly accounts link the processes of modern internationalism to *ressentiment* and trauma explicitly. According to Wendy Brown, for instance, a number of related processes have brought us to our contemporary interest in reparations and redress and have suffused them with the odor of *ressentiment*. In her view, these include: first, 'increased global contingency' combined with 'the expanding pervasiveness and complexity of domination by capital and bureaucratic state and social networks' which have intensified the sense of 'impotence, dependence, and gratitude inherent in liberal capitalist orders and constitutive of *ressentiment*'. Second, she points to the impact of secularization and 'desacralization', which undermine the ability of Nietzsche's ascetic priests to cause guilt and depravity not only in the disprivileged but in the powerful as well. And third, redolent of Weber, she highlights the destruction of intermediate associations as protectors of the isolated individual from the inability of liberalism to follow through on its promise to protect individuals.[37]

Each of these explanations certainly contributes to the overall picture of the rise of *ressentiment* in and with modernity, particularly within liberalism, though we can think of a number of other contributory processes as well, including dynamics not addressed within the universe of this Weberian scheme of rationalization, secularization, and atomization. Emile Durkheim's account of the rise of individualism, for instance, provides, we believe, a still-convincing account of the non-contractual elements of contractual obligation necessary for a complex commercial system. As the division of labour in European societies increased, according to Durkheim, these societies saw the progressive disappearance of segmentary organization (according to Scheler, the kind of social organization least conducive to *ressentiment*). The increasing efficiencies of industrial production also required vast new supplies of labour, which meant that people migrated into cities, leaving behind their taken-for-granted social solidarities.[38] With large numbers of different people with different traditions, different languages, different stories, and different jobs living next to each other, individualism became the predominant ideology and common sense, requiring new forms of exchange, standardization, and commensuration.[39] In commerce as well, a new moral universe was necessary, because contractual relationships multiply as the division of labour increases and segmentation declines. But in order for contracts to be binding, there needs to be an agency of enforcement. This agency is both institutional – the law and its agent, the state – as well as cultural, what Durkheim again calls the 'non-contractual elements of contractual obligation', which involve such intangibles as trust and an expectation of recourse. In this way, new commercial arrangements not only give rise to the statistical gaze described by Quetelet (discussed in our first paragraph) but to the institutions of compensation. According to Durkheim, restitutory law, in contrast to penal law, is the hallmark of a complex society.[40] In our view, this kind of an explanation goes a long way to explicating the relations between institutions of compensation and the rising experience of trauma, which authors like Wolfgang Schivelbusch have explained in terms of the denaturalization of temporal experience with the advent of mechanized travel: 'In the railroad journey, the traditional experience of time and space was demolished the way the individual experience of battle in the Middle Ages is abolished in the modern army (and the individual craft activity is abolished in manufacturing and industrial production)'.[41]

Durkheim's and Schivelbusch's accounts contribute, we believe, a great deal to the sociology of trauma, rather than merely to the descriptions and diagnoses we outlined above. But clearly they do best with a particular point in time, the late nineteenth century, just as Levinas and Ulrich Beck do better with the twentieth century. Yet other theories – not least Hannah Arendt's account of the rise of ideology in the French revolution – do better for earlier periods, though it seems useful to treat these theories as explaining different moments in an overall process. Other theories, moreover, date the seminal stages of this process even earlier than Arendt. Nietzsche's theory is vaguely ancient in reference – though neither historical nor sociological. Discussions of theodicy often go back to the Book of Job and then spend a great deal of time and attention, for the obvious reason that this is the source of the term, with Leibniz's 1710 treatise, *Theodicy*, and then Voltaire's scathing satire *Candide* after the Lisbon earthquake of 1755, in which Voltaire's Leibniz – defender of God at all costs, in face of all reason, by explaining evil as the 'best of all possible worlds' – earns the name Pangloss, which subsequently becomes an adjective (panglossian) for excessive, even stupendous, optimism. Something clearly happened between the world for which Leibniz was really too late, and the one Voltaire helped articulate.

One further set of theories deserves at least brief mention here – namely those that address the decline of religious eschatology that prepared the rise of rationalism and the birth of modernity – because they describe clear preparations a century earlier for the ideas Arendt identified as operative in the French Revolution and Weber and Scheler, among others, found operative at the end of the nineteenth century. Reinhart Koselleck, for instance, writes that before the modern era '[t]he future as the possible end of the World is absorbed within time by the Church as a constituting element, and thus does not exist in a linear sense at the end point of time. Rather, the end of time can be experienced only because it is always-already sublimated in the Church'. In contrast, '[t]he experience in a century of bloody struggles was, above all, that the religious wars did not herald the Final Judgment ... this disclosed a new and unorthodox future'. There is thus a stark contrast between a world of prophecy, in which 'events are merely symbols of that which is already known', where 'apocalyptic prophecy destroys time through its fixation on the End', and one of prognosis, which 'produces the time within which and out of which it weaves'.[42]

Combining this attention to the crisis of eschatology with a consideration of technological factors, Lutz Niethammer describes a similar decline of existential security with the invention of the prognosticative chronotype:

> It eventually became apparent that there were worldly reasons to change the basic conditions of existence and to detach them from the cyclicity of nature. Once new discoveries burst the limits of the world, and trade, technology, and institutionalized relations of power

> freed part of society from direct ties with the sequences of nature, elements of total explanation of the world could be transferred from the jurisdiction of salvationist history to the scientific processing of experience ... Out of the various histories through which men and women reached agreement over the origins and institutions of their group ... a new universal history had to come into being, with a perspective that would provide an understanding of the cosmos to replace the religious world-view.[43]

This account thus synthesizes the religious explanation with technological factors and the increased capacity for abstract thought due to the spread of print culture, which theorists like Benedict Anderson have described.[44] It offers a powerful explanation for the rise of philosophies of history in the nineteenth century, as well as for the more mundane institutionalization of empirical historical discourse.

Interestingly, the philosopher of history Frank Ankersmit reverses the causal logic of this account, though in the processes reinforcing the association. According to Ankersmit, quoted at the top of the chapter, the susceptibility to collective trauma cannot be explained by the objective qualities or amounts of pain and suffering. (In this regard, Ankersmit must disagree with Levinas, who seems to place a great deal of explanatory weight on the nature of the injuries – or accumulation of injuries – in the twentieth century). Ankersmit suggests that '[i]n the West a shift may be observed from collective pain to an awareness of this pain and ... this is how this peculiar Western capacity for suffering collective trauma originated'. As such, Ankersmit reinforces Niethammer's attribution of causal power to the rise of abstract thought. In this sense, Améry's positive existential valuation of resentment is part of thinking made possible by the modern capacity to translate suffering into trauma. In Ankersmit's sketch, moreover, '[t]he historian's language originates in the "logical space" between traumatic experience and a language that still had a primordial immediacy and directness in its relationship to the world – and that pushes this language aside'.[45] Here, however, one can note the limits of the entailed logical links in providing moral history. Améry's hold on resentment reminds us of just that, as it renders both progressive temporality and modernity's downplaying of primoridalism to be inefficient contexts for rehabilitating the trauma of the Holocaust.

It is unclear to us whether Ankersmit thinks traumatic consciousness gives rise to History, or whether he is implying that both are caused by a wider set of transformations. It also seems plausible to make the case that historical consciousness *preceded* traumatic consciousness and that the linear, progressive temporality of History – and its individual corollary, biography – are part of the conditions that increase the likelihood of trauma and traumatic interpretations of suffering (this is certainly clear in Arendt's account of the politics of pity). This discussion of the rise of progressive temporality, which instructs individuals as well as collectivities how to understand their experience, is obviously one of the conditions for the experience of trauma because it is precisely this capacity that is disrupted by the kinds of experiences one has in industrial civilization.

Here, then, is yet further support for the belief that trauma is a novel modern disease, though two caveats must be stressed. First, the argument here is that the interpretive category – progressive temporality – gives rise to the syndrome rather than that the syndrome – trauma – gives rise to a new framework of interpretation. And second, being far from uniform, the process of modernity presents limits, even contradictions, to the moral repercussions of trauma. Given that the discovery of equivalence is still expanding conceptually and geographically – statutory law, described by Durkheim as national law, has only partially turned into international law, whereas the latter has hardly included with any efficacy broader moral claims, at least until very recently – trauma became politically relevant in world politics without as yet having become a strong norm.

Finally, we take no small inspiration from the account of German philosopher Odo Marquard who, following Vico, traces the history of compensatory culture as follows: 'First, in the age of religion, God sat in judgment over humankind; then, in the age of theodicy, humankind sat in judgment over God; finally, in the age of critique, humankind sat in judgment over itself.' This latest stage, according to Marquard – following Nietzsche – involves what he calls an 'overtribunalilzation' of history, not a positive condition. In Marquard's account, three new philosophies – the philosophy of history, philosophical anthropology, and philosophical aesthetics – which all emerged in the period after about 1750, are efforts 'to compensate for a human loss of "life-world" '. They are, he says, 'attempts to compensate for this overtribunalization by an "escape into unindictability" '.[46] Nevertheless, it is clear from the conceptual history we undertook above that this escape has been temporary and that judgment day has arrived, if it is now a self-judgment – and indeed condemnation – of Man by Man. Following Marquard, the older compensatory systems no longer suffice. Insurance and reparation are rather thin shoulders to carry the burdens of theodicy, though it is interesting that in the wake of the January 2005 South Asian tsunami, it was governments and industry in the dock, not God.

V.   Conclusions

In conclusion, we offer a somewhat more differentiated historical typology, before flagging the implications of this body of thought for contemporary politics, domestic as well as international. First, the end of eschatology gave rise to linear temporality and History, thus placing Man at the center of the moral universe. As a result, and because of the concomitant decline of supernatural beliefs (matched by what Weber has to say about the social location of Salvationism, which does not attract the new middle class), theodicy lost its efficacy (witness again Voltaire's response to Leibniz). Second, this centering of Man in History gave rise to the revolutionary ethos sketched by Arendt, in which humanitarianism provides powerful tools with which to vent *ressentiment*. Here redemption comes through a vision of the future, which provides *ressentiment* with a constructive goal.[47] Third, rise of industry and speed generated a new kind of randomness to injury coupled with a denaturalization of temporal experience in travel and electronic communications (i.e. telegraphy). The stochastic nature of these injuries gave rise to a new form of outrage – why me! – because of the obvious amoral quality to the injury; it is no longer possible to believe, in any but the most illusory or metaphorical fashion, in just desert. Combined with the 'statistical' worldview that arises to confront and control this randomness, insurance, psychiatry, and law collude to generate a new moral universe of compensation. This connection between modern injury and rational compensation is also expressed in the dehumanizing experience of mechanical death in the First World War and in the social welfare programs that states developed – first and foremost to care for veterans – in its wake. And finally, 'useless suffering' reaches its apotheosis in the middle of the twentieth century, with the stunning combination of genocide in the heart of Europe and the capacity for the nuclear self-abnegation of humankind. What possible compensations could there be left to the cowering individual, who has learned to internalize risk as a basic feature of personality?

In sum, we have moved, we propose, through a developmental trajectory characterized by the progression (decline?) from eschatology and theodicy, to revolution, to accident (which used to mean coincidence) and insurance, through therapy to reparation. In this light, it seems as if ours is the proper age – as implied by Améry – for *ressentiment*. What kind of money is there left that isn't blood money? *Ressentiment* is only a delusion and weakness if we do not embrace and understand it, as Améry seems to have done. As a result, we worry less than Brown and others that the demand for reparations as part of identity politics and international relations is an undesirable, even sordid attitude.

Part II

5

Remembering Relationality
Trauma Time and Politics
Jenny Edkins

> I have nothing to say – no words
> stronger than the steel that pressed you into itself; no scripture
> older or more elegant than the ancient atoms you
> have become.
> And I have nothing to give either – except this gesture,
> this thread thrown between your humanity and mine:
> *I want to hold you in my arms* and as your soul got shot
> of its box of flesh to understand, as you have done, the wit
> of eternity: its gift of unhinged release tearing through
> the darkness of its knell.
> > Toni Morrison, 13 September 2001[1]

I. Introduction

Memories of traumatic events can be seen, to borrow Toni Morrison's phrase, as a 'thread thrown' between the dead and those who survive: to hold the dead in our arms is an impossible gesture of solidarity and compassion in the face of 'the wit of eternity'.[2] What is being remembered, or perhaps more accurately re-constituted, is relationality, that radical interconnectedness that has been so shockingly betrayed in and through the violence of trauma. In one sense, it seems that it is not so much death that is traumatic as survival, or at least survival in the face of particularly brutal or incomprehensible deaths. Morrison's poem reminds us how those killed on 11 September disappeared. No remains were found: those who died became nothing more, or less, than 'ancient atoms'. They became dust, breathed in by their fellow New Yorkers.[3] Earlier in the poem she reminds us how by the time her words were composed the deaths of 9.11 had already become entangled in talk of 'nations, wars, leaders, the governed and the ungovernable ... armour and entrails'. She seeks to 'freshen' her tongue, 'abandon sentences crafted to know evil – wanton or studied; explosive or quietly sinister; whether born of a sated appetite or hunger; of vengeance or the simple compulsion to stand up before falling down'. Instead she addresses the dead in terms of a relationality that has nothing to do with 'blood', 'a false intimacy' or 'an overheated heart'. It is a relationality in the face of death's 'gift of unhinged release'.[4]

The connection between memory and a radical relationality that trauma betrays is the subject of this chapter. I shall seek to demonstrate how this link can be central to thinking about international politics, and particularly to rescuing it from its confinement in talk of nations, wars and leaders. In the face of terrorist attacks it has become increasingly clear that those who suffer such assaults are precisely not nations or leaders, but people: it is people, in their physicality and their vulnerability, that experience the trauma, both bodily and psychic, and it should be to them that the memories belong.[5] Memories of trauma are, potentially, a mode of resistance to a language that forgets the essential vulnerability of flesh in its reification of state, nation and ideology. What this chapter presents, then, is an argument that addresses the relationalities at stake in memory, and traumatic memory in particular. This radical relationality is what national and international politics, so poorly named in these hegemonic terms, should more properly be about.

At the end of the twentieth century and the beginning of the twenty-first century, the memory of the organized violence of genocides, slaveries, wars, famines, and latterly terrorism has become an important site of political investment. Writers in cultural studies, comparative literature, anthropology, history and sociology are involved in analysing not only the commemoration of such events,[6] but also the practices of retribution, recovery and reconciliation that follow in their wake.[7] The concerns of politics, and particularly of international politics, have always been at the forefront of these debates, which is not surprising considering the subject matter such discussions centre around. A number of authors focus specifically on the memory of wars,[8] or genocides;[9] others examine the relation between collective memory and cultural or national identity.[10] Some focus on the way in which memories are used to shape state policy, both domestic and foreign.[11] The wealth of interest in memory outside academia has been noted, and it has even been argued, somewhat unconvincingly, that the increasing emphasis placed on memory is symptomatic of a victim culture and provides evidence not of concern but selfishness.[12] Some of the contributors to this volume, however, concur that the current interest in and emphasis on memory has its limitations.[13]

In this chapter, I want to suggest the opposite. I shall argue that an analysis of memory and particularly traumatic memory can be central to an understanding of forms of political authority. In other words, the study of memory and commemoration is even more important than it appears. It is not a self-contained topic: memory is not an add-on to the study of politics. Memory, and the form of temporality that it generally instantiates and supports, is central to the production and reproduction of the forms of political authority that constitute the modern world.[14] It is not just that ceremonies of remembrance are supportive of nationalist sentiment, or that heroic narratives are fundamental to the imagined community that is the western, imperial nation.[15] It is not a question of identity in other words. It is rather that the form of political authority that the nation represents is intimately tied up with, and made possible by, the way in which it invokes its memories, and with what it remembers and why. A study of practices of memory thus provides an insight into political community, and the forms of temporality and subjectivity that necessarily accompany contemporary forms of political authority. This chapter will propose an approach to memory that involves a study of time or temporality, and the way in which time is implicated in politics. Thinking about practices of memory is a way of thinking about notions of time.

Questions of time and temporality do not only relate to political authority – or to forms of power relation – they also relate to the question of resistance. The way in which events such as wars, genocides and famines are remembered is fundamental to the production and reproduction of centralized political power. However, memory is central not only to the production of these forms of power but also to their contestation: certain types of memory, the memory of catastrophic events, for example, provide specific openings for resistance to centralized political power. Ways of remembrance then are not only a site of political investment but also a site of struggle and contestation. What is at stake is the continuing existence of a particular form of power relation: sovereign political authority.

In this chapter I discuss why this is the case, and how examining the relationship between memory and the political can be helpful in understanding both. I consider what it is that is specific about memories of wars, genocides and famines that leads to these consequences, and what this can tell us about contemporary national and international forms of political authority. I pay particular attention to the way in which memory provides openings for resistance and consider what might count as opposition in contemporary global politics. In the discussions that follow, I draw on examples from my research on memory and traumatic memory in the aftermath of 11 September 2001 to illustrate the arguments being made.[16]

The question at stake is what memory has to do with politics, particularly international or post-colonial politics. It is widely accepted that 'memories' can be used to further particular political and global political aims, and that 'memory' influences the actions of particular actors in world politics, including elites. It is recognized that the way in which memories are exploited can be crucial in the construction of nationhood and in cultures of nationalism. However, the question as interpreted here is a much broader one. This chapter is concerned to explore the extent to which what we call politics, and the form of authority that is generally regarded as legitimate in the contemporary world, relies on a particular conception of time and a certain form of 'memory', and how these settled understandings can be and are being challenged, particularly through what are called 'traumatic memories'.

To address this question, the first part of the chapter begins by examining notions of subjectivity and the political in two bodies of work that can be fruitfully juxtaposed: Lacanian psychoanalysis, specifically Lacanian notions of subjectivity and the social order, and Derrida's thinking on politics and ethics in his work on the force of law and responsibility. Lacan and Derrida both take radical relationality as central. The allusions to trauma and traumatic memory contained in these two bodies of work are identified in this discussion. The second part turns to the question of what we call trauma and traumatic memory specifically. Work on trauma, particularly that of Cathy Caruth, is read alongside Lacan and Derrida, and the political implications of trauma theory are drawn out. Practices of traumatic memory can be considered as potentially both productive and destructive of sovereign power. The notion of 'trauma time' as the time of the political is introduced. It is argued that trauma can be seen as betrayal (both in the sense of giving away and of revealing radical relationality) and that the concept of trauma can usefully be extended to the idea of indistinction. In the third part Foucauldian notions of power relations, resistance and sovereign power, particularly as elaborated and expanded by Giorgio Agamben, are discussed. Agamben's work on distinction/indistinction leads back to the questions of radical relationality with which we began and a further examination of the possibility of resistance. Finally, in the conclusion, Derrida's notions of futurity, friendship and the ethico-political bring the discussion back to the question of the present time as an impossible political moment, which memory, of 'the future' or 'the past', obliterates.

II. Subjectivity and political order

Lacanian notions of subjectivity and social order

When psychoanalytic perspectives are used in political analysis, the question often arises as to whether the individual level of analysis is appropriate for a discussion of the collective, seen as synonymous with the political.[17] However, the approach taken here, drawing on Lacanian thinking, is one that refuses the distinction between the individual and the social.[18] Lacanian analysis is not, I contend, best understood as situated within a framework, or at a level, of the individual. In many ways it does not make sense to talk of the level of the individual as a starting point: the idea of the pre-existing individual is rather a product of particular representations of the world. In the discussions here, psychoanalytic concepts will be used to theorize *the political*, and in particular *political community*, but community will not be treated as something that is made up of a collection of separate individuals, in the manner of much political theorizing. Indeed many of the problems of political theory arise precisely because it makes this separation in the first place. Once a separation is assumed, the political question becomes: how do people join together to form communities? Beginning rather with a view of the subject or person that sees the subject and the social as mutually constituted, neither one coming before the other but both being produced together, leads in different directions. In this view, the social, or society, is brought into being by a precipitate gesture, an act that assumes that the social already exists. This constitutive act brings into being the social at the same time as it produces within the social a place for the subject. The subject only exists in relation to other subjects and in relation to language or the symbolic or social order.

The Lacanian account provides several takes on this relationality. In the first place, the subject, or strictly speaking what will become the subject but at this stage is undifferentiated, sees itself in the eyes of other subjects. To these other eyes, it appears to be whole, complete, separate and individual. This is what Lacan calls the mirror stage[19] The subject mistakes this image for reality, and continues thereafter to look for an imaginary wholeness. Later, the subject encounters the symbolic order, a framework within which there are always already a series of subject positions that can be occupied. However, none of these positions will provide a place that fully 'fits' the subject: there will always be a lack or an excess. Finally, the symbolic order, or language, is itself incomplete or partial. There is always something that a language cannot quite express, and what language does express is never quite fully expressed, so that again there is a lack or an excess. This reflects what psychoanalysis calls the real.[20] In this view, which draws on psychoanalytic and specifically Lacanian approaches, both the subject and the social order are radically incomplete or impossible: they are structured around a lack or an antagonism.[21]

In this view, and importantly for the discussion of trauma that follows, what we call 'social reality' is more accurately thought of as social fantasy. In this fantasy, the social world is complete, contained and secure. It appears as though we have the answer to most of the questions we need to ask, or at least we are happy (or pretend to be happy) to assume that we do. We choose to *forget* those that we have no answers to – the awkward questions about life, death, survival. Once the social order is in place, these questions disappear: they can no longer be seen. What we call social reality is structured around what Lacanians call a 'master signifier', something that conceals the lack or the excess, and provides answers to awkward questions: God, the Nation, Communism, the Jew, for example.[22] When the master signifier is in place, the lack or antagonism around which the subject and the social order are constituted is concealed or hidden: they are *forgotten*. In retrospect, retroactively, it appears that the social order has always existed, or rather that there is some completely plausible account of why it exists in the form it does. The social order is held together by the 'master signifier', which quilts the sliding signifiers and makes sense of the whole social field. In the past 'God' has fulfilled this role, or 'science'. The 'nation' has a similar symbolic function. A narrative comes into being that can explain everything, and that gives no space for the lack: the social field is totalized and made to appear impregnable.

The force of law and responsibility

In Derridean thinking we find similar ideas expressed somewhat differently. Derrida draws our attention to what he calls 'the mystical foundation of authority'.[23] In his essay on the force of law, he points out that the law has an intimate relation to force or violence in two distinct ways. First, law has to be enforced: the very notion of the law implies the ability by what we call the state to use force to make sure that the law is obeyed, and, importantly, makes that force or violence appear to be legitimate. Generally, perhaps because its legitimacy is not challenged, the violence that is an inherent part of the state as a form of authority or type of power – sovereign power as we shall see it called later – goes unrecognized and unquestioned. Second, the violence of the law becomes visible in the moment in which the state and the legal system that accompanies it are founded. This is what Derrida calls a non-founded founding moment: a moment that is foundational (it marks the beginning of the new state, after a war or a revolution) but that in itself has no foundations.[24] It cannot justify itself. There is nothing that provides a legitimating framework at the moment of foundation: the legal system that the state will produce is not yet in existence. Those who will lead the state appear still as revolutionaries, terrorists or guerrilla fighters.

Of course, as soon as the new state is established, it begins the process of producing a point of origin, through a legitimating narrative that takes the form of a heroic memory of struggle, the violence of which appears both inevitable and justified in relation to the foundation of the new authority. At this point ceremonies of remembrance come in: they tell tales of sacrifice for the greater good, for the community. Of course the sacrifice is on behalf of a community that the narrative itself produces: a community that only comes into being after the fact as it were; a community that only ever *will have been*, to use a Lacanian phrase.[25] If the revolution or the coup fails, then those involved remain terrorists; they are executed or imprisoned.

This mystical foundation of authority does not only occur at dramatic points such as the foundation of states in the aftermath of wars. The system of laws that is put in place by the *coup de force* of state foundation has a complex relation to the question of the ethico-political act and to justice. Although the social order may appear to dictate actions that should be taken, or at least to affirm what actions should be considered appropriate or just, this is not in fact the case. The social order and its legal rules are pitched at a level of generality; they are meant to be applicable to all manner of cases. However, once it becomes a question of specific action in particular circumstances, then the rules are not quite so clear. Questions always arise as to which rule is applicable, to what extent and how, in any particular case. According to Derrida it is never clear after the action whether the rules have been merely applied, in which case what has happened is a technology, a mere application of rules or formulaic action, or whether rules have been invented or re-invented. There is something like a black hole which has been gone through – or what Derrida calls an aporia – the aporia of the undecidable. Looking back, it is impossible to tell whether there has been an ethico-political decision or whether, on the other hand, there has been a technical action, involving no ethics, politics, or justice.

For an action to involve ethics, politics or justice, for Derrida, it must be an action that is radically groundless or unsecured, without foundation in law or practice. It must involve what is called a decision. This is not a choice, because choice is between two or more possibilities that are presented within already given frameworks. A decision is something radically different. It involves the invention of a rule, or the presupposition of the social order and hence its production in new ways, to use the Lacanian terminology.[26]

Once the action has taken place, it is literally impossible to know whether what has taken place is an action that is without grounds, or whether, alternately, the action is merely rule following, because, once the action has happened, if it has, it will have produced its own grounds. Again we have a strange reverse or retroactive temporality, the production of a ground after the event, which we saw in the case of the Lacanian production of the social order and of subjectivity. Both are produced together and both *only ever will have been*. In the following section, these ways of thinking the political and social order are used alongside and linked with a discussion of trauma and traumatic memory.

III. Traumatic memory and sovereign power

From the discussion so far, we have seen that in psychoanalytic approaches the subject and the social order (what we call social reality) are always incomplete or structured around a lack. This lack is concealed, hidden, or forgotten, by the ideological field or fantasy that is centred on a 'master signifier'. From Derrida we can add to this the way in which this forgetting conceals not just a lack but violence. The violence that takes place when a new social reality or a new symbolic or legal system is established is forgotten. This violence is often very real: wars, revolutions and genocides often accompany the founding of new forms of sovereign authority. From Derrida, we also have the notion of the political moment as a moment that has to go through the aporia of undecidability: anything less than an encounter with traumatic ungroundedness is not an ethics or a politics but a technology.

Already, in both these thinkers, we can discern the idea of trauma: as the traumatic lack around which the subject is structured in Lacan, and as the aporetic or traumatic moment of decision at the heart of the political in Derrida. We also find in these approaches the idea of traumatic memory, or, rather, the way in which the traumatic moment is forgotten, or indeed is invisible. This can be linked to work more specifically focussing on trauma, to which we will turn now.

Trauma

What does it mean to call something 'traumatic'? The term indicates the response to a shock encounter with brutality or death, or, as Cathy Caruth puts it, 'an overwhelming experience of sudden or catastrophic events, in which the response to the event occurs in the often delayed and uncontrolled repetitive occurrence of hallucinations and other intrusive phenomena'.[27] It is 'the confrontation with an event that, in its unexpectedness and horror, cannot be placed within the schemes of prior knowledge'.[28]

In this notion of trauma are two ideas we have already come across in the discussion of subjectivity, social authority and the political. First we have the idea of a distortion of temporality: a retroactivity in which trauma is not experienced at first, in the present, but only afterwards. Second, there is the idea that what we call traumatic is an event that cannot be placed within prior schemes or frameworks. It is a confrontation with an occurrence that is not part of the symbolic order and hence that cannot be predicted or accounted for: there is no language for it.

In this sense, trauma can never be a purely individual event, in the same way as there cannot be a private language, because it always already involves the community or the cultural setting in which people are placed. I will return to this in a moment. First, I want to pursue the question of memory and forgetting in relation to trauma, and introduce the notion of 'trauma time' as the time of the political.

Trauma time

Trauma is clearly disruptive of settled stories. Centralized, sovereign political authority is particularly threatened by this. After a traumatic event what we call the state moves quickly to close down any openings produced by putting in place as fast as possible a linear narrative of origins. We have seen already how this happens after a non-founded founding moment. Ceremonies of remembrance after wars produce a heroic narrative of sacrifice, and constitute the state as the object of that sacrifice. In the case of 11 September 2001 we found remembrance being invoked by President Bush before the events that were to be remembered had unfolded. In his press conference in Florida at 9.30 am that day, he called for a 'moment's silence'. At that time there was anything but silence in New York, in Washington, and on board the plane headed for a field in Pennsylvania. People were calling relatives, fire-fighters were rushing into buildings, passers-by were watching in disbelief as the towers burned. Meanwhile, the president was already invoking commemoration of the about-to-be-dead as a way of reconstituting the nation.[29]

However, some people want to try to hold on to the openness that trauma produces. They do not want to forget, or to express the trauma in standard narratives that entail a form of forgetting. They see trauma as something that unsettles authority, and that should make settled stories impossible in the future. I have proposed that it might be useful to call this form of time that provides an opening for *the political* 'trauma time', as distinct from the linear, narrative time that suits state or sovereign *politics*.[30]

In New York after the destruction of the World Trade Center this form of time was seen in the way in which people abandoned their day-to-day activities and took to the streets. Obviously the relatives of those missing were engaged in an endless and increasingly desperate search, but others too were circling what became known as Ground Zero in an attempt to offer help or gathering in public places to express their grief, shock and numbness. There was a remarkable openness to discussion, and public gatherings took place around hastily constructed shrines. People wrote on sidewalks and on rolls of paper laid out in Union Square. Time was suspended: everyday life no longer took place. Meanings were open, and could be held that way, or closed down. Street life was articulated more to openings than to closure.[31]

There are two important footnotes to this discussion. First, it is necessary to recognize that memory can be associated equally well with *either* those who want to close things down, or in other words to remember through linear narratives of nationhood and the like, *or* those who want to keep things open and to remember the traumatic moment as a political moment of openness. It is an undecidable.

Second, in these discussions, 'the political' is seen as distinct from 'politics'. Politics is the regular operation of state institutions, elections, and such like within the framework of the status quo. In other words it does not challenge existing ways of doing things. The political on the other hand is the moment where established ways of carrying on do not tell us what to do, or where they are challenged and ruptured: in traumatic moments, for example. There are problems with these distinctions. For one thing, even 'politics' is not really ever settled, finalized or complete. It might make more sense to talk in terms of *processes* of politicization or re- and de-politicization. And for another, maintaining 'politics' itself requires moves that could be called 'political'.[32]

Trauma as betrayal

As I have argued, trauma always already implicates the community, language or symbolic order in which it is set. In one sense, it seems that what we call trauma involves a betrayal, both in the sense of giving away and of revealing radical relationality. This idea is elaborated in this section.

It seems that trauma is more than a shock encounter with brutality or death; in an important sense, trauma is the betrayal of a promise or an expectation. Trauma can be seen as an encounter that betrays our faith in previously established personal and social worlds and calls into question the resolutions of impossible questions that people have arrived at in order to continue with day-to-day life: 'what we call trauma takes place when the very powers that we are convinced will protect us and give us security become our tormentors: when the community of which we considered ourselves members turns against us or when our family is no longer a source of refuge but a site of danger'.[33]

So what trauma or a traumatic encounter does, then, is reveal the way in which the social order is radically incomplete and fragile. It demonstrates in the most shocking way that what we call social reality is nothing more than a fantasy – it is our invention, and it is one that does not 'hold up' under stress. When it comes down to it, for example, what we call the state is not a protector, the guardian of people's security. On the contrary, it is the very organization that can send people to their deaths, by conscripting them in times when the state is under threat and sending them to fight in its wars. On a different level, the 'realities' of combat demonstrate that ideas of invincibility and good training only go so far. Ultimately, they do not protect: flesh is shown to be vulnerable after all.

As Annie Moore has pointed out, the word 'betrayal' in this context has two distinct meanings: it means both to give away or abandon and to reveal.[34] What is betrayed, as she puts it, is our radical relationality. It is betrayed in two senses. First there is a betrayal of trust that threatens that relationality: relationality expressed as national or family belonging turns out to be unreliable, for example. Second the radical relationality that is normally forgotten is revealed or made apparent. In the next section, I unpack this notion of betrayal further by extending the idea of relationality. This brings us to questions of resistance and indistinction.

Trauma, indistinction and resistance

In this part of the chapter I discuss the link between what I call drawing the line and trauma. I examine trauma as indistinction, and argue that resistance could be seen as a refusal to draw the line, or, in other words, a recognition of radical relationality.

Trauma is often seen as an injury. First the word meant an injury to the body, but now it is more commonly taken to mean an injury to the psyche, or even the community, the culture, or the environment.[35]

What happens if we think this differently? Perhaps it is possible instead of seeing trauma as involved with an injury to an object – when a sharp object enters the skin, for example, or a shock encounter to the psyche – to see trauma as something to do with the crossing of distinctions we take for granted, the distinctions between psyche and body, body and environment, for example. It is perhaps this obliteration of distinctions that is horrific, and that prompts us to describe an event as 'traumatic'.

What is important about something that we describe as traumatic then could be not just that something is injured, but that the very possibility of the thing itself, its very separateness as a thing, is threatened. For example, the way in which the body is generally regarded as distinct from its surroundings is called into question. The radical relationality of bodies, and of bodies and other 'things', is revealed; traumatic events 'tear us from ourselves, bind us to others, transport us, undo us, implicate us in lives that our not our own, irreversibly, if not fatally'.[36] However it is not just, as Judith Butler argues, that we are all vulnerable, it is rather that this vulnerability consists in and is comprised of our radical relationality.

In the events of 11 September in New York, the trauma lay not only in the incomprehensibility of the way in which civilian aircraft were flown deliberately into skyscrapers, with living passengers incorporated as part of an explosive weapon. There was another aspect to the events of that day that redoubled the traumatic impact. The unanticipated collapse of the twin towers and the way in which 'the steel ... pressed' the occupants of the towers 'into itself'[37] revealed the indistinguishability of flesh and metal. In addition, buildings seemingly intended to protect betrayed their inhabitants. Mark Wigley has pointed out how such corporate buildings are never intended mainly as a protection: their architects design them to perform other functions for capital and the corporate client.[38] The collapse of the towers revealed this generally hidden agenda too.[39]

A traumatic event is one that entails the blurring of the very distinctions upon which everyday existence depends, upon which people rely to continue their lives. It may be clear that some or even all of these distinctions are questionable: we 'know' for example, as in Toni Morrison's poem, that our bodies are made of the same chemical or atomic constituents as the rest of the world. Yet on the whole we prefer to forget these questions. We prefer to think of buildings as solid, of home as a place of safety, of ourselves as separate from our neighbours, and of our bodies as made of living flesh not inorganic atoms. A traumatic event demonstrates how untenable, or how insecure, these distinctions and these assumptions are. It calls for nothing more or less than the recognition of the radical relationality of existence – both living and dead.

IV.   Radical relationality and the refusal of distinctions

In this final section, I bring in Agamben's ideas of radical relationality and his refusal of distinctions. This is a refusal that Derrida calls for too, and in the conclusion I return to Derrida's ideas of openness to radical alterity and of the future to come, and relate these to the discussion of trauma time and the political.

Distinction/indistinction

In his study of testimony, 'Remnants of Auschwitz',[40] Agamben examines the extremes to which people were brought in the Nazi death camps. He draws our attention to the way in which it becomes impossible in this situation to make a satisfactory distinction between the human and the non-human. We cannot call those who became like animals as a result of their treatment non-human. Although they no longer cared whether they lived or died, and in a sense their 'humanity' was extinguished, to call them 'non-human' would be to repeat the gesture of their persecutors. The survivors of the camps were on the whole drawn from the ranks of those who in one sense retained their 'human' dignity: they did not become mindless, unfeeling animals. However, the survivors were also generally the ones who stole, collaborated, or were lucky, in other words, the ones who in a very important sense were inhuman.[41]

Agamben points out that the form of political authority under which we live, which he calls sovereign power, produces exceptional zones, or what he calls 'zones of indistinction', like the concentration camp, where distinctions disappear. In an apparent contradiction, sovereign power has relied since its beginnings on making a distinction between bare or naked life (the life of the home) and politically qualified life (the life of the public sphere). Only politically qualified life has any say in politics. At the same time as relying on these distinctions, sovereign power has maintained itself through the production of zones of indistinction on its borders, where these same distinctions between bare life and politically qualified life are suspended. Eventually, Agamben argues, zones of indistinction have extended to become all-encompassing, and politics is replaced everywhere by biopolitics. Life is no longer politically qualified. Sovereign power administers bare life, life that has no political voice.

Once the zones of indistinction that were exemplified in the concentration camps extend to all political space, sovereign power as Agamben describes it can perhaps no longer be seen as a relation of power in Foucauldian terms, because there is no longer a question of resistance. It is rather a relation of violence.[42] This violence is, as ever, concealed. According to Foucault relations of power entail resistance. Without resistance we would not be talking of relations of power. Relations of violence do not involve this resistance. The only way to challenge relations of violence might be to try to find a way to make them revert to power relations, or, in other words, to attempt to regain the properly political. Two possibilities can be suggested: the refusal of distinctions, and the assumption of bare life.[43] The former entails a refusal to make any of the distinctions between forms of life, or even between life and death, that are constitutive of sovereign authority. It means refusing, for example, to take on the authority or authorization that goes with the status of academic, whether historian or political scientist or whatever. The latter, the assumption of bare life, is not a passive acceptance. On the contrary, it is an active taking on of bare life, as a challenge to the form of violence that refuses it recognition. It is seen in protests where mere life, in all its vulnerability, is asserted in the face of violence.[44]

Toni Morrison's poem of 13 September can be seen as such a refusal of distinctions, and as a call for an assumption of bare life. She refuses all talk of categories such as 'evil', and all distinctions on the basis of 'nation', 'revenge' and the like. Instead, she addresses 'the dead' directly, as bare life, from the location of her own bare life. This is an acutely political challenge to the incorporation of the dead into narratives of heroism and sacrifice. Other examples of such challenges can be found in the aftermath of 11.9.2001. One example might be the action by a group of artists around a hundred strong who staged a protest against the way their shock and sorrow (and that of others) was being co-opted by the federal government and translated into a call for revenge.[45] Dressed in black with white dust-masks over their mouths, they stood in silence in a semi-circle. Around their necks hung placards reading 'Our grief is not a cry for war'.[46] The symbolism was interesting. The figures were voiceless: they stood with their mouths gagged, speechless in the face of trauma perhaps, but also rendered dumb by the rhetoric of war and its attempt to silence dissent through a summons to patriotism and revenge. Speechlessness and what Agamben characterizes as 'bare life' go together: language and voice are a feature of politically qualified life, the life of the citizen. The activists, in the silence of their grief, stand up for their right to a political voice, in opposition to others claiming to speak for them. They both emphasize their bare life and use it politically. They are rendered silent by their grief, but it is *their* grief, and they lay claim to the right to speak of it, or, rather, in this case, of what it is not.

V.   Conclusion

Resistance to come

Finally, I want to return to Derrida, and in particular to his notion of openness to the unconditional future, the 'to come'. In French the word-play is obvious: the *avenir*, which translates from the French as 'future' and the *à venir*, which translates as the 'to come', sound exactly the same. With this notion of the 'to come', Derrida is bringing the future into the present as part of his call for an openness to absolute otherness. In other terms this could be read as an openness to the encounter with the real or an openness to trauma, such as trauma survivors call for.

In some sense Derrida is saying that there 'is' only the present. Of course, there is no possibility of a present in so far as this means an existing present or a present that has *presence*. Deconstruction challenges the notions of existence as presence that characterize western metaphysics. What this might be saying then perhaps, to put it differently, is that 'there is only the present' in so far as 'there is no past' and 'there is no future' in the way that we generally think of 'past' and 'future'. In other words, notions of past, present and future succeeding one another in a sequence are peculiar to one way of thinking. It might be helpful to think in terms of a different idea of time, an archaeological time perhaps, where past, present and future are all present in the present[47] as in a geological core that cuts through layers of time that have been sedimented one on top of the other.[48]

Thus Derrida's notion of futurity challenges us to rethink linear notions of time and temporality, and their bed-fellow, prescriptive thinking. The final paragraphs of *Politics of Friendship* (in the English translation) make precisely this point. The future 'is' in the present: it is in the here and now, that very here and now that we cannot locate, that is an aporia.[49] At the end of a book that discusses at great length the concept of friendship from the Greeks onwards through a reading and re-reading of a single phrase, 'O my friends, there is no friend', Derrida himself addresses us directly, and in the present, with the call: 'O my democratic friends ...'[50]

The time of the political then, which I have called 'trauma time', is the aporetic time of the present, the moment at which no decision is assured, nothing is certain, the time in which responsibility is called for, and the time of the precipitate gesture. This is the time of resistance, the time in which the drawing of lines must be resisted and yet political engagement grasped fully.

Toni Morrison's piece 'The dead of September 11', with which this chapter began, speaks directly to the dead in an attempt to hold open the moment of awareness after the events of what is now called 11.9.2001. She insists that she cannot say a word until she has set aside all she knows or believes 'about nations, wars, leaders, the governed and the ungovernable'.[51] She has to purge her language, freshen her tongue, and 'abandon sentences crafted to know evil', whether they come from the privileged or the exploited. She has to create a space of silence amidst the cacophony of claims for revenge, the talk of attacks on America and sacrifice. She has to forget what nationalities, leaders and governments are and remember only one thing, the 'thread thrown' between the humanity of those who died and her own. For Morrison, this thread is a shared mortality, or what Derrida calls 'the gift of death'. She must remember her mortality in the face of their deaths. They do not sacrifice themselves for her: she still has her own death to die when the time comes. In the moment of trauma, their death betrays (in both senses) their absolute singularity and ours and, as Derrida says, 'it is from the site of death as the place of my irreplaceability, that is, of my singularity, that I feel called to responsibility. In this sense only a mortal can be responsible'.[52]

There is an intimate relation between the memory of nation or sovereign state, and the time it instantiates, and ordinary forms of politics. The political, that is, a challenge to settled or sovereign politics, is impossible without a forgetting of these ties, a rejection of this time and an opening up to responsibility and to singularity. It is only with the abandonment of the drawing of lines and the assumption of bare life that responsibility and political engagement is possible. An international politics starting from here would make very different demands. In place of a search for ever more refined categorizations and delineations of norms (for intervention, humanitarianism, defence, aggression, equality and the like) and types (failed states, developing countries, terrorists, partners, citizens, genuine asylum seekers and so forth) there would be an acknowledgement of the inevitable openness of possibilities, and the impossibility, and risks, of attempts at closure. As international relations scholars we would need to 'freshen' our tongues, purge our language 'of hyperbole; of its eagerness to analyse the levels of wickedness; ranking them; calculating their higher or lower status among others of its kind',[53] and abandon our vocabulary of good and evil, security and terror, in favour of the recognition of radical relationality and the inevitability, and indeed the necessity, of vulnerability. We do not stand outside, looking in. As scholars we are already intimately engaged. We cannot prescribe from outside (or inside, for that matter) without denying the relationality we attempt to analyse. This chapter has argued that the study of memory and time is one way of revealing, but hopefully not betraying, this relationality.

6

Bewitched by the Past

Social Memory, Trauma and International Relations

K. M. Fierke

I. Introduction

The twentieth century saw two world wars, the Holocaust, Hiroshima and Nagasaki, as well as ethnic cleansing in the Balkans and Rwanda, to mention only some of the worst atrocities. As John Wilson notes, the litany of war, civil violence and nuclear attack produced more trauma, mass destruction and death in a limited time frame than any other period in human history.[1] Trauma has also become a feature of political discourse, most evident in recent history in the relation to the attacks on the World Trade Centre and Pentagon on 11 September 2001.

There is a growing literature on trauma and war that crosses disciplinary boundaries.[2] This literature tends to be dominated by Freudian notions of trauma and repression, which presume a concept of the unconscious focused on the individual. Another stream creates distance from any notion of the unconscious, emphasizing instead the political expediency of trauma discourse. An example of the latter is Peter Novick's *The Holocaust and collective memory* (1999). He draws on the work of the French sociologist, Maurice Halbwachs, who, through a concept of collective memory, explores how present concerns determine what past we remember and how we remember it. In this theory, collective memory is ahistorical in so far as it simplifies and is impatient with any kind of ambiguity, reducing events to mythic archetypes. Memory in this conception denies the 'pastness' of its objects and insists on their continuing presence. A memory once established defines an eternal truth and identity for members of a group.[3] Novick argues that present concerns determine what is remembered and when. He rejects the role of unconscious trauma, focusing on the 'chosenness' of collective memory. However, this presents a conceptual problem. On the one hand, he denies the explanatory role of trauma, given its close connection to a concept of the unconscious. On the other hand, he speaks of past traumas as chosen for their political useful-ness, which locates the trauma more in discourse than political experience.

If 'chosen' trauma is merely an expression of politically expedient discourse, arguably, it is not dependent on the actual experience. This chapter approaches the relationship between trauma and political dis-course from a different angle, based on a rethinking of the former and its entailments, i.e. repression and the unconscious. By detaching trauma from a Freudian concept of the unconscious, I argue that past trauma can be manifest in the habitual memory of a culture. Action within a culture may continue to be bound up in the linguistic boundaries of a past world, thereby reproducing patterns of speech and behaviour from the past trauma in the present. This introduces a performative element to Halbwach's narrative account of social memory.

In part I, I lay the groundwork for the analysis by examining Wittgenstein's critique of Freud's concept of the unconscious, which provides a basis for shifting from an emphasis on the individual mind to social meaning. In part II, I relate this to a theory of action, arguing that a concept of political trauma necessarily replaces the distinction between unconscious and conscious mind with a distinction between habitual memory/action and reflexive action. This is illustrated in rela-tion to a number of examples. In part III, I further develop these themes in relation to a concept of political denial or repression.

II. Freud, Wittgenstein and the unconscious

Freud and Wittgenstein, at first glance, may seem an odd combination, aside from the common origin of the two thinkers in the Viennese culture of the early twentieth century. Freud, a psychoanalyst, developed a theory of the unconscious, while Wittgenstein, the philosopher of language, argued that there is nothing 'hidden' to exhume, that everything is in principle immediately accessible to the surface.[4] It is precisely this differ-ence that makes Wittgenstein's critique of interest in this case. The con-cept of social memory is distinguished by its focus on the political uses of memory, as distinct from the supposedly 'hidden' nature of trauma.

One similarity between Freud and Wittgenstein is also important. Both thinkers gave impetus to the postmodern critique of the autonomous rational agent.[5] Freud's theory of the unconscious displaced the cen-tral role of consciousness. Wittgenstein recognized that language and social meaning are prior to individual intentionality. Thus, while both presented a fundamental challenge to the notion of individual autonomy, they did so in quite different and, arguably, conflicting ways. Freud claimed to have developed a scientific theory built on a concept of the unconscious. Wittgenstein was critical of Freud's ontology and questioned the claim that behaviour has unconscious causes.

In stating that nothing remains 'hidden', Wittgenstein recast the dichotomy between conscious and unconscious in terms of degrees of 'perspicuity' or clarity regarding the *reasons* for our action.[6] What was most intriguing about the process of psychoanalysis, for Wittgenstein, was that it provided an opportunity to work on 'one's way of seeing things'.[7] He saw this as a model for a more 'therapeutic' approach to philosophy. He shared with Freud an emphasis on the meaning of what was being said in the therapeutic environment, as well as the tendency to be bewitched by our own assumptions. He was critical of Freud's inability to see the extent to which he was himself bewitched by his own theoretical constructs, in particular that of the unconscious.

Use of the word 'unconscious' often refers to mental processes that are not present to consciousness at any given moment, but are not excluded from it in any permanent sense. For Freud, the concept was more far-reaching. Unconscious processes refer less to those thoughts that are presently outside consciousness, than processes that cannot be perceived because something is *preventing* the thought from rising to the surface, because the subject does not want to know. The repressed thought in the unconscious is predicated on observable behaviour and mental effects, for example hysteria is a manifestation of repressed childhood trauma. Freud used the metaphor of two rooms (the conscious and unconscious) with a doorkeeper standing between them who exercises control over the movement of ideas from the first to the second and decides whether or not to grant passage.[8] This suggests a place for storing and maintaining mental objects that is inaccessible to perception but present in a way that can be felt by effect. Consciousness, he says, is a 'spectator at the end of the second room'.[9]

From Wittgenstein's perspective, Freud resorts broadly to a grammar of conscious processes to describe unconscious processes and the unconscious mechanism, while the latter obeys principles that are completely different.[10] The one is transparent and intentional while the other is opaque and repressed. Freud suggests that the unconscious is a cause of behaviour, which is distinct from the reason given for an act. Wittgenstein argues that what Freud says about the unconscious is merely one means of representation or notation, rather than the discovery of a new region of the soul.

To suggest that an action, for example, laughter, has a cause outside consciousness is to suggest that the reasons for the laughter are not available to the person laughing. By contrast, within a Wittgensteinian framework, Freud's theory provides one way, among others, of representing the laughter. In Freud's language, the laughter is explained within a conceptual apparatus including concepts of 'Unconscious' and 'Repression', in which the cause of the laughter (e.g. a desire to slander someone) is hidden to the person who laughs. Many of us would freely use an explanation of this kind, given that these words have become a part of our everyday language. But this is distinct from the actual existence of an unconscious against which this claim could be empirically tested. It is unclear how a test would be conducted, given the source is, by definition, hidden.

Rather than searching for hidden causes, Wittgenstein focuses on the reason for an act. The person laughing may draw on a Freudian conceptual apparatus to explain the laughter. Alternatively, they may know the reason and lie about it. It may also be that the reason for laughter is not completely transparent to the agent, that is, he or she does not grasp its meaning. The laugh may have emerged out of a juxtaposition of meanings, which have not acquired coherent sense. He or she may, by looking more closely at the meanings, see its sense more clearly. Rather than caused by an unconscious desire, one might say the laugh is constituted out of a variety of meanings that have shaped the background of the individual. This is consistent with much contemporary research on human memory. Memories are not like computer files, retrieved from the unconscious, but are always constructed by combining bits of information selected and arranged in terms of prior narratives and current expectations, needs and beliefs.[11] Wittgenstein, in sum, shifts the emphasis away from something hidden and repressed to the reasons for an action, which may be more or less transparent to the actor.

The question of meaning is at the heart of Wittgenstein's critique of Freud, but is also what he found most intriguing in the psychoanalyst's work. The critique focused on Freud's assumption that he was creating a scientific theory when he was merely creating a conceptual apparatus for describing a certain type of experience. At the same time, it was Freud's emphasis on meaning and perspicuity in the therapeutic process that resonated with Wittgenstein's own efforts in philosophy.

There were several ways in which meaning played a central role in Freudian therapy. First, the notion of free association relies on allowing the patient to spontaneously express him or her self. The words, dreams, thoughts of the patient and their meanings, provide the material for analysis.[12] Second, Freud recognized that the meanings presented by the patient are in a sense more important than the actual experience of trauma. He argued it was not the experience itself that was the source of trauma, but its delayed revival as memory after the individual had entered sexual maturity and could grasp its sexual meaning.[13] As old scenes are recovered, whether through flashback or through memory therapy, they become invested with meanings that they did not have at the time they were experienced.[14]

These ideas resonate with Wittgenstein's own work in philosophy. He argued that we need greater perspicuity about our use of words. This requires looking more closely at our own grammar and language games, and what they assume, rather than creating new conceptual vocabularies. Because this language is overly familiar, because it is constitutive of our selves and our social world, we often cannot see it clearly. We are often 'bewitched' by our own assumptions.[15] While Freud recognized that his patients were often captive of their own assumptions, and that speaking provided a way to see those meanings in a new light, he was unable to see the extent to which he was himself bewitched by his own theoretical categories.[16]

III.   Traumatic versus narrative memory

Wittgenstein's critique of Freud provides a basis for situating the question of social meaning and language at the heart of traumatic memory. The shift is counterintuitive, however, given a distinction in the psychological literature between traumatic memory and normal memory, which builds on a theory of the unconscious. Traumatic memory, in this view, lies outside verbal-semantic-linguistic representation and involves bodily skills, habits, reflex actions and classically conditioned responses. Whether through repression, dissociation or neurological shutdown or the impossibility of representing horrific events, the trauma is not available to consciousness or speech. The experience of trauma thus becomes fixed or frozen in time. It refuses to be represented *as* past, but is perpetually reexperienced in a painful dissociated traumatic present. This assumes a distinction between conscious representation and unconscious repression. By contrast ordinary memory is declarative or narrative. It involves the ability to be consciously aware and verbally narrate the events that have happened to the individual.[17] Therapy has traditionally been seen to involve the transition from traumatic memory to narrative memory. The individual masters the traumatic experience by narratively mastering an account of it, in which the event is located in the past.[18]

In a genealogy of the concept of trauma, Ruth Leys presents a tension or opposition that has shaped the history of trauma studies and the treatment of traumatic memory. The first pole of this opposition, which relies on Freud's concept of unconscious, is a mimetic tendency by which the traumatized imitate and identify with the aggressor. This locates the problem of trauma in the individual unconscious where it is dissociated from the conscious self and contributes to the acting out of the traumatic scene, which is only available to recollection under hypnosis. Mimetic theory has had an appeal in so far as it explains the victim's suggestibility, but it also threatened the ideal of individual autonomy and responsibility. A competing antimimetic tendency reestablished a strict dichotomy between the autonomous subject and an external trauma, regarding the latter as if it were a purely external event imposed on a sovereign if passive victim. This has lent itself to positivist or scientific interpretations of trauma, which focus more on the body. Neurobiological theories of trauma fit this category.

Leys argues that there has been a continuous tension and oscillation between the two paradigms, from mind to body, which has generated a range of paradoxes and contradictions. Both have contributed to a conception of trauma, shared, in contemporary debates by neurobiologists as well as post-structuralists, in which the literalness of trauma is beyond representation.[19] My purpose is not to criticize this claim, but to shift the focus away from representation to action and practice. The literal experience of trauma may be beyond representation, but in the imitation or acting out of the traumatic event, the victim reproduces the linguistic boundaries of the past experience. Trauma is consequently part of a cultural package involving a range of speech acts, patterns of relationship and assumptions. The key difference between traumatic memory and declarative memory is thus not one of the presence or absence of language but rather the degree of *perspicuity* with which the traumatic event is expressed. Acting out is a phenomenon by which the traumatized individual or group continues to live within the linguistic boundaries of a past world. This can be distinguished from a narrative account that reflexively identifies the past as past.

The notion that trauma is beyond representation rests on an assumption that it is inside the individual mind and cannot be communicated to others. This does not presume that the traumatized person is mute and incapable of speech, only that she is unable to speak of the traumatic event or locate it in the past. However, there is a sense in which the meaning of the trauma comes to be expressed, as suggested above, in the habits, behaviours and conditioned responses of the individual victim or a culture that has been traumatized by war. Paul Connerton argues that this represents a form of habitual memory and that this type of memory has largely been ignored in the psychological literature. Acting out is a compulsive repetition of the past in which actors deliberately place themselves in distressing situations. But, in the repetition, the agent forgets the prototype of the present action, feeling themselves fully determined by present circumstances. As he states, 'The compulsion to repeat has replaced the capacity to remember'.[20]

Forgetting in this argument is less a function of repression or dissociation than the habitual nature of the act.[21] Habitual memory, which he distinguishes from personal or cognitive memory, consists in the production of a performance. For instance, reading, writing, driving a car or riding a bicycle all have the marks of a habit, in that the actor largely forgets the rules on which the habit was built. Or, more specific to the political world, leaders, in a crisis which they do not wholly understand and where the outcome is unforeseeable, may have recourse to rules and beliefs that rely on assumed knowledge and embed actions in a taken for granted background narrative. Rules cease to function as rules or be recognizable as such once a pattern of behaviour or action becomes habitual.

From this perspective, social memory as a *narrative* recollection may be no less habitual than habitual behaviour. There can be a habit of remembering a unique event. The words used to capture that event may become habitual.[22] Vaclev Havel provides an example of this:

> Twenty or thirty years ago, in the army, we had a lot of obscure adventures, and years later we tell them at parties, and suddenly we realize that those two very difficult years of our lives have become lumped together into a few episodes that have lodged in our memory in a standardized form, and are always told in a standardized way, in the same words.[23]

In this respect, the habit of remembering is also a habit of forgetting in that the memory becomes tied to a specific narrative that focuses selectively on elements of the past. Habits of behaviour are learned in much the same ways as habits of language, that is, from 'living with people who habitually behave in a certain manner'. The practical knowledge of rules entailed by a command of language or behaviour is impossible until we have forgotten that they rest on rules and we are no longer tempted to turn speech and action into the application of rules to a situation.[24]

Acting out is expressed in language, yet distinct from narrative memory or recollection. The psychiatrist James Glass provides a very moving account of how a Holocaust survivor passed on a set of meanings and relational patterns, acquired in the concentration camp, to his daughter, Ruth.[25] As Ruth was growing up, she was never allowed to express suffering or pain. If she did, she was told that her suffering could never compare to that in the camps and was thus of little consequence. The father also replicated the communicative patterns of his Nazi tormentors in relating to his daughter, ordering her to 'perform this, do that, be obedient, stay invisible, don't get in the way'.[26] As a result, she never experienced home as a place of safety or security. She dealt with this acquired worthlessness by dissociating the ideal public self she presented to the world from the miserable human being she felt herself to be. The two selves are not distinguished by conscious and unconscious. Instead, they are two conflicting self-representations, in which the public self is dissociated from the private self. By the time she was hospitalised for psychosis, she had entered into the world of 1943, without ever having been there physically. The beds of the hospital became barracks, the staff were SS guards and Kapos. Her therapist was Josef Mengele, waiting for the right moment to do experiments on her brain.

Ruth's narrative while in hospital reveals how the world of 1943, learned from her father, structured the linguistic boundaries of her world:

Can't you see, all these people, these Nazis – the Holocaust – the Holocaust – it's ugly, the cold/hot water torture – boiling alive ... leave quickly before you're caught in it – stripping flesh from my bones, throwing the raw meat to their dogs – snarling bastards – Did you hear what happened to me? The CAT scan machine – they lied – told me it was for my own good – do you think I believed them? – It was an experiment – Mengele's henchmen sending rays into my brain, popping little blood vessels to see if I could have a stroke – But then they took out needles, sticking them – everywhere – all over my body – deep – I'm in such pain! It's horrible! Make them stop, please! Do you see the guards over there, the beatings ... I saw hooks in the ceiling – plans to string me up using electrodes and cattle prods to do God-knows-what – Papa told me they hung Jews up with wires in their cold-storage rooms – by their toes from meathooks and whipped them until their skin started peeling off and finally the flesh lay loose off the bone like a fresh piece of meat – Speak about punishment! I deserve to be punished – My evil, it smothers me – it won't go away. Please kill me before they start with the tortures – I'm as bad as those Nazi pigs. Is it 1983, 1943? Does it make any difference? – Is anyone around here human?[27]

The purpose of this example is not to suggest that trauma is equivalent to psychosis, or that all Holocaust survivors or their children are psychotic or that all individual victims of trauma turn into aggressors, which they obviously do not.[28] My point is the role of socially acquired *meaning* and *action* in constructing the world not only of a Holocaust survivor but his offspring. As Cushman notes, in the transgenerational reproduction of trauma, what is re-enacted is a cultural package that relies on a particular configuration of self-other relations[29] – the general stuff of daily life that, in this example, shaped and moulded the prisoner's reality orientation in the concentration camp. This is a social world peopled with characters and voices from the past, from a world where people lived and interacted.[30] The victim in the one world later does to himself and to others what was done to him, as a way of staying involved with a (now absent) perpetrator or reproducing a (now absent) abusive terrain.[31]

That the daughter could enter into her father's trauma, as if she were reliving the Holocaust itself, was a function of the pattern of interaction he had passed on to her. The traumatized father had placed himself in the position of his tormenters and imitated their attitudes in relation to his own daughter. She became the victim, the invisible, the humiliated, the less than human. This shaped her private sense of self, as she projected an idealised and opposite image to others around her. The father did not narrate the story of his experience in the camps as past; rather he continued to live within the linguistic boundaries of that world.

Public and private, in these examples, might be translated into the categories of Freud's theory of unconscious. The patterns of behaviour and the conditioning of camp life were passed on from father to daughter, from unconscious to unconscious, while the daughter's public presentation was at the level of consciousness. However, it seems more obvious in this case that the father's acting out of his earlier trauma was situated within the linguistic world of the concentration camp, structured by a particular kind of relationship, that is, of dominance and humiliation, and particular speech acts, such as ordering. This differs from a narrative account of the past in so far as the past continues to be alive and is reproduced in the present, rather than recognized as past.

As the Israeli psychiatrist Moses Hrushovski notes,

> Traumatized people ... relive the event as though it were continually recurring in the present, not only in their dreams and thoughts, but also in their actions. Often they reenact the traumatic moment ... wishing thereby to change the traumatic encounter retroactively, so that they can, as it were, overcome it differently this time.[32]

In 'overcoming it differently' the father steps into the position of his Nazi tormenters and his daughter becomes the humiliated victim. In this respect, the traumatic past was so overwhelming that it continues to shape interactions in the present. Far from being forgotten, the past is continually relived in the present. At the same time, as this past world becomes habitual, there is a forgetting of the uniqueness of the original event. This contrasts with narrative memory where the self stands outside the past, in the present and provides a representation of events gone by.

In Connerton's argument, social habits, unlike purely individual ones, rest on conventions for interpreting behaviour as socially legitimate. This provides a backdrop for thinking about how a past trauma can provide the basis for social practices resting on habitual memory. The traumatic experience of a culture may provide the performative context or the cultural package in which a habitual memory contributes to the reproduction of the past in the present. Political trauma can be understood as a state in which fear and hypervigilance become habitual.

IV. Habits of social memory

James Fentress and Chris Wickham argue that a memory can only be social if it can be transmitted and this requires its articulation. Social memory is articulated memory, not only in speech but in ritual. It is not only put into words but is acted out.[33] Much memory, they argue, is the memory of context dependent information. As long as actors remain in a context they will be surrounded by clues that prompt a memory. Events in the present, which may or may not by themselves be traumatic, induce a repetition of the traumatic event, like an imprint which casts the boundaries of future action, constraining the space within which it is understood and performance enacted. Narratives of the event provide a sequencing of images and logical and semantic connections that are retained and repeated, becoming the container of memory. These stories not only provide a representation of particular events, but connect, clarify and interpret them.[34]

Social remembering and forgetting, that is, the narration of memory, as distinct from its habitual performance, may coexist in a dialectical tension. For example, 'Hitler' is a central component of social memory in the West which transcends any one specific culture. There exist narrative memories of who Hitler was and how he relates to who we are. This may be *deliberately* remembered in commemorative acts, which re-enact the past as a part of public ritual, such as the various celebrations in May commemorating the end of the Second World War. But this memory may also be re-enacted with less perspicuity or clarity about the role of the past in shaping a present performance. When foreign leaders are depicted as 'like Hitler', the present encounter becomes an encounter with the past. Interactions may subsequently become a re-enactment of a habitual performance in which the identity of various participants, as victims, tyrants or liberators is reinforced.[35]

The 'like Hitler' argument would seem consistent with Novick's claim about the political expedience of trauma discourse, detached from the traumatic experience. As a tool of American foreign policy in particular, which remained salient until 11 September 2001, there seems little connection to the actual experience of post-war generations. Idith Zertal's study of the use of the Holocaust in Israeli discourse brings the problem closer to the direct experience of trauma.[36] Like Novick she recognizes the silence surrounding the Holocaust in the decade following World War II, even in Israel. She highlights the focus there, prior to the trial of Adolf Eichmann in 1961, on trials of Holocaust survivors who 'collaborated' with the Nazi regime in the brutalization and elimination of European Jews in the camps.[37] Both of these established a distance in the Israeli psyche between those who experienced the Holocaust and those Jews involved in building the new nation.

In her argument, the Eichmann trial was the beginning of change in Israeli discourse, by which Ben Gurion mobilized the memory of the Holocaust in the construction of Israeli nationhood. In this new discourse, 'the total helplessness of European Jewry in World War II could now directly serve as the "counter metaphor" to the discourse of Israel's omnipotence and also as its ultimate justification'.[38] The construction process involved several discursive moves. First, a direct link was constructed between Arab enemies of Israel and the Nazis. As she states:

The transference of the Holocaust situation on to the Middle East reality ... was done, before and during the trial, in two distinctive ways: first by massive references to the presence of Nazi scientists and advisers in Egypt and other Arab countries, to the ongoing connections between Arab and Nazi leaders, and to the Nazi-like intentions and plans of the Arabs to annihilate Israel. The second means was systematic references – in the press, on the radio, and in political speeches – to the former Mufti of Jerusalem, Haj Amin El-Husseini, his connections with the Nazi regime in general and with Eichmann and his office in particular. In those references he was depicted as a prominent designer of the Final Solution and a major Nazi criminal. The deeds of Eichmann – and other Nazi criminals – were rarely mentioned without addition of the Arab-Nazi dimension.[39]

Second, lessons were derived from the trial regarding what can happen in the absence of a defense force, giving new meaning to the fight against Arab enemies, and the possibility of death in this fight as a vindication of past helplessness in the face of the Nazi enemy.[40] Third, this established the basis for articulating an existential threat to Israeli identity, given the potential for the Holocaust to recur. As Ben Gurion stated in his nationwide broadcast for Independence Day in 1962:

On this holiday it is our obligation to warn the people of Israel that the independence we gained thirteen years ago is neither complete nor guaranteed. The hatred for Israel that brought about, twenty years ago, the extermination of two-thirds of European Jewry, who had not sinned or done wrong; this hatred is still simmering among the rulers of our neighboring countries, plotting to eradicate us, and dozens of Nazi experts are their tutors and advisers in their hatred for Israel and the Jews of the world.[41]

The experience of the Holocaust was woven into Israeli identity, rather than distancing it as in the past. The dangers confronting Israel remained essentially Nazi dangers and any military threat to Israel would mean a new Holocaust.

Similar themes have been evident in other societies that have experienced trauma. In the Balkans, the Serbs established a link between past enemies, such as the Croat Ustasa, who were puppets of Hitler or the Ottomans, and contemporary enemies, that is, the Croats and Albanian Kosovars, respectively. This was the basis for the naming of an existential danger and a resolve, as famously claimed by Milosevic, never to be beaten again. Hitler himself called on the trauma of defeat in the First World War and the humiliation of the Versailles Treaty, in mobilizing an existential threat to German society, to the end of making Germany great once again.[42] The United States Bush administration, post-11 September 2001 and leading up to the invasion of Iraq in 2003, made a discursive link between Iraq and the terrorist attacks, a link which lacked evidence in fact. This was part of articulating an existential threat to America itself, despite, as was later revealed, the absence of any weapons of mass destruction capability on the part of Saddam Hussein. While these are very different contexts and by no means equivalent, they all relied on similar semantic and logical connections that were retained and repeated and became the container of past memory.

In the Israeli case, the discursive moves, as Zertal notes, relied on a high degree of misperception and disortion, which highlights one issue at stake in discussing these political phenomena in terms of trauma. The compulsion to repeat relies on the continuous appropriation of the past as a feature of the present. While distorted, the salience of the discursive move is dependent on a context of past experience. Zertal argues that collective anxiety is never purely a product of elite invention or manipulation, although there is an element of this. The discursive moves are only effective if they respond to deep and genuine social concerns in a time of general malaise, that is, a population has to be receptive to manipulation.[43] For instance, while US plans for an invasion of Iraq may have existed prior to 11 September 2001, the execution of these plans became possible in a context where Americans had recently experienced the terrorist attacks on the World Trade Center and Pentagon.

The transition, in the case of Israel, from a situation shrouded in silence, to one in which the Holocaust became defining of Israeli identity and politics, highlights the process by which a social memory is assimilated in the performative acts of a culture, such that the underlying rule is forgotten and becomes constitutive of ongoing practice. Avi Shlaim's analysis, *The Iron Wall* (2000), illustrates the continuing legacy of the Holocaust. Shlaim argues that since its inception, Israeli policy toward the Palestinians has been defined by the need to build an 'iron wall' of military force to protect the new state.[44] While stated explicitly in terms of military security, the link to the traumatic experience of the Holocaust is unmissable. While this link was first constructed by Ben Gurion, as Zertal demonstrates, it was reproduced by future generations of Israeli leaders.

Shlaim refers to the Israeli memory of the Holocaust as a powerful psychological force, akin to a 'collective psychosis' that deepened the feelings of isolation and accentuated the perception of threat.[45] An inflexibility and intransigence among many leaders severely limited perceptions of the Arabs. They 'were' the Nazi aggressor incarnate. There was a predominant view, particularly among traditional Zionists, that the impenetrable wall of Arab hostility presented them with a situation of *ein breira*, of having no choice regarding the pursuit of peace.[46] The logic of acting out was expressed by an American Zionist leader, Nahum Goldman, following Israel's military victory of 1948:

> The victory offered such a glorious contrast to the centuries of persecution and humiliation, of adaptation and compromise, that it seemed to indicate the only direction that could possibly be taken from then on.[47]

Israel, comprised of the 'new Jew',[48] stepped into the position of victor vis-à-vis another dispossessed and homeless people. This was complemented by a view that Israel was isolated, surrounded by hostile Arab states, and unable to rely on the United Nations for its security. The social memory also included an idealized mission of a greater Israel for the chosen people.

Intransigence, the perception of having no choices in a hostile world, the acting out of an earlier relationship, the perception of isolation, hypervigilance to recurring threats, and an idealized mission, are all expressions of a habitual memory of past trauma, which was larger than the sum of traumatized individuals, and became a structural feature of the context. As Shlaim rightly notes, in his discussion of the Begin regime, these are also characteristics of what is more commonly referred to in the International Relations (IR) literature, as the 'security dilemma':

> the trauma of the Holocaust produced a passionate desire to procure absolute safety and security for the Jewish people, but it also blinded him to the fears and anxieties that his own actions generated among Israel's Arab neighbors. By invading Lebanon in 1982, Begin thought he could turn the corner, defeat all Israel's enemies once and for all, and achieve perfect security for his people. But there are no corners in a vicious circle.[49]

In the realist literature in IR, the security dilemma is primarily motivated by fear for one's survival. Arguments in this genre focus, alternatively, on a pessimistic view of human nature or on the absence of an overarching authority to enforce, mediate or protect.[50]

In the realist prescription it is egoism and self-interest, generated by fear, which propels conflict. Misperception may result from problems of interpretation, given the fine line between defensive and offensive action. A politics of trauma deepens the dynamics of that fear. Fear, rather than contributing to rational action, severely constrains the perceptual field within which reasons for action are defined. Any positive potential other than a hostile, dangerous world is blocked out, given a perception that the past is continuously recurring in the present. As a result, it becomes impossible to recognize the present as a distinct set of political and psychological forces that require a distinct response. It is not purely the present threat, but the experience of the present as like the past and a constant hypervigilance, that propels the security dilemma. Shlaim provides several examples, of cases where more peaceful opportunities were interpreted in hostile terms, leading to a strengthening of the Iron Wall, and a failure to see how Israel's own actions increased the fears and anxieties of the Arabs or Palestinians.

The Middle East is only one example of the on-going influence of a social memory of past trauma, as revealed in the examples of the former Yugoslavia, post-First World War I Germany, and the United States post-9/11. The troubles in Northern Ireland involved similar dynamics, as have conflicts in other parts of the world. To recognize the role of traumatic social memory in these widely varying contexts is to highlight the relationship between the past suffering of a people and the process by which this experience comes to shape a set of practices that reproduce both war and the traumatic experience.

Traumatic memory is not hidden in a social unconscious. Rather it may be constitutive of a world of habitual action, which often reveals a lack of awareness of the effects of these actions on others. The 'therapeutic' potential resides in greater perspicuity regarding the traumatic dimensions of a conflict. A concept of habitual memory adds greater nuance to Halbwach's depiction of collective memory. In Halbwachs' theory, collective memory is obviously expressed in language as it is a social property. In his argument, the idea of an individual memory absolutely separate from social memory is an abstraction devoid of meaning. In the example of Ruth's father or Israeli foreign policy, habitual memory of the Holocaust is inseparable from a social memory. Social memory does not place trauma in the past. As Halbwachs said, 'memory denies the pastness of its objects and insists on their continuing presence'.[51] The narrative of social memory, like traumatic memory, gives an account of past as present. As such, the boundaries distinguishing traumatic and narrative memory, as expressed in the psychoanalytic tradition, are blurred. Narrative memory presents the past as present, and legitimates a field of performative action.

Halbwachs fails to link collective memory of the past to a performative element or to explain how collective memories are passed on within a social group from one generation to the next.[52] A concept of habitual memory or acting out makes explicit the role of communication between individuals in the transmission of memory as well as the role of social memory in constituting social structures of action and communication.

V.   Memories and exclusions

Habitual memory constitutes interactions with present others on the basis of a memory of the past. The re-enactment of the past takes place in a relationship to others. But there is also an 'internal' relationship in Freudian theory between the conscious and unconscious, which is expressed in concepts of denial or repression. In the political world, denial, rather than a function of unconscious repression, can be understood as a political act for the purpose of creating a unity of interpretation.[53] For instance, as Gieko Muller-Fahrenholz points out, the Nazi's wiped out any differentiation within Germany, melting the German people into an integrated whole, which required the suppression of alternative narratives. [54]

While this process involved an element of repression, it did not require psychological denial. What is repressed is difference, debate or alternative narratives of the past. As Catherine Merridale argues, repression or censorship and the silence it engenders, can be attributed to state violence and the threat of arrest or demotion.[55] It is less the case that your average person in a situation of war engages in psychological denial; rather what can be said in public is dissociated from what can be said among trusted friends or what one thinks. Individuals may be inclined, in a repressive situation, to adopt an *interpretation* akin to that of the authorities, in order to survive or avoid conflict, but this is not the same as repression in an unconscious.

Political denial may come to be embedded in everyday action, such that one hardly recognizes it as denial. It becomes part of the habitual performance. Vaclev Havel provided the example of the greengrocer who had a slogan in his window stating 'Workers of the World, Unite!'[56] The greengrocer never thought about the meaning of the slogan; hanging the sign was just a normal act in the context of communist Czechoslovakia. But in doing so he participated in living a lie, as did all of his neighbours. If he were to stop and consider what he really thinks and whether he believes this claim, he would become dangerous. If he stops putting up the slogan he breaks the rules of a game by exposing it as a game. He will have become reflexive about the reasons for his action.

Adam Michnik made a similar point about Eastern European communism in Poland:

> What do I mean when I say that the Poles allowed themselves to have a language imposed upon them after 1945? One example is the attitude toward the German question. The role of Stalin in the annexation of territories and in the victory over the Germans was only mentioned positively. To do so was to accept a language that was compromised. One was free to say many things of Stalin – whether it was true or false was irrelevant – as long as the rhetoric was positive. To be sure, those who played this game (journalists, for example) understood full well that it was a game with rules. Their readers, however, were not always so well informed. Due to the long habit of covering Stalin's real face with a mask, the mask seemed more real than reality.[57]

Michnik's point is that these language games did not necessarily involve lies, although they might; rather, playing the game involved knowing the rules and what could and could not be said in relation to any particular subject. Language and behaviour become intertwined in a game, which provided social legitimation for certain acts, while often 'forgetting' that these rest on rules. Behind the habit of denial, Stalin implemented a regime of terror. The idealized image of a communist state in which worker's unite, masked brutal practices of repression against those who would dare to offer a different interpretation. Political denial can take many different forms and become a normal practice. The repression is less a matter of banning unwanted material to the individual unconscious, than the repression of alternative interpretations of reality that would threaten the existing order.

What then constitutes political trauma, if anything? Arguably, it is less censorship or repression, in and of itself, whether by self or others, than the *assimilation* of a past context of trauma such that it comes to structure identity within a linguistic world of action and interaction vis-à-vis others. It is less the existence of a repressed memory than the habitual acting out of the life world of the past in the present, mirroring a past experience of humiliation and destruction. Political denial, for instance, of the brutal consequences of these acts, goes hand in hand with a single interpretation of 'reality' composed of a perpetrator and victim. This represents a form of political 'illness' that resides in a faulty relationship between speakers and their language, or as

Wittgenstein says, 'the bewitchment of our intelligence by means of language'.[58]

The 'illness' resides less in the presence of the picture than captivity to it. In not recognizing the picture as one representation of reality, the agent is powerless before it – and thus not an agent at all – experiencing the confusion that arises from taking it literally. Held captive by the past, the actor is bound to one way of looking at the present and is thus unaware of the role of his or her actions in reproducing that past. This powerlessness is contrasted with the 'power of the powerless', articulated by Havel, in which the greengrocer comes to recognize that what he assumed to be part of the world as it is, is in fact a game, in the sense that it rests on habitual rules, which are no more necessary than any other. In the grip of the picture, the agent loses agency and becomes invisible, an impotent observer of the way things are. Like the fly buzzing in the fly bottle, he is powerless to escape suffocation. The object of therapy is to create the conditions for reflexivity and thus a certain freedom within and from the picture. To recognize a picture as a picture, and even more hopefully, to recognize the possibility of alternative pictures, is to be freed from captivity. To recognize the picture as more than a representation of reality as it is, but as legitimating habitual performative acts, is to transform it into a game with rules that can be broken. With greater clarity, comes a conviction that things need not be one certain way.

VI.   Conclusion

Social memory, as a picture of past trauma, may, at one and the same time, take a narrative form and provide a script for re-enacting a cultural package inherited from the past. Both help to bind together the identity of the group. What is reproduced is less an identical set of practices than a relationship between victim and perpetrator, which in 'acting out' is reversed. The experience of humiliation or betrayal sets the stage for the dissociation of a realist logic of survival and an idealized mission of the future. The latter is an expression of the intent to reverse the trauma of the past; in practice the realist logic is reproduced.

Novick makes a distinction between collective memory and trauma. The purpose of this chapter has been to illustrate how the two can be mutually constitutive rather than existing purely in a relationship of political expedience. This requires an understanding of trauma as a socio-political concept, which, unlike Freud's concept of the unconscious, assumes 'nothing remains hidden'. Social memory blurs the distinction, found in the literature on individual psychology, between narrative and traumatic memory. Trauma may be expressed in the habitual memory of a culture, providing social legitimation for performative acts. While reproducing the linguistic boundaries of a past world, the pastness of the present may be obfuscated by the habitual nature of the acts and the 'forgetting' of the rules on which they rest. Denial is less repression of memory in an unconscious than repression of dissent. In this respect, political denial may be constitutive of habitual memory. It may contribute to the 'forgetting' that is at the core of the habitual re-enactment.

7
Mourning, Melancholia and Violence*

Larry Ray

I. Introduction

During the past decade there has been renewed attention in sociology to the relationships between memory, commemoration and (especially national) identity. There is presently a passion for the recovery and discovery of collective and individual 'pasts', which are brought into the service of constructing and maintaining identities in a new memory politics. As Jeffrey Prager notes,

> Today the past has achieved a kind of iconic, even sacred status. Remembering the past is now widely understood as a valuable activity in and of itself; ... We have become a society of 'memory groups' where one's claim to group membership typically goes unchallenged because a common past ... constitutes an area of discourse that cannot be contested.[1]

This chapter examines one aspect of these relationships – the relationship between memory, remembrance of the dead, and national/ethnic conflicts.

The formation of nation states and territorially based entities involved a process of pacification and the formation of a *civil* society. Norbert Elias argued that the process of internal pacification in pre-modern societies, associated with increased personal restraint and mannered conduct, was facilitated by developments such as the growth of trade and towns, a complex division of labour, and the collection of taxes. The longer and denser the networks of interdependence, the more people are obliged to attune their action to those of others and the less their interactions will be marked by overt violence. However, this paradigm has been criticized. Zygmunt Bauman has argued that the 'civilizing process' as a depiction of the emergence of modern societies is a myth and that violence, genocide, and the Holocaust were made possible precisely by the formal bureaucratic procedures of modern societies.[2] But the civilizational paradigm does not present a rosy view of a future without violence and Elias used his theory to shed light on Nazism.[3] He argued that a peculiar conjuncture of circumstances following the First World War established a 'de-civilizing process' – a resurgence of warrior values, a decay of the state's monopoly of force, middle class resistance to the Weimar Republic, and an escalating double-bind of violence and counterviolence that ended in Hitler's rise.[4] Attempting to reconcile Bauman and Elias, Abram De Swaan argues that state organized violence involves a twofold movement of rationalization-bureaucratization *and* regression, breakdown and barbarism.[5] Following Elias he argues that this happens as a result of 'disidentification' between ethnic groups along with a campaign to strengthen identifications among the rest of the population, thus creating increased polarization. He describes the result as a 'dyscivilizing' process in which society is compartmentalized into areas where 'peaceful' everyday life continues and those such as the camps, where extreme violence is perpetrated against the targeted group.

How does this bear on understanding the internecine violence that appeared in the 1990s and beyond, especially in some post-communist countries? These conflicts have many causes and the present chapter will focus on one in particular: the relation between collective memory, commemoration, and the mobilization of ethnic violence. I will suggest that in order to understand the links between modernity, identity and violence we need to examine the different ways in which memory and mourning can be mobilized into genocidal hatred. The affective dimension of this is central. One of the criticisms of such arguments is that they are overly clinical. Daniel Goldhagen comments that they misrepresent the 'phenomenology of killing' – they miss the emotional components, failing to convey the horror and gruesomeness of events in which blood, bone and brains are flying about and onto to the perpetrators, accompanied by the cries and wails of people awaiting slaughter.[6] To understand the spiral towards a process of dyscivilization we need to examine the conditions in which it is possible to mobilize national, ethnic or other identities in ways that promote the violent exclusion of supposed enemies. In a context of dramatic social upheaval communities can externalize dangerous experiences onto 'enemies' with whom they were previously intimate.[7] The collapse of Yugoslavia into genocidal war, for example, involved extricating and mobilizing national and ethnic identities that had in many cases been merged into a more diffuse if always contested 'Yugoslavian' identity.[8] The civil war, reflecting a crisis in bonds of social solidarity and civil society, created an obsession with enemies within and with what Julia Kristeva calls 'familiar foreigners'.[9]

This chapter examines the processes of memory, narrative and cultural formation in an era of globalization. It begins with a discussion of the resurgence of memory studies in the context of relationships between modernity, nationalism and memory. It then highlights the particular relationships between commemorations of the dead in war within a framework that draws on Freud's distinction between mourning and melancholia. Finally, the discussion will elaborate these issues with reference to the use of the myth of Kosovo Polje in Serbian national mobilization.

II.   The resurgence of memory

Memory has recently become a major scholarly theme, and while this is not in itself a new topic in sociology, the collapse of time, space and territoriality associated with globalization change the dynamics of memory and identity. Knowledge now inheres not in 'consciousness' but (for example) non-linear textuality, discourses and electronic archives, film and video. Kenneth Gergen talks about the postmodern 'multiphrenia' of memories that are exteriorized in print, film, photograph and cinema – these are not based on common experience but 'parallel memory'.[10] In web-based archives, the linearity of text and narrative memory gives way to non-linearity in virtual time offering multiple levels and entrances, simultaneous presence and virtual 'experience'. Thus between the 1920s sociology of memory – exemplified by Halbwachs – and the present lie the various postmodernist and cultural turns that frame our current understandings. As the idea of a subject that 'possesses' memory has given way to one in which memory inheres in texts and archives, so the politics of memory has taken on increased significance.

Nonetheless, one insight from Halbwachs' work that we should keep in mind is that while monumental space draws people together and 'exudes timelessness'; its meanings will shift according to contemporary concerns. Furthermore, despite the digitalization of memory the 'resurgence of nationalism throughout Europe ... has been substantially based upon ... an unleashing of primordial sentiments and attachments at the local, regional, national or continental levels, exposing the fractured and dispersed structure of the imaginary basis of intolerance ... as well as the defensive rejection of ambivalence and uncertainty in the context of globalization'.[11] The nation is a mnemonic community whose *raison d'être* derives from both remembering *and* forgetting, especially where the past poses a threat to the unity of the nation. Thus memory and its appropriation have become central issues in societies emerging from the erasure of public memory and the survival of counter-memories. While these counter-memories acted as a focus of resistance to the official re-writing of history, they can also have deadly consequences – as in the Yugoslavian wars.

III.   Modernity and commemoration

In modern societies the transmission of collective memory is not a continuous process but is subject to dislocation. By establishing post-traditional values and practices modernity erased traditional forms of cultural transmission while generating a sense of dependence on the past, especially through public memorials that engendered a distinctive form of memory and commemoration. Increasingly significant among these were war memorials. No longer living within memory embedded in communities – where memory installs remembrance within the sacred – modern forms of memory are radically different to those experienced in archaic societies.[12] Merging personal and collective identity and memory, monuments replace the real site of memory while shaping the past within a struggle for supremacy.[13] The differentiation of a specialized religious field, the gradual pluralization of institutions, communities and systems of religious thought, correspond historically to the differentiation of total social memory into a plurality of specialized circles of memory. Two consequences follow from this. First, memory becomes subject to homogenizing processes – mass communication and media image production lead to saturation and focus on a perpetual present. Second, an increasing fragmentation of collective memory occurs as individuals and social groups attempt to construct their pasts in various ways.

Industrialization along with the rapid pace of technological and commercial change brought about a rupture of collective memory, as the intergenerational transmission of social knowledge and its relevance were dislocated. In this context the problem of social integration itself became a central topic of social and political reflection, and indeed a central theme in early sociology.[14] Architecture, monuments and public rituals played important roles in creating an external memory along with for example medals, postage stamps, statuary and festivals.[15]

Mona Ozouf argues that the French revolutionary festivals, such as Bastille Day, were the first attempt to tie public festivals to a national calendar.[16] These involved the transference of sacralty from religious to political objects – the tricolour cockades, liberty trees, red liberty caps and the goddess of liberty.[17]

The rupture of cultures of transmission brought about by political revolutions and industrialism engendered a sense of detachment from the past. In the process, calendrical time was invested with progress and narrative, as a shell through which events moved. The theme of deliverance – having been saved from foreign invasion or internal subversion – was supplemented by public rituals and festivals around monuments and memorials, punctuating the movement of time as markers that looked backwards and forward. Nineteenth-century monumental architecture often harked back to classical antiquity, connoting a depth of time and distant origins. The Roman standard for a victory monument was the triumphal arch, evident in modernist triumphalism such as the Arc de Triomphe and Marble Arch in London. But these were not simply replicas of classical triumphal arches; within the Arc de Triomphe, for example, were inscribed the names of hundreds of Napoleon's generals, with those who died in battle underlined, and as such the status of the arch as a memorial dedicated specifically to war was established. These were in part memorials to rulers, but they also served to engender a sense of collective identity, while expressing the aspirations of a self-confident bourgeois order. Memory processes have been imagined and communicated through a variety of spatial and visual metaphors that construct an architecture of internal memory places.[18] Monumental solidity offered resistance to the possibility of everything melting into air, creating instead the appearance of timelessness and solidity.

The rise of nationalism was central to this process, since rapid social change and the loss of cultural remembrance paved the way for new forms of imagined community.[19] Landscape is essential for national imagining, since territory becomes inscribed with history and temporality. Landscape is external – it is a visible and palpable synthesis of time and space, a fusion Bakhtin describes as a 'chronotope', the intrinsic connectedness of temporal and spatial relationships.[20] In this sense landscapes and monuments are chronotopes in which time has been condensed in a space symbolically arranged and invested with myth and identity. This occurs in official commemorations, such as battlefields, monuments and special days, but it is also evident in unofficial practices. Yet these external memories require continuous mobilization and enforcement, since monuments can become invisible and fade into the background. Much reinforcement of national identities is 'banal nationalism', that is, the routine ways of instilling a shared sense of a collective past inscribed into everyday events, such as saluting the flag.[21] Even so, banal monuments are not innocent since they are often the sites of conflict between competing (often incompatible) histories and unstable in that they are subject to competing meanings.

Add to this, though, the role of globalized technologies in creating and sustaining 'memory' and the process of their transmission identity is complex. Postmodernists tend to emphasize the fluidity of 'memory' while others seek to identify real sites of cultural transmission. Anthony Smith in particular has argued that the ancestral land links memory to destiny.[22] By contrast to the emphemerality of 'memoryless' global culture, Smith argues, the 'obstinate fact is that national cultures, like all cultures before the modern epoch, are particular, time bound and expressive and their eclecticism operates within strict cultural constraints'.[23] In particular, he says, national cultures share memories of specific events and display both a sense of continuity across generations and a common destiny.

Smith implies that ethno-memories are the repository of a definable and stable group (similar to the older sociology of memory). But two issues are relevant in challenging this claim. First, national identities are not stable and primordial, but unstable hybrids of conflicting passions, as 'scraps, patches and rage of daily life must be repeatedly turned into the signs of a national culture'.[24] Maintaining a personal narrative that instantiates and affirms a collective memory continually suppresses the irredeemably plural nature of modern identities. Second, an important issue here is how collective memories are transmitted, stored, mobilized and made relevant to present concerns and projects. They are never just 'there' and the sources of modern identity lie in multiple histories, media and archives that are subject to revision, mobilization and recombination according to contemporary cultural shifts and politics. It is true that commonly shared pasts create a necessary component of identity and history, providing an answer to the question 'who are we'? But this always seems to rely, as Slawomir Kapralski notes, on the question of 'who we were' and the existence of the group's collective identity makes real a particular construction of the past.[25] While Smith is right that the living transmission of cultural memory is an important component of national identity, it is also the case that the existence of national groups constructs collective memories so there is a self-sustaining process of remembering and collective identity. If this line of argument is correct then Smith may be exaggerating the extent to which national-ethnic identities are primordially derived. Or at least, even if fragments of ethnic memories are primordial, their recombination may be mediated by electronic technologies which impose their own structure on the content.[26] This suggests collective memory has undergone a transformation in its mode of recall and representation.

The meaning and appropriation of public sites of memory is subject to contestation and struggle. 'Memory is social because every memory exists through its relation with what has been shared with others: language, symbols, events and social and cultural contexts'.[27] Memories are organized around places and things that imprint effects on topography and space. This contestation has extended across post-communist Europe. Kapralski points out that in the wake of the collapse of 'official' commemorative activities the field has opened for often-bitter conflicts, illustrated by the clashes over the rhetorical ownership of Auschwitz.[28] Kapralski argues that for Jews, Auschwitz symbolizes the Holocaust, the event that condensed a history of antisemitic persecutions and therefore a symbol of Jewish uniqueness in the face of annihilation. This is in a context in which the specifically Jewish significance of the site was largely denied during the communist period and the deaths of Jews de-emphasized in favour of the 'Struggle Against Fascism'. It has been suggested that for American and western European Jews going to Auschwitz involves passing through a secular ritual that confirms their identity as Jews.[29]

For the Poles, Kapralski claims, Auschwitz symbolizes the Polish tragedy during the Second World War, which was a condensed history of German attempts to subordinate and eventually destroy the Polish nation. Polish nationalists denied a chance to express national identity freely outside state-designed channels redefine identity via the memory of Auschwitz as a solely 'Polish' place and a national-religious symbol. These conflicts came to a head in the early 1990s with the dispute over the Carmelite nuns at the site who had appropriated a camp building and erected more than 100 crosses.[30] This resulted in a fifteen-year conflict amidst accusations of the Christianization of Auschwitz, which seemed doomed to remain unresolved. Although the convent was eventually moved outside the camp's boundary, a large wooden cross that had been erected at the height of the convent crisis in 1989 remained at the site. Both sides have now agreed that the cross will remain in perpetuity and some Jewish groups find this strangely appropriate, regarding it as a symbol of divine abandonment, in accordance with Jesus's cry, 'My God, wherefore hast Thou forsaken me'. Thus its presence at Auschwitz may be seen as a testimony to the absence of divine intervention that has so exercized theologians since the Holocaust.[31] As the collapse of communist official control over their interpretation and commemoration of the past disappeared, such memorials have been subject to struggles for appropriation especially by peoples in the past marginalized in a process that asserts claims to contemporary national formation.[32] Competing historical narratives and the commemoration of genocide are bitterly contested around landscape and monuments.

IV. Nationalism and death

Auschwitz is a powerful symbol, in many ways the Ur-phenomenon not only of the Holocaust but also of twentieth-century genocide. Sites commemorating mass death are especially potent since the rhetoric of national identity emerges particularly through the pathos of remembrance. But these meanings are never fixed and there is interplay between elite and popular uses of the monuments. The graphic memorials to the victims of concentration camps in Père Lachaise Cemetery, Paris, emphasize the role of resistance brigades rather than Jewish civilians. In one monument a skeletal figure is represented in redemptive pose, suggesting resurrection, flight (transcendence) suggesting therefore a future in which hope is possible. This could be seen as a gesture of national solidarity, of the shared fate of Jews and others that transcends particular identities. But it could alternatively be viewed in more critical terms as an inability to confront the specificity of antisemitism in which the Jewishness of victims is lost beneath an essentially nationalist rhetoric of struggle against foreign occupation. Such monuments are open to both readings because the architecture of commemoration encodes political constructions of the past and is therefore an always-unstable hybrid of conflicting identities and memories. Diverse social groups invoke the commemorative power of public objects and spaces such as war memorials, statues and street names in different ways. Nationalism can be seen as a way of repairing the rupture in collective memory brought about by industrialization, but nationalism is linked to death in that the industrial age was par excellence the age of the movement of weapons, troops and populations through time and space, which were depleted by modernity's mass 'democratic' war machine.[33]

With the erection of war memorials national identity appealed to a putative community of the living and the dead. The commemoration ceremony of remembrance – 'they shall not grow old as we who are left grow old' – has the mnemonic effect of summoning the 'presence of absents' and inviting participants to join with an imagined community encompassing the living and the dead.[34] The inscription of names on monuments speaks to a transcendence of forgetting that is poignant and disturbing and links individuals to the nation across generations. The externalization of memories of mass death occurred particularly after the First World War, though they had precursors in war cemeteries such as Gettysburg National Cemetery.

The scale and scope of the First World War had deprived survivors of the capacity for memory in the sense of relating encompassing narratives accounting for their experiences. Walter Benjamin claimed that the war was a cataclysm that had left people without conditions for telling stories in that mechanical warfare, hyperinflation, the vast movements of population, and the scale of destruction wrested the events from the grasp of individual life histories.[35] Leo Lowenthal argues that memory's most serviceable reminder was landscape, and memorials and monuments locate the imagined or remembered past in the present landscape.[36] Jay Winter believes that spatial memory (as distinguished from visual memory) transforms latent memory into active ('flash-bulbs lighting up') memory when an individual occupies a site associated with a ritual or event.[37] Both further claim that warfare, particularly in the twentieth century, is a time of dramatic and unique experiences, which leave dense memory traces, both social and individual. Witnesses of warfare, whether surviving soldiers, family members of those wounded or killed, surviving civilian victims or their relatives, were all involved in memory work – that is, in a public rehearsal of memories. They acted in order to fill in silence, to struggle with grief, to offer something symbolically to the dead.

The effect was a particularly modern form of public memory that became a sacred experience, the purpose of which was no longer to marvel but to mourn.[38] These war memorials further reflected the rise of mass culture and democratization. Earlier war memorials, where they existed at all, had commemorated only officers and royal leaders. Now each fallen soldier was commemorated by name, or at least regiment, in standardized format without personalized inscriptions. This was a form of official, public memorialization that was no longer unambiguously progressive. One purpose of the war memorial was to serve as the centre of rituals of mourning which bind together the putative national community in a sense of collective wrong. But the silent horror and pathos of the First World War memorials, such as Vimy Ridge near Arras in northern France, is open to various meanings. War grave commemoration has elided the unambiguous meaning of national sacrifice to admit to the possibility that this was meaningless killing – emphasizing for example (as at Vimy Ridge) the closeness of the German and

Commonwealth lines, separated year on year by a few metres. Over the years the landscape of the Western Front and the imagined landscape of sites that attracted travellers altered. The scenes of death and destruction to be found on the battlefields were, as David Lloyd says, initially the centres of attraction for many travellers. When much of the devastation and most of the wartime aspect of the battlefields was removed by reconstruction, the travel objective shifted to the cemeteries and memorials built by the Allies, and the few remaining battlefield sites. Increasingly for travellers the imagined landscape was perceived within the context of the war's wider meaning, which shifted between on the one hand, concern that the horrors of war needed to be remembered and avoided to, on the other hand, an appreciation of the heroism and sacrifices made. Lloyd shows how this dichotomy led to debate: did it sanitize, even glorify, war, or was it a lesson in peace? After the war, the first travellers to the Western Front were confronted by a landscape that denied not only order, but also civilization. Lloyd points out that an important theme of battlefield travel in the 1920s was sacrifice. In particular this was associated with the memorials and cemeteries that came to dominate both the actual and the imagined landscape during the 1920s and 1930s.[39]

It would be hard to argue that the war memorials and cemeteries are overtly patriotic structures that were designed to celebrate a major national triumph and mask the war's horrors. The sheer scale of the loss commemorated means that to lionize the dead and glorify war was both distasteful and inappropriate. The commemorative landscapes of the war was invoked frequently by Britain's inter-war peace movement, but these landscapes were not unequivocally anti-war statements consciously designed to indicate modern war's futility and waste.[40] A shift towards the demystification of heroic death in public commemoration has been accompanied by a falling military participation rate in most western societies along with the technologization of mass death, which is no longer labour intensive.

V.   Mourning or melancholia?

So far, I have suggested that memorials embed within landscape and ritual discourses of national collectivity complex processes of remembering and forgetting. But they are also ambiguous and open to diverse meanings. This very ambiguity enables the process of memory to be mobilized in the service of national formation, but it can also trigger the release of violence in the name of unexpiated historic wrongs. It may be useful to bear in mind Freud's distinction between mourning – memory work that enables reconciliation with loss – and melancholia, where the loss is continually revisited, is vital, intrusive and persistent. The latter becomes a metaphor of modernity in which genocide cannot be presented within traditional historical perspectives.[41] This helps us understand the dynamics of civil conflict in the post-communist world. Death and genocide evoke powerful responses and it is crucial whether these take the form of reconciliation with the past (mourning) or melancholic repression of grief followed by the repetition of trauma that cannot be expurgated.

The ways in which people remember their past is dependent on their relationship to their community, public discourses of legitimation, and the contestations between these. For Halbwachs memory was social in that its content is intersubjective (we remember interactions with others), it is structured around social reference points (such as rituals and ceremonies), and it is shared (rehearsal of memories is associated with high levels of affect).[42] But he did not address collective processes of *communication*.[43] Celia Lury has further shown how self-identity and memory are redefined through the manipulation of personal and public photographic images.[44] It is not the remembered so much as the forgotten that provides the key to 'rewriting the soul'.[45] Again, 'remembering and forgetting are ... locked together in a complicated web as one group's enfranchisement requires another's disenfranchisement'.[46] In particular the notion of trauma provided the point of entry into the 'psychology of the soul' through which the forgotten could be therapeutically remembered.[47]

Commenting on Freud's theory of aggression, C. Fred Alford argues that 'hatred is egostructuring. It can define a self, connecting it to others, anchoring it in the world, which at the same time acting as a fortress ... Hatred creates history, a history that defines the self and provides it with structure and meaning'.[48] Moreover, 'loving recitation of harms suffered and revenge inflicted, constitutes the single most important, most comprehensible and most stable sense of identity'. If this argument is valid, then alongside mannered interactions and civility, civilization also shifts powerful and disturbing emotions and experiences from the centre of life to the periphery. In this process, public rituals and symbols of commemoration inscribe a collective narrative memory into individual life histories. Narrative emphasis on continuity and development leads to a unity of the self as a project with access to personal and collective memories. Being a member of a national community often involves taking ownership of a public, historical narrative

that typically defines a degree of difference and sense of a nation belea-
guered. In her interviews with survivors of the Latvian deportations of
the 1940s, Vieda Skultans found that respondents often drew no temporal distinctions between the deaths of immediate family and historical
events, such as the death of Namijs, the thirteenth-century Latvian
chieftain who resisted a German invasion.[49] Personal loss is shaped by
and is located alongside textual memories adapted from school history
and literature lessons.[50] Furthermore, terror does not necessarily destroy
civilizational values. Rather, witnesses to genocide say they cannot
describe these experiences and when they find their way into narratives
they are no longer direct expressions of the past but draw on cultural
resources to give their descriptions meaning.[51]

An important contrast here lies in the way memories are communicated and the dispositions to which coming to terms with the past give
rise – through mourning and memory-work or melancholia. One theme
within the emergence of modern, post-traditional worldviews has been
what Jürgen Habermas calls the 'linguistification of the sacred', in which
the 'spell-binding power of the sacred' is eroded by the collapse of binding worldviews and the argumentative functions of language.[52] On a
more practical level, it is possible that open and reflexive discourse
enables participants to confront the complexities and ambiguities of
their identities and pasts in ways that diffuse violent emotions and effect
reconciliation between antagonists. This at any rate is the idea behind
practices of mediation and reparation and institutional processes such as
the South African Truth and Reconciliation Commission.

By contrast, many public commemorative ceremonies close off any
open or reflexive reconciliation of past grievances. Durkheim pointed
out the extent to which sacred public rituals re-affirmed collective solidarity through commemorative rites that relive the mythical history of
ancestors and sustain the vitality of beliefs by rendering them present.[53]
One might imagine that modern values deny credence to the idea of
life as a structure of celebrated recurrence, but commemorative rituals are
dependent on calendrical time that enables the juxtaposition of profane
time with the sacred return marked by anniversaries.[54] Furthermore, the
sacredness of public commemoration (such as remembrance parades) is
dependent on a highly ritualized language in which stylized and stereotyped sequences of speech acts contrast with the linguistification of the
sacred. Commemorative speech does not admit any interrogation of its
discursive properties because its meanings are already coded in canonical
monosemic forms (oaths, blessings, prayers and liturgy) that bring into
existence attitudes and emotions. For example, the words 'they shall not

grow old as we who are left grow old' does not admit discursive interrogation. Listeners are not invited to reflect on the benefits of immortality within a putative national community against the cost of premature death on the battlefield. The particular speech variant of commemorative and other public rituals is important because they close off possibilities for the reflexive examination and juxtaposition of identities.

Special but crucial cases of public commemoration are what Durkheim labelled 'sad celebrations', that is, piacular (expiatory, atoning) rites which fuse mourning and melancholy with sacrifice and violence.[55] Their effect is to generate anger and the need to avenge the dead and discharge collective pain, manifesting in real or ritual violence. Victims are sought outside the group, especially among resident minorities 'not protected by sentiments of sympathy', and women serve more frequently than men as objects of the cruellest rites of mourning and as scapegoats. The context for piacular rites is often a social crisis and the pressure to bear witness to sorrow, perplexity or anger. Participants imagine that outside are evil beings whose hostility can be appeased only by suffering. Thus piacular rites involve mourning fasting, weeping, with obligations to slash or tear clothing and flesh, thereby renewing the group to a state of unity preceding misfortune. The more collective sentiments are wounded, as Durkheim suggested, the greater is the violence of the response.

VI. Memories of Kosovo Polje

Commemoration then may take the form of mourning in which subjects are able to confront and effect reconciliation with the past; alternatively it can take the form of melancholia in which grief and anger predominate. Melancholia was to play a significant role in the Yugoslavian civil wars. We see something of this in the mobilization of Serbian national myths in the late 1980s. Despite the efforts in pre- and post-war Yugoslavia to fashion a unified federal state, national countermemories kept alive old hatreds in popular consciousness. In her account of travels in pre-war Yugoslavia, Rebecca West quotes her Serbian guide in 'Old Serbia' (Kosovo) in the 1930s:

> We will stop at Grachanitsa, the church I told you of on the edge of Kosovo Plain, but I do not think you will understand it, because it is very personal to us Serbs, and that is something you foreigners can never grasp. It is too difficult for you, we are too rough and too deep for your smoothness and your shallowness.[56]

National identity is public (shared and reinforced through public affirmation and commemoration) yet private to the putative community of those who share the particular imagined historical memory. 'Roughness' (Serbian *surovost*, connoting also rudeness and brutality) is contrasted with the cosmopolitan superficiality of those who can never participate in the ethnic-cultural community. In this case, where the traditional blessing for the new-born is 'Hail, little avenger of Kosovo' one is born with the weight of unexpiated vengeance.[57]

Between 1987–89 Slobodan Milosevic conducted a carefully orchestrated campaign of nationalist hysteria focussed on Kosovo but widening gradually to conjure up for Serb audiences an unholy alliance of Albanians, Slovenes and Croats. Milosevic made the six hundreth anniversary of the Battle of Kosovo in June 1989 the focal point of this 'anti-bureaucratic revolution' to displace political opponents within the Serbian ruling party – especially Ivan Stambolic (who was abducted and murdered in 2000). Milosevic's speech in June 1989 invoked the 'heroism' of 1389 in a theme of betrayal and lack of unity, linking the historic defeat first with Serbia's occupation by Germany in the Second World War and then with the subsequent 'weakness' of Serbia within the Yugoslav Federation. Now he claimed that Serbia was a victim of Albanian 'fascists and secessionists' who threatened the Serbian nation with 'genocide'. The nature of this threat had been made clear in the 1986 Serbian Memorandum signed by 212 academics and artists which complained that the Albanians of Kosovo were pursuing a policy of 'genocide' against Serbs. The threat of 'genocide' was demographic – it claimed that the proportion of Serbs to Albanians in Kosovo was rapidly declining, from 23 and 67 per cent respectively in 1961 to 90 and 10 percent in 1991.[58] But this imagined threat of 'genocide' tapped into and mobilized cultural memories of past Serbian 'sacrifice' and suffering.[59]

A classically piacular ritual signalled the escalation of national mobilizations prior to the Yugoslavian civil war. This was the Serbian commemoration of the battle of *Kosovo Polje* (Field of Black Birds) in 1389, where the last Serbian prince, Lazar was defeated by the Turkish Sultan Murat. That this defeat is celebrated in Serbian national narrative as a 'holy and honourable sacrifice' illustrates an important point about national mythologies – defeats, because of their affective and sacrificial power, may be more central than the 'faked up glories and imagined pasts' of standard national rhetoric.[60] In Serbian legend the sacrifice of Lazar who (according to a Serbian poem) 'chose a heavenly kingdom' was also a sacrifice for Christian Europe, allowing Italy and Germany to survive. This became the cornerstone of modern Serbia's national mythology. The uprisings at the beginning of the nineteenth century were represented as the revival of the Serb's struggle against the Ottomans at the end of the fourteenth century. Through these poems and songs, modern Serbia claimed a vital continuity with a romanticized past as a means of underscoring its claims to disputed territory. Most of the songs contained stark moral messages.[61] Martyrdom became a theme in Serbian propaganda, and the Serbian Network (a website maintained by the Serbian Government) claims that it would be wrong to assert that the defeat at Kosovo prevented Serbia becoming a great nation. On the contrary, 'It was [defeat] that made us a great nation. It is our Golgotha; but it is at the same time our moral resurrection'.[62] The 'coffin' (with the alleged remains of Lazar) toured every village in Serbia followed by huge black-clad crowds of wailing mourners. Serbian nationalists regard the autonomous province of Kosovo, with an Albanian-Islamic majority population, as lying in the 'heartland of our nation'. In the meadow of Gazimestan the monument to Lazar expresses vengeful sadness and defeat:

> Whosoever is a Serb and of Serbian birth
> And who does not come to Kosovo Polje to do battle against the
>   Turks
> Let him have neither a male nor a female offspring
> Let him have no crop.

In contemporary nationalist symbolism, 'Albanians' in Kosovo and other Islamic minorities elsewhere in the former Yugoslavia, especially Bosnia, have substituted for 'Turks'. In both the Serbian and Croatian national imaginations, the civil war was a replaying of ancient conflicts between west and east, European and Asiatic, 'civilization' and 'barbarism'.

The anniversary commemorations began the revolt against the Yugoslav federation as nationalist violence spread throughout the country. The affect encoded in the Lazar memory informs contemporary discourses of violent conflict. During the fighting in Kosovo early in 1999, the Serbian Democratic Movement (nationalist and close to the Orthodox Church) claimed,

> We Serbs are a proud people who have endured throughout history –
> and still our homeland suffers the agonies of war. We respond with
> pride and courage. Never have we needed it more … .It is a coura-
> geous sacrifice. Before the Battle of Kosovo Prince Lazar told his

gallant knights that it was better to die heroically than to live under the enemy yoke. More than ever, we must hold Kosovo dear for all the world to see, for it is a testament to the courage of our people.[63]

This and similar statements drew their meaning from the particular politics of memory in the Yugoslav Federation in which the Second World War had been 'memorized' through education and public discourse as a people's liberation war – a struggle of class rather than ethnic or national aspiration.[64] The language of socialism had not permitted an open discourse nor subjected Yugoslav history to unrestricted discussion. With the collapse of the Federation the Party lost control of memory and secret histories of trauma and ethnic hatred were opened up. This coincided with a process of 'recounting the dead' on all sides of the conflict prior to the civil war. The history of German occupation and conflicts between the Croatian Ustashe and Chetniks (Serbian partisans) had left largely suppressed historical memories of mass slaughter. The collapse of Federal and Communist rule was accompanied by the uncovering of (semi) hidden massacres followed by new commemorative funerals, which provided a 'supreme moment for transforming ritual into political theatre'.[65] Each subsequent antagonist in the civil war could mobilize the unexpiated trauma of suppressed memories. The Communists were mass murderers (of Ustasas and Chetniks); the Croatian (fascist) State of 1941–5 murdered Serbs; the Muslims were collaborators with Nazi genocide; while the new Croatian state under Tuðjman diminished the extent of Ustashe genocide thus provoking further trauma-rage. Each collective participant imagined themselves victims of unavenged historical wrongs that could be expiated only through the elimination of the enemy.

The ensuing conflict took on the proportions of what René Girard calls 'violent contagion' which was exterminatory and potentially unlimited.[66] This arises, in his view, from an unresolved primal conflict. Mimetic desire to acquire the wholeness of the other (which is experienced as a lack or incompleteness of oneself) leads to a feud between incompatible rivals. By simultaneously taking the other as a model and obstacle they form 'violent doubles' locked in mutual destruction. Violent doubles are characterized by incommensurable identities – to be X is to fear Y; to be Y is to fear X – locked in a confrontation in which one's enfranchisement requires another's disenfranchisement. This is resolved, temporarily, by sacrifice, where potentially violent doubles discharge mimetically generated violence onto an arbitrary and innocent victim whom they scapegoat, by attributing to it the violence they have just committed. The scapegoat mechanism establishes in-group/out-group differentiations that maintain the communities' structure and cohesion. For Girard, this sacrificial expulsion is the basis of all social order and ritual through which communities gain control over their violence. Myths bind communities and symbolically discharge rage while disguising the original sacrifice-murder but a crisis in the social order, what Girard calls a 'sacrificial crisis', can release the violent desires once renounced.

Girard's thesis may illuminate the dynamics of bitter and intractable national conflicts in which both sides claim exclusive rights over identical social and territorial space. One excludes the other, yet both share the same space and are destined to be enemies, until the spiral of violent contagion can be broken. In the Yugoslav case, a patchwork of competing national identities entered fields of struggle over incommensurable desires for national homelands. In a triadic pattern, minorities struggled with titular states for a national homeland that was the goal of each. The Krajina Serbs, looking to incorporation in a Serbian homeland, resisted Croatia's nationalizing desire, while Milosovic insisted that Croatia could be independent only without Krajina. In Kosovo the Serbian minority, backed by the Serbian army, resisted independence and the desire for unity with an Albanian homeland. The conflict in Bosnia was particularly exterminatory because it was a field of multiple doubles – Serb/Croat, Islamic/Serb, Islamic/Croat – each struggling for incommensurable spaces.[67]

To understand this and similar ethnic conflicts we need to understand the processes of the construction and mobilization of collective memory. The Kosovan conflict took place on a landscape of sacred territory, which was an object of mutually exclusive desires for the rectification of historical wrongs. Both sides legitimated exterminatory desires with reference to historical memories. Kosovo was alternately the spiritual home of Serb Orthodoxy, marked by holy sites, monasteries and forced evacuations, both following Prince Lazar's defeat and again led by Patriarch Arsenije III Carnojevic in 1690; or for centuries populated predominantly by Albanians periodically subjected to Serbian genocide. 'Ethnic cleansing' is not new to these landscapes. In accounts from both sides commemorations and rituals demonstrate the loving recitation of harms suffered and revenge inflicted. The massacres and removals of Kosovans by Serbs in 1999 had had many precedents, such as the expulsions of Albanians during the second Serbian-Ottoman war (1877–8).

Melancholia and grief, then, are of particular importance because they constitute the basis for the desire for vengeful justice. Grief and loss may prove to be significant in discourses authorizing violent actions.

Unresolved grief does not allow accommodation or reconciliation but perpetuates stereotyped repetitions of thought and behaviour. Further, state control and sanctification of national rituals of remembering will both preclude open confrontation with the past and encourage the formation of counter-memories that likewise will not be discursively examined. In this way conflicts become intractable, and an exterminatory violence resulting from friend/foe enmity in which the very presence of the other sustains yet threatens each identity.

Nonetheless, we should note two further points. First, for both Durkheim and Girard (in different ways) piacular rites and mimetic scapegoats should operate to *contain* and limit violence. But they do not necessarily do so; on the contrary they may act as catalysts and authorizations for further violence. In the examples cited above expiatory-sacrificial rituals were the prelude to violence that spilled into communal destructiveness. Furthermore, whilst the symbolic discharge of violence may serve to dissipate actual violence the border between the symbolic and real is unstable and under conditions of crisis the former may spill over into the latter.[68] But whether violence is symbolically discharged (thereby being contained) or is real, is of critical importance, and we need to know how this line gets crossed. Rather than containing violence, the kinds of ritual memory discussed here generate an unstable process of national identity formation, which requires continual affirmation. National identity is not fixed or stable but an unstable hybrid. Maintaining a personal narrative that instantiates and affirms a collective memory continually suppresses the irredeemably plural nature of modern identities. The more the maintenance of a unisonant self is threatened by the presence of competing identities, the more likely that inner conflicts will take the form of paranoid projections. Secondly, however, Girard believes that sacrificial violence is transcended through the 'non-sacrificial' Christian gospels, which by revealing the sacrificial process render it ineffective. A different, sociological approach would be to argue that post-traditional reflexive forms of communication themselves undermine sacred bonds thereby weakening the effectiveness of sacrificial violence.

VII.   Conclusion: collective memory and identity

National memories are not only the repository of definable and stable groups. Rather, they are unstable and constructed as a hybrid of conflicting passions that are actively assembled into a narrative of 'nationhood'. Attempting to maintain a personal narrative that instantiates and affirms a collective memory continually suppresses the irredeemably plural nature of modern identities. Against this background of instability and reconstruction nationalism is an allegory of irresolution, an expression of fear of the transient nature of the nation.[69]

Social transformation risks increasing instability, with multiple forms of social identification and rethinking a past that was often subject to official controls. In particular, the collective memory of trauma, of counting the dead and the construction of a narrative community with the dead, can invest collective memories with a pathos that under certain circumstances legitimates expiatory violence. The Serbian case shows the potential for violent conflict following from the mobilization of cultural memories where these are the object of melancholic grief rather than memory-work.

A crucial factor in authorizing violence, then, is the availability of languages of rationalization and legitimation, which draw on the affectively charged pathos of collective loss. These may be inscribed into cultural memories in ritualized ways and are therefore not open to discursive examination. In response to social stress, such as state failure, piacular rituals expiate memories of collective injustice. These have the potential to spiral into a process of 'disidentification' between ethnic groups (for example Serbs and Albanians) along with a campaign to strengthen identifications within the population. The resulting 'dyscivilizing' process gives rise to a society that is compartmentalized into areas where 'peaceful' everyday life continues and those such as the camps, or the whole area of Kosovo, where extreme violence is perpetrated against the targeted group. These are likely to be most severe where they involve unmediated mimetic conflicts between similar actors competing for an identical object, such as incompatible national homelands. These are extreme cases of routinized processes of commemoration and identity formation. Yet at the same time, 'memory' is becoming less officially and publicly sanctioned and more constructed and consumed in an individualized way. One consequence of this is the detachment of identity and place, as diasporic communities sustain national 'belonging' via global systems of communication. Various sides in the Yugoslavian civil war mobilized support among diasporic communities, particularly via the Internet.[70]

In post-communist countries we witness rhetorical battles over the appropriation of representations and commemorations. The collapse of the Soviet version of high modernity has given way to more individualized forms of commemoration that are unstable and contested as the media of commemoration diversifies. There is lesson here with wider applicability. This is that the way communities address the past and work through historical grievances is crucial to the chances for the formation of communicative civil societies that are able to learn and mediate diversity. This chapter has contrasted on the one hand forms of commemoration based on incantations of closed quasi-sacred language with communicative communities that are able to subject identities to reflexive examination. What further complicates these issues though is the transformation of 'memory' itself – from public narrative to hybrid forms of individualized and publicly contested 'memories' that are subject to mobilization via multiple media of communication. The problem is not so much being condemned to relive the past because of failing to remember it – more that the way of remembrance involves a compulsive attachment to unrelieved trauma. In order to understand the dynamics of ethnic and national conflicts as well as ways of resolving them we need to understand the dynamics of commemoration and remembrance.

Part III

8

Trauma Culture
Remembering and Forgetting in the New South Africa

Lynn Meskell

I. Introduction

In the past few decades we have witnessed an emergent debate about the relationships between history and memory. Underlying this debate is a critical 'disturbance not just of the relationship between history as objective and scientific, and memory as subjective and personal, but of history itself and its promises'.[1] What is increasingly being contested here is not simply an upheaval around notions of the past or the role of the past in the present, but a crisis in our imagining of possible futures. Here memory is understood as an active remembrance, a recognition of past ideas and events, the power to reproduce the past in both symbolic and material terms and the creative entailments following on from these practices. For many memory and trauma have been inextricably linked, yet this does not have to be the case. In Huyssen's view, this linkage is often predicated by the fact that trauma as a psychic phenomenon is located in the threshold between remembering and forgetting, seeing and not seeing, experience and its absence in repetition. And it is in this connection that the two discourses are so heavily imbricated in the context of South Africa, as I will argue in this chapter. In South Africa public memory discourses might ideally allow individuals to break out of traumatic repetitions. Human rights activism, truth commissions, and juridical proceedings are powerful methods for dealing with historical trauma. Again following Huyssen, I demonstrate that another powerful arena is the constitution of cultural productions including objects, memorials, museums and public spaces of commemoration.[2] It is thus critical that in the urban spaces of daily life, particularly in contexts such as South Africa, we can analyse how memory and forgetting pervade the public sphere and the world of things.

The past occupies an ambivalent role in post-Apartheid South Africa. For some it is seen as a vast reservoir of trauma and loss, while for others it can be mobilized as a source of pride and redemption. In fact there are many constructs of the past at play: the deep past of prehistory, the colonial past of named individuals and events, and the unforgettable apartheid past. Not surprisingly, due to decades of institutionalized racism South Africa has a very complex and contradictory relation to its past and the subsequent remembering of that past. At this unique juncture, the category of memory is being reworked in South Africa, as many of the political and cultural elite urge their fellow citizens to forget the past and look forward to a new future. Put simply, there is often a state-sanctioned willingness to suspend disbelief and focus on the united aim of moving forward and healing the nation. In this chapter the Voortrekker Monument forms the first critical locus for a historical analysis of the making and remaking of Afrikaner identity. The monument betrays the difficult and disturbing loss of memory regarding colonial history, as it is relegated to a generic history, and its archaeological underpinnings. Next, I discuss more recent sites of cultural production including the Apartheid Museum in Johannesburg and the Hector Pieterson Museum in Soweto that form potent and much needed examples that actively remember the recent past and the scaring specificities of apartheid. Another focus is the practice of trauma tours for economic development, specifically the initiatives of Western Cape Action Tours (WECAT). These too have been successful in sustaining the memory of recent history and recent trauma. Taken together, each of these productions has been forged around sites of intensely 'negative heritage'.

II.   Negative heritage: the past is past

As I have argued previously, negative heritage is a particular type of cultural production that operates as a site of memory occupying a potentially dual role.[3] Negative heritage can be mobilized for positive didactic purposes (e.g. Auschwitz and Hiroshima) or, alternatively, erased if such places cannot be culturally rehabilitated or otherwise resist incorporation into the national imaginary (e.g. Nazi and Soviet sites). Monumentality is intimately tied to memory, whether active remembrance or purposeful forgetting. South Africa exhibits one the most complicated relationships with its past of any colonial society, more so than Australia or the United States, and here we witness the potential re-writing of any prediscursive linkage between memory, trauma and empowerment. The aim of this chapter is to engage with these tensions, to document sites that are inflected with negative heritage, and to track how groups and individuals are currently re-working history for perceived social imperatives. Through this analytic lens I offer a close reading of new heritage practices at an important juncture, at a time when South African heritage agencies are reassessing their role and mandate in a new political climate and when newly commissioned museums and heritage sites are proliferating at an increasing rate.

Any such discussion of memory and trauma is necessarily framed by the spectre of the Truth and Reconciliation Commission (TRC), its place in South African society, and its general underpinnings of amnesty, forgiveness and the desire to move forward as a nation. That spectacle of trauma and memory is shot through with the interventions of globalization and the impacts of world media, making it a rather different prospect to the entanglements of memory in the past. However today, as in the past, memory and identity are inseparable experiences. José Zalaquette, a member of the Chilean Truth Commission, cautions that identities forged out of half memories or false memories easily lead to future transgressions.[4] By not fully recognizing the past – and in this instance I am concerned with the longer historical experience and effects of colonialism – a post-1994 society might simply concentrate on its end product, apartheid, as an aberration. To contextualize apartheid as one logical (evil) outcome of the colonial encounter in Africa generally,[5] is an integral step in addressing the larger historical framing of individuals and collectivities, the politically motivated construction of tribal identities and the fractures and fault lines that continue to haunt the nation. We need to actively 'discriminate among memory practices in order to strengthen those that counteract the tendencies in our culture to foster uncreative forgetting, [and] the bliss of amnesia'.[6] My fear is that the larger edifice of forgetting will elide the specificities of a history that can still to a large degree be documented and told, and in the process the ingrained effects of colonialism will be naturalized and their didactic fictions will retain their residual power. This is the challenge of a responsible and ethically aware archaeology, anthropology and history.

Throughout South Africa there is a proliferation of sites redolent of mourning and memory, so much so that negative heritage is ubiquitous. And yet South Africans have chosen a very specific path to reconciling their entwined histories, a strategy which is at variance with that of Europe and the Middle East. There were no forced removals of statues, no erasures on the scale we have witnessed in the overthrow of the Iraqi regime in 2003. And yet the spaces and potentialities of the past and of heritage in general wield significant political force. South Africa is, moreover, considerably different to other settler societies that have survived the brute forces of genocide and colonization, including the United States, Canada and Australia: the place of the past is built into the very fabric of the new post-apartheid constitution.[7]

> We, the people of South Africa,
> Recognise the injustices of our past;
> Honour those who suffered for justice
> And freedom in our land;
> Respect those who have worked to build
> And develop our country; and
> Believe that South Africa belongs to all
> Who live in it, united in our diversity.

South Africa is in many ways trying to reinvent itself by rewriting its' history – a strategy that goes hand in hand with the didactic contours of nationalism. Building a new national history entails forging a national culture: a self-conscious fusion, combining shreds of regional cultural legacies and international symbols.[8] As evident in South Africa, to be compelling and successful it must form an assimilative tradition, drawing upon the knowledge of particular ethnic groups to enlarge them, thus creating a broader national embrace. I hope to show here that the past has now become a nodal point within high profile cultural productions that recursively connect materiality and sociality. Ebron's notion of an 'imaginative project' for the South African context, rather than reductively suggesting that we are witnessing the proliferation of 'imagined communities', is particularly attractive.[9] Because imaginative solutions have been adopted in many cases, rather that addressing the harsh specificities of the past, there is a strong seam of reworked and re-imagined pasts that run through these new narratives of nationalism. The desire to fabricate and reinterpret colonial history, whether in the name of racial harmony or the creation of a more progressive future, can lead to a tendency to forget or embellish past atrocities, retaining the spectre of potential slippage. The nation might then continue to make a virtue out of colonization and oppression, under the rubric of the rainbow nation narrative, a blurred and ultimately void construction that might superficially look appealing, but which fails to address the historicity of the past. In their desperate attempts to forget the past and move forward, South Africans must also remember and make sure that this never happens again.

Negative heritage can be seen as a specific configuration of materiality, cultural production and social experience, yet more generally it is redolent of, and a signifier for, a broader construction of trauma culture. In the South African context, 'trauma can be unspeakable and unrepresentable ... because it is marked by forgetting and dissociation' and thus '[t]rauma puts pressure on conventional forms of documentation, representation and commemoration, giving rise to new genres of expression, such as testimony and new forms of monuments, rituals and performances that can call into being collective witnesses and publics'.[10] In the process of the remaking of heritage, trauma challenges common understandings of what constitutes an accurate archive. Often it can demand an unusual archive whose materials are frequently ephemeral productions, much like trauma itself. A good example would be the so-called trauma tours that are now proliferating around major cities, townships and slums that constituted the sites of violence under apartheid's regime of terror. As Cvetkovich reminds us, the memory of trauma is embedded not just in narrative but in material artifacts, whether image or monuments that are themselves material storehouses for an archive of feeling.[11] Memory and forgetting as experiential substrata 'pervade real social space, the world of objects and the urban world we live in becomes crucial'.[12] Hence, a material culture perspective is an important vector of analysis in the understanding of memory practices.

III. Traumatic productions

Trauma cultures and their cultural productions enable new practices and publics, as evidenced in post-apartheid South Africa. In that imaginative process trauma raises questions about what constitutes a public culture, and in the case of South Africa it also constitutes what counts as history and whose history, a re-writing of the history of the nation, a re-contextualization of deep history in the service of a rainbow nation narrative. There is a clear relationship between public culture and the therapeutic strategies they choose to enact: archaeology is used as a therapeutic measure in South Africa and is called upon to labour in the service of both individuals and state.[13] Heritage is utilized repeatedly in the rhetoric of politicians like Mbeki and Valli Moosa to help pay for the socio-economic depredations of the apartheid regime and to forge a new, more humane and more prosperous South Africa for all its citizens. Thus we need to expand the category of 'heritage' beyond the confines of traditional understanding, to see heritage as a form of therapy, as the past labouring in the service of a better future, a progressive and productive benefit to all, but specifically for the disempowered, dislocated and disadvantaged. An archaeological past and its concomitant heritage operate very specifically within South Africa's political economy, they have become salient as therapeutic loci. And yet the socioeconomic hardships faced by black South Africans have hardly been ameliorated, and moreover, evidence points to the fact that small-scale ventures around heritage tourism and self-sustainability are tenuous at best.[14] Trauma cultures may be doing the work of therapy, in a collective sense, but also in an inherently political one. South Africans are being educated through various cultural productions about what is best remembered and what is best to forget. The very recent past and its horrors can be foregrounded, yet the longer, more complex colonial history of the country, and the reasons why apartheid was successfully entrenched in the first instance, are subsequently downplayed. This is reflected in the very constitution and fabric of the state and is part of the presidential mandate for a new South Africa.

Despite this willingness to forget, there are undoubtedly good reasons why national solidarity must be fabricated at all costs: 'trauma histories are frequently taken up as national urgencies, histories that must be remembered and resolved in order for the nation to survive a crisis to sustain its integrity'.[15] After the 1994 elections South Africa could have witnessed greater violence and bloodshed. Even now there is an increasingly optimistic atmosphere of looking to the future, of possibility; as one national motto proclaims, 'South Africa is full of potential'. Yet there are still dangers in relegating the specificities of the past – distant or recent – to the realm of forgotten histories. As Ndebele argues, this jostling of past and future requires constant wrestling, for the ambiguities and choices remain difficult: 'Now we want to throw off the psychological burden of our painful past; now we want to hold onto it. We know that death may be a very real consequence of throwing off the burden altogether in one big heave.' Furthermore, he underscores the significance of the past, the connectivities of history that 'intricately binds us to the rest of the world'.[16] Thus while there are demons to exorcize, there are also achievements that must be recognized, resulting in a complex mosaic of present pasts and imaginative futures. These structures of feeling, and their material corollaries in the form of sanctioned heritage, can bring into being alternative cultures and histories. They are the structures of affect that constitute cultural experience and serve as the foundation for public cultures.[17]

In South Africa, as elsewhere, the project of nation building is essentially oriented toward the future. Here building the nation and constructing culture are deeply enmeshed. As Ebron encapsulates the process, talking directly of African nations, this requires the forging of a national community that draws in local loyalties in a self-conscious fusion, combining shreds of regional cultural legacies and international symbols and conventions.[18] She argues forcefully that it must be syncretic and transformative, mobilizing an assimilative tradition that draws on the forms and knowledge of particular ethnic groups to enlarge them, creating a broader national embrace. Finally, this must be the kind of culture that is not trapped in tradition: history must be forwardlooking. Creating a broader national embrace is key in the South African context, given the diversity of people, histories, nationalities, colonialisms, languages and so on. The therapeutic strategy employed is one of assimilative rhetoric, cultural syncretism and ultimately, the goal is transformation. The South African past was impelled to confront the present through settlement, not revolution, exemplified by the TRC and other cultural institutions.[19] Like Ebron, De Kok identifies the accompanying rhetoric about moving forward through the process divined as nation building. The installation, itself a cultural event, is unclear and should be re-done as "The Political inaguration of the motto, *One Nation, Many Cultures*, attempted to forge out of the fragmented ethnic cultural expression a notional celebratory narrative called 'one nation'". Archbishop Tutu's famous phrase to describe South Africa, the 'rainbow nation', encapsulated the euphoria, and the fiction, of the moment. Memory and representation were deemed crucial in the narratives and practices of reconstruction.[20]

We must also remember that it was Nelson Mandela who preached forgiveness to the nation, most notably in his 1994 'Free At Last' speech: 'This is the time to heal old wounds and build a new South Africa'. And he has been a major figure in creating the myth of the rainbow nation at home and abroad. Lesley Wits has focused on both black presidents, Mandela and Mbeki, particularly upon their political rhetoric surrounding the imaginings of rainbow culture, specifically in the context of colonial histories.[21] One evocative example involves the positioning of the historical figures, Jan Van Riebeeck and Maria de la Quellerie. Within ten years of the overthrow of apartheid it was possible for both presidents to put a positive spin on historical figures associated with the beginnings of white colonization (read the origins of apartheid) and deploy this in the service of the rainbow nation. In 1999, President Mbeki pointed out that the great racial divide began when the first commander of the Dutch East India Company's revictualling station at the Cape of Good Hope, Jan Van Riebeeck, planted a hedge of 'almond and thornbush ... to ensure the safety of the newly arrived white European settlers by keeping the menacing black African hordes of pagan primitives at bay'.[22] This was the genesis of apartheid, where 'Black and White had to be kept apart, circumscribed by an equation which described each as the enemy of the other, each the antithesis of the other'. However, the colour of Van Riebeeck and de la Quellerie, as Wits demonstrates, has moved from that of supreme whiteness to that of a rainbow hue, forged in the new language of multiculturalism and diversity. Almost inconceivably, and in a remarkable display of spin, this enabled Mandela to affirm Jan Van Riebeeck as founder of a component of the new South African nation. In such originary myths, narrations of nationhood may be deemed necessary for the security of a new South Africa, yet they seem perched on the dangerous precipice of fabrication. These could be seen as similar to the various racist fantasies, of fundamental rites to appropriate another's country, at the very roots of colonialism, thus forcing indigenous constituencies into celebrating their own oppression.

While the implicit strategy in South Africa is one of incorporation and a willing amnesia, which has effectively ameliorated the threat of violence and revenge in a post-apartheid setting, what has been compromised is the accurate reflection of deep historical events and their ultimate repercussions. Here we see a notable disjunction between the spheres of cultural memory and individual memory. Cultural memory refers to the operations of public life in political and social arenas, which include the performance of culture and heritage. In South Africa, political rhetoric in a climate of confession and forgiveness asks that certain pasts are kept alive, others are glossed over, and still others are relegated to the shadows of prehistory. Questions remain about what constitutes trauma history, or a suitable trauma history, and what sentiments can be expressed in the national public sphere. The Voortrekker monument is a tacit example of a monument in which the past is glossed or inflected with a conscious misreading. Its counterpart, Freedom Park, potentially allows the haunting of apartheid, although its focus is very much one of reconciliation and forward movement.

IV.   The Voortrekker monument

Many cultural commentators fear that South Africa's past will lose its intrinsic historical complexity as well as the ability to critically inform the present if framed paradoxically as both a remedial encounter with living communities and the key mechanism for developing knowledge about the nation. There is a real danger is this conflation and blending, that the historicity of the past will be elided and that with forgetting comes the potential for future fallbacks.

Here I want to offer a potent example of this willing suspension of disbelief, or the desire to forget or rework negative heritage in the present. The Voortrekker monument is a site built in the 1930s outside Pretoria that was, and perhaps still is, completely enmeshed with National Party ideology. Many of those prominent in the National Party had links with the Nazis and other fascist groups, a fact which is betrayed in this edifice where the eternal flame of white progress still burns. Its original purpose was to commemorate the Great Trek, which took place in the late 1830s, when a group of white farmers of mixed European descent sought to escape the encroachment of English settlement by moving from the relative safety of the coastal regions of South Africa into an interior dominated by indigenous populations. David Bunn suggests that early twentieth-century Afrikaner memorial traditions effectively set themselves against themselves, against rival African kingdoms, and against the forces of British imperialism.[23] In 1838, closely knit bands of farmers, later known as the Voortrekkers, reacted against oppressive British rule and the emancipation of the slaves by moving out of the Cape in search of new land and political autonomy. The Great Trek consisted of ox-wagon migrations into territories already destabilized by the success of the Zulu state and internecine warfare. The trekkers found themselves in bloody fighting and eventually were victorious against the Zulu in the battle of Blood River. As Bunn outlines, the monument and a large amphitheater nearby constitute a site of extreme contestation. It provided the 'staging ground for rallies of Afrikaner extremists opposed to extending equal citizenship rights to blacks on the eve of South Africa's first multiracial election. Many now assert that the site should be erased because it symbolizes the roots of racial oppression and the ideologies of apartheid'.[24]

Bunn asserts that the Voortrekker monument exemplifies the fraught histories of colonial monuments more widely and that their celebratory architecture bears the burden of several racially specific contradictions. The structure was originally likened to the pyramids, Great Zimbabwe, the Mausoleum of Halicarnassus, Les Invalides, the Taj Mahal, and the Great Wall of China.[25] By invoking these buildings and their concomitant cultures of greatness, Afrikaner culture sought to take its place alongside them. And like those celebrated cultural survivals, the creators of the monument hoped that the values embodied in it would also be memorialized. 'Imagined as a white tradition, it is though to surpass the ethical understanding of native communities, for which it is an obscure promise of future independence; at the same time, white monuments run the risk of becoming invisible or being neglected, because they rely on the memorial practices of an embattled minority group of settlers and their children'.[26] This paradox has general implications for the symbolic functioning of all monuments in the contemporary setting, particularly because monuments such as the Voortrekker can never be receptacles of collective meaning, or even mourning. They are inflected with contradiction because of their reluctance to imagine the idea of citizenship outside the boundaries of race.

This is an easy monument to deconstruct on so many levels, but here I want to focus upon one very recent display in their museum, a set of illustrated panels that rationalizes the colonization of South Africa. Intended as an explanatory framework for global 'migration', the display reiterates the old narratives that European settlers arrived at the Cape at much the same time as other African groups were entering South Africa from the north. There were so many ethnic migrations that the European entry was simply one of many. These texts couch the overt invasion of the country in the language of migration, a harmless movement of people from one place to another. Ten years after the overthrow of apartheid, meanwhile, the dangerous myths perpetuated through Bantu education remained intact.[27] Archaeologically, we know that Bantu speakers were in South Africa well before the arrival of colonists, some 2000 years ago, and this information is now well circulated. One has to question why that set of correctives has not been implemented? As Dubow, Hall, and Shepherd have respectively shown, archaeology and anthropology as related disciplines were deeply imbricated with the National Party strategy of institutionalized racism in South Africa.[28] These deeply flawed constructions of history and culture have had a lasting legacy, felt to this day, but most palpably felt over the apartheid years since they were used to create racial hierarchies and structure living experiences for both black and white South Africans.

The museum actively presents a picture of 'tribal interaction' (so popular under apartheid) as a set of historical fractures and fault lines that cannot resist the interventions of external colonial forces.[29] Moreover, the devastating impacts of contact were absent: regimes of brutality, disease and the decimation of indigenous populations, exploitation of resources and so on. As an Australian, educated in the language of invasion, rather than colonization and certainly not migration, this struck me as the perpetuation of an appalling lie, largely in the service of a rainbow nation narrative. It is a dangerous fabrication, presumably embedded within a new political sensitivity toward an integrationist and healing policy. Furthermore, we are all implicated in the narrative through the citation of other areas across the globe where 'migration' took place throughout history. For example, the movement of Austronesian speaking people across the uninhabited islands of the Pacific was considered a migration, and so it was. But directly underneath the Austronesian example is a similar claim of 'migration' by Europeans to Australian shores, which were definitely not *terra nullius*. Within this very neat, palatable scenario South Africa conveniently implicates the rest of the world, and its history, in its national shame. It conflates history, erases specificity, and abnegates responsibility for the ensuing policies of apartheid. One has to ask how much has really changed? Consider an earlier text which argues that the 'Great Trek was not an armed invasion into the vast open areas of South Africa, but a trek in search of a new home, a homeland of promise … it was a climax of a gradual development towards national independence'.[30] As Smail concludes, 'they helped in the opening up of Southern Africa to habitation by civilized peoples and by their combined efforts they opened up new areas of settlement, paving the way for the development of the land and the proper cultivation of the soil'.[31]

More generally, the Voortekker Monument is a marker of systemic violence and a material signifier of events that sedimented the policies of institutionalized racism. The political significance of the 1938 trek was its invention and affirmation of white nationalist traditions.[32] It celebrated a newfound unity and created the illusion of a collective identity through the political staging of vicarious spectacle – some might suggest it has continued to fulfill its task.[33] The monument's immense materiality still exerts social and political energy, ostensibly doing the work of perpetuating the colonial fantasy of superiority and suppression.

Despite the enshrining of racist propaganda, the Voortrekker Monument will not be erased; instead something called Freedom Park will be built on a large hill directly opposite. The concept is a 'one-stop heritage precinct', where 'Freedom Park shall strive to accommodate and chronicle all of the humanity's experiences. It will be an international icon for humanity and freedom and serve to inspire people all over the world to rediscover their humanity.'[34] Destined to provide a therapeutic context for healing and reflection the rationale is explicitly to 'address the gaps, distortions and biases and provide new perspectives of South Africa's heritage'. Reinforcing this healing vision of the past for the future, the hope is that the 'Freedom Park should be a spiritually uplifting and inspirational experience for its visitors.' In retaining the Voortrekker monument (still visited by hoards of tourists and students, black and white) and mirroring it with Freedom Park, we have another example of the willingness to incorporate, rather than erase negative heritage, within the rainbow narrative. Because as Mandela himself has noted: there has to be white in the rainbow nation.

V. Trauma tours

Since it has long been debated whether collective memory resides in the monumental realm or in the sphere of performance, it is instructive to examine another active dimension of cultural production.[35] Trauma tours are embodied and economic responses to the violence and social injustices of apartheid. They are in the very business of keeping recent memories enshrined and specifically focus on the lineage and legacy of oppression and resistance. Their mandate is to facilitate former members of *Umkhonto We Sizwe* (MK), the military wing of the ANC, taking visitors through townships and sites of political violence in an effort to explore and understand the fault lines of South Africa's recent past. Trauma and memory are at the stated forefront of their initiative: 'Ours is the struggle of memory over forgetting, of hope over hopelessness, through laughter and tears.' The Western Cape Action Tour Project (WECAT) was started in 1997 and is now run under the auspices of the Direct Action Centre for Peace and Memory. WECAT is also part of the Survivor Support Initiatives that is directed at overcoming the isolation many former combatants and survivors of torture experience by breaking both personal and public silence and dealing with the psychological effects of war and conflict upon the lives of ex-political prisoners and former combatants and their families. I remember reading the testimony of WECAT's co-ordinator, Yazir Henri, in Krog's deeply disturbing transcripts from the TRC, *Country of My Skull* (1998). It seemed all the more poignant having met someone who actively fought in the armed liberation struggle and was subsequently wrestling with trans-generational trauma. As Henri says himself, 'whilst lives of pain and histories of excision have been called upon to rewrite the kinds of histories that discursively contour new possibilities of national belonging they have very often been displaced as they are simultaneously inscribed in a new national memorial canon'.[36]

Through leading these tours their objective is to provide the opportunities for new life and vocational skills, providing the space for creative self-expression, intellectual reflection, and discussion. The members of WECAT are effectively using the past and their traumatic memories of it to frame their own cultural, and economic production, to create new forms of subjectivity and citizenship.

> In celebrating the liberation struggle of our country we, as veterans of MK, have undertaken to appreciate and commemorate histories that are as yet unrecorded.

On our City and Sites of Memory tours, we invite Capetonians as well as visitors to Cape Town to journey with us into these histories. In many cases, our story-telling – during the tours of our city's neighbourhoods and townships – is the only memorial for the people, many of them very young, who lost their lives in the struggle against Apartheid and oppression.[37]

For initiatives like WECAT, and from my experience, such tours are burgeoning: forgiveness does not entail forgetting. These individuals have a vested interest in seeing that the intimate spaces and places of apartheid repression are revisited, both literally and metaphorically. Trauma pilgrimages are new responses to the long-term effects of disempowerment and their concomitant spatial economies. As Henri argues 'When we commemorate those who died, it is not to drive us back into the past. It is for the future so we can appreciate the valuable things they did.'[38] Through their tours WECAT aims to bridge divides, offering safe spaces for transcultural dialogue, interpersonal encounters and non-exploitative exchanges between visitors and locals. By bringing different communities together, specifically their diverse backgrounds and experiences, everyone is challenged to work towards reconciliation and understanding. Yet there is a haunting danger that these initiatives might only embellish the standard township tour of old, one that sought to exoticize a world of cultural difference.[39]

Townships form the central locus for trauma tours, since they represent sites of violence and places of repression. As such they have also been sites requiring memorialization for both individual victims and entire communities such as Thokoza, Mamelodi, Tembiza, Kagiso and Wilgispruit. Inscribed upon many of these memorials are the names of the victims of the apartheid regime, especially those of well-known activists. Family members saw this as a validation of their ultimate sacrifice and a material commitment to peace. Others remain nameless monuments. Understandably, specific individuals in various townships have been outspoken about the remembering of certain names and the forgetting of others, which they see as an explicitly political move. As one researcher optimistically claims 'memorials contain an element of reconciliation' and that '[d]ivided communities can strengthen the vulnerable stability and continue the process of reconciliation (e.g. Thokoza), through the establishment of monuments. Monuments constantly remind them that violence is an unworkable strategy to solve their differences'.[40] Their materiality provides the bedrock for psychological healing, proffers a form of recognition, represents social values, and consolidates the role of the victims within the new nation. Sadly, some have become sites of negative heritage and been subject to desecration, reinforcing the inherently political nature of memorializing trauma.

VI.   Historicizing trauma

We have long recognized that monumentality is intimately tied to memory, as evidenced for decades particularly in Europe. It is similarly a material expression reflective of the immaterial, highly emotional processes of forgetting and moving forward. Yet some have charged that by preserving the monument the social obligation to engage in more active remembrance is partially removed, for its inherent exteriority affects the internal experience. Museums in South Africa, both historical and archaeological, have enormous social obligations to fulfil in the responsible and accurate recording of the South African experience, replete with its horrors and struggles, its diversity and social differences. Given the national sentiment of progress and unity, they must also herald new forms of social being within a multicultural, multiethnic understanding of the nation.

I would suggest that specific cultural sites such as the Apartheid Museum in Johannesburg and the Hector Pieterson Museum in Soweto are socially regarded as suitable and contained national sites of memory and trauma; one built with private monies, the other by government funding. Their primary focus is the recent past, the apartheid years and the ensuing struggles for democracy and an end to racial segregation and violence. Trauma is a form of mediation, connecting past and present through the pain of memory, the material expressions of loss, and it is monumentalized through the cultural production of shared histories. Like memory, the museum itself operates as a mediator between past, present and future.[41] However, these sites enshrine sanctioned memory, they are cultural edifices that sediment certain versions of the past and serve as an anchor for specific memory practices. Their resilient materiality serves to both remember and forget, juxtaposing the dual processes of inclusion and exclusion.[42]

The Apartheid Museum is attached, rather incongruously, to the Gold Reef City Casino outside Johannesburg. That the museum was a token project when it was first conceived says much about the nation's recent mindset. The privately owned museum was built because having a 'socially responsible project' was one of the conditions of winning the bid for the casino license. Its design is redolent of apartheid's brutality; concrete, red brick, rusted and galvanized steel. The shock of being arbitrarily assigned a racial classification at the museum's entrance gives you the first taste of what it meant to live under state-sanctioned racism.[43] A multi-disciplinary team of curators, filmmakers, historians, archaeologists and designers was assembled to develop the exhibition narrative which sets out by means of large blown-up photographs, artefacts, newspaper clippings, and some extraordinary film footage, to graphically animate the apartheid story, but also to ground aspects of this recent history with the deep past. Archaeologists from the Rock Art Research Institute also contributed to a film that recounts the events of conquest and colonization from the perspective of indigenous people. That being said, the main focus is upon the struggle and the later years of the apartheid regime. As the director reminds us, 'It is not only important to tell the apartheid story, but it is also important to show the world how we have overcome apartheid', reinforcing this desire to move forward rather than focus on the specificities of the past.[44]

Designed by the same architects, the Hector Pieterson Museum is an impressive red-brick building with irregular shaped windows placed in a haphazard pattern in keeping with the Sowetan landscape in which it resides. One is made uncomfortable at all possible opportunities within the museum and its environs, rusting iron, dripping water, confined spaces, uncomfortable seating, all designed to inflect visceral horror through phenomenological means. The museum highlights and commemorates some very specific historical moments that devastated the community and took the lives of its most precious, its children. Some 566 people were killed on 16 June 1976, when students from three schools planned to march to the Orlando Stadium. But before they got to the present museum location, the police met them, in Moema Street. Hector Pieterson, a young boy, was shot and his image, and that moment, was preserved in Sam Nzima's now-legendary photograph. Only with the sacrifice of hundreds of young lives in a single day was world attention finally captured, thus exposing the injustices of apartheid to a long overdue international scrutiny.

Like the Apartheid Museum, it was opened in 2002 at a cost of 16 million Rand, donated by the Department of Environmental Affairs and Tourism, and a further 7.2 million Rand from the Johannesburg City Council. But unlike the Apartheid Museum, this museum is situated in the township, with the landmarks visible from the museum windows, only two short blocks from where Hector was shot and fell. The most haunting reminder is a scarring line, gouged into the cement outside, visible there and from the museum windows, which traces the line of the bullet that killed the young Hector Pieterson. A potent physical reminder of a fatally wounded child and an equally damaged nation, a persistent scar on the Soweto landscape. Both museums reflect the concerted efforts of South African historians to revise the official version of their country's tortured past, specifically for the 1948–94 period when the apartheid system of racial segregation treated nonwhites as inferior beings. At the opening of the Hector Pieterson Museum, Pumla Madiba, chief executive of the South African Heritage Resources Agency, stated that 'There are going to be many more monuments and buildings like this one, as we take stock and gradually rewrite our history.'[45] However, the museum has not been free from controversy: Hector's mother recently accused politicians of enriching themselves through using her son's name. She argued that she should receive a share of the profits gathered from museum charges.[46]

In South Africa, archaeologists are effectively historicizing and interrogating the socio-political experience of 'heritage', particularly through the lens of interdisciplinary scholarship devoted to the entanglements of identity, place, politics, memory, and tourist economies. A series of small museums and interpretive heritage centres have been more successful in highlighting the salience of colonial contact and exploitation, thereby historicizing the full spectrum of a history that hurts. Interestingly, but perhaps not surprisingly, these centres have placed archaeologists and archaeological materials at the forefront. Several chose to emphasize the plight of San communities that were almost exterminated by a government-sanctioned policy of genocide.[47] This work has been conducted largely under the auspices of the Rock Art Research Institute at the University of the Witwatersrand in Johannesburg, led primarily by Ben Smith and Geoff Blundell. At the sites of Game Pass in the Drakensburg and Wildebeest Kuil in Kimberly,[48] Smith and Blundell have worked with indigenous communities, their representatives and other specialists to establish new heritage practices and representations of pre-settler African lifeways. The rock art of both regions, highly distinctive and dramatic, is the vehicle through which tourists, both local and global, are educated into indigenous symbolism, ritual belief and social systems. Overlain upon this is another rich strata of contemporary ritual and social life, that of modern communities, whether San or Zulu, that are similarly connected to these landscapes. Inserted between these stratigraphies of deep time and contemporary connectivity is the painful recognition of colonization and genocide, and the trauma and loss subsequently inflicted upon generations of individuals. At both Game Pass and Wildebeest Kuil heritage centres, newly commissioned video documentaries detail the historical events and effects of European invasion and colonization, replete with the long-term residual inequities, attitudes and subsequent laws that formed the nexus of the apartheid state.

Yet other museums focus on a longer and more complex set of intertwined histories that feature both San and black communities as they were confronted by the forces of European mercantile expansion. The Macgregor Museum in Kimberly is an example of one such responsible recording of the nation's history. Not shying away from the region's brutal history of black exploitation in the famous De Beers diamond mines, the museum traces the history of inter-ethnic conflict as the borders of commerce were advanced further north and east. It also takes seriously its role in educating the public about the importance of archaeology, and thus that past, as a vital resource for the future. A deepened understanding of the nation's history generated through the disciplines of archaeology and history is much needed as it moves forward in a desired spirit of mutual respect and co-operation. As Ebron suggests, the most successful ways of combating the negative effects of the past and moving forward in the process of nation building ultimately rests with the incorporation of regional cultural histories and legacies. Instead of focusing on the recent past it must be broadly inclusive, enfolding many historical experiences within its remit. As we are already seeing, groups such as the KhoiSan already feel marginalized within a post-apartheid South Africa and have mobilized their own identity politics around historical figures such as Krotoa and Sarah Bartmaan, and the furor over the San Diorama at the South African Museum,[49] to both empower and remember. This reiterates Ebron's observation, that an explicitly assimilative tradition that draws on the histories and knowledges of various groups to enlarge them successfully creates a broader national embrace.[50]

VII. Conclusion

Memory has played a key role in the reconstitution of South Africa, specifically in restoring a sense of continuity and unity within the experience of trauma culture.[51] Memory practices have significant potential for creative re-working and re-negotiation: memory is always more than the prison house of the past.[52] In the main, the mnemonic devices relating to pre-colonial African culture, whether the landscape itself or the material residues of cultural practice, have been erased or dramatically modified. Thus it requires imaginative measures to reinstate those social and material linkages. Heritage discourses including archaeology and history are productive avenues to pursue. What we have seen in South Africa is the assimilative rhetoric of heritage around notions of primordial culture and narratives of rainbow unity, while at the same time there is a fracturing of heritage production replete with the negative valences of complexity, controversy and contestation.[53] A critical deconstruction of the Voortrekker Monument provides an obvious example of negative heritage. So too do the more recent cultural productions such as the museums in Johannesburg and Soweto, as well as smaller provincial centres. Here I have argued that the full sweep of history requires recognition and recall, not simply of the atrocities of the apartheid past alone but also of the colonial engagements that led to its establishment with Van Riebeek's line of almond and thornbush.

In South Africa history and memory have struggled in fraught relationship since the onset of colonization. Memory is characteristically selective, comprising not only acts of recovery but also practices of suppression. During the apartheid years memory was materialized as a reshaping history around the largely imagined national consciousness of the Afrikaner, and was constrained to forget large tracts of the South African past. Some potent examples of this are the 'shaping of the Afrikaans language in the mouths of slaves; slave revolts; the enslavement of indigenous people; the role of Coloured and black labourers in the service of Boers in the Great Trek; collaboration between black nations and Afrikaners on the Eastern frontier during the nineteenth century; the part played by women in conserving certain standards of education and morality'.[54] Dangerously, it may also prove possible for post-apartheid society's memory to elide or underplay other events and characters in the overall narrative. For those involved in decision making about appropriate memorialization, the clear challenge will be to keep the multiplicity of pasts alive, to support various experiences and interpretations of the past and not to privilege one particular master narrative. We see the dangers of this with the rainbow nation narrative, despite the fact that its ultimate goals are inherently positive, forward-looking and broadly assimilative in its rhetoric. That understandable desire for unity should not be compromised by the fears surrounding the dissonance and fracturing of memory: they are the hallmarks of trauma culture and the necessary constituents for a broader social understanding. This is part of the rationale provided by the WECAT tours, a didactic performance that traces the sites of violence, as narrated by the victims themselves. Suturing the very personal desire to remember and the collective need to move forward simultaneously is a fraught, if not impossible, endeavour.

What we risk by forfeiting our tactics of remembering is the break out of further traumatic repetitions. In South Africa today, most people undoubtedly wish to avoid a compulsive attachment to the grievances of the past that might ultimately invoke vengeance or self-destruction. But there also exists an argument that denial of the facticity of the past might conjoin the nation to that history of grievance, and to the reproducing of that history, even more powerfully than revenge might. If the project of reconciliation is to succeed, the nation and its citizens require the physical evidence of suffering and complicity to be accurately represented.[55] Modernity has been very effective at space/time compression. In a South African setting such a collapse may prove inherently treacherous from a political, postcolonial perspective. Alternatively, modernity has also re-imagined the borders of local, national and international imaginaries, which have become central to understanding the long-term histories of oppression and the subsequent production of trauma cultures. We might recall Mamdani's salutary warning that 'in the aftermath of conflict, healing is not a foregone conclusion'.[56]

9

Memorials to Injustice

Stephan Feuchtwang

I. Introduction

It is normal to find an event of great loss at the foundation of a nation. It is an occasion of sacrifice in the physical assertion of dignity against its denial. For instance, the first nations, as famously pointed out by Benedict Anderson, were composed of South and North American colonial settlers, revolting against their subordination and waging wars of independence against their distant sovereigns.[1] At the same time they were blotting out their own violent suppression of native and slave rebellions. There is typically, as argued by Ernest Renan, a disavowal or a silenced sub-plot of collective violence at the origin of national stories.[2] Historical enquiry prompts and can satisfy calls for adequate recognition of such suppressed catastrophes.[3]

Claims about the justness of civil and international wars are a commonplace of state nationalism. Behind and beyond them are other senses of injustice and demands for recognition, registrable in courts or by states making apologies and authorizing compensation. In this chapter, I will explore how such senses of injustice are transmitted and what kinds of recognition they demand in the course of transmission. I will describe a case that arose from the violent detention and arrest of mountain villagers by Nationalist troops in the last throes of the civil war between the Nationalist and Communist Chinese. It took place in Taiwan in 1952. It was a suppressed incident until the revision of Taiwan's history took place alongside an opening out of Taiwanese politics and its 'Taiwanification' in the 1990s. Cases like this question and are capable of transforming the stories that states tell about themselves. We shall see how in this case, as in others, such transformations have consequences for the international order and for world organizations such as the United Nations (UN) since it is to their founding principles that appeals for just recognition are often made.

II. Memory and transmission

'Memory' is a useful and convenient way of relating levels of increasing scale between the emotions felt by individuals, the immediate social institutions within which people learn their habits and the stories they tell themselves, and more distant institutions and their centralizing and encompassing authorities. But it is only useful if it does not obfuscate the quite distinct processes that occur at each level, within the human body and beyond.

'Memory' refers to three broad and very different processes. Two of them are located in the realm of individual psychobiology: the *registration* of experience and the *recalling* of past experiences. The third is social. To make the link, let me start with the most biological and move up. *Registration* enables the moment-by-moment recognition and anticipation that is behind all practical learning and action outside consciousness. Split-second mini-narrations of recognition and anticipation are distinguished by psychologists and neuro-biologists into a core self and an autobiographical self. The core self is an integration of neural representations of what is and has been sensed. The second, autobiographical self is the extension of this integration in secondary representations over long durations, some of them conscious. It is what turns sensations into emotions and furthermore into the feeling of emotions. Memory is always feeling-laden.[4]

Psychologists distinguish procedural memory, what is learned as bodily skill and habit, from declarative memory. Declarative memory is neurologically divided into short- and long-term memory. So the memory with which we must be concerned is autobiographical and long-term declarative. And here lies a critical distinction for social scientists of all kinds, namely that between episodic and semantic memory. Episodic memory is memory of events while semantic memory is what is learned about the world, including history, by which social meaning is given to those events.[5] Both are involved when *recalling* memories into consciousness, usually called 'remembering'. Remembering can of course be entirely voluntary, spurred by some need or demand. And it can be entirely involuntary, as a syndrome of trauma. But it is most often partially voluntary. Whether voluntary or involuntary, remembering is determined by the signals and demands of the situations that trigger it. Recalling adds a new record to the chains of association that link memories. It is a performance that has an effect on them. It is the occasion by which social meanings that have already been learned are also recalled and to which adjustments are made in that moment.

Most memory is not recalled. Consciousness is a very limited facility compared to all the sensations and feelings the body has registered and the brain has recognized and synthesized. Aside from this limitation, it is important to distinguish forgetting as sheer erasure and forgetting as the result of censorship, where memory remains but is repressed. Between erasure and censorship there are lapses and failures of recall related to both. Erasure is neurological damage to the brain. Self-censorship is made up of habitual blocks to recalling memories of certain kinds because they cause acute embarrassment, are profoundly at odds with what has been learned as permissible, and are threatening to the constant process of self-integration that already contains ambivalent and conflicting desires and different senses of self.

Practical and relatively unconscious ways of learning semantic memory and self-censorship predominate over conscious learning. They include childhood participation in family life, seeing and hearing how people are addressed and treated, participating in the special occasions that create daily and longer calendrical times, and hearing stories read and told. From hearing and being told how to address different people and from being addressed in different ways by different people at different times, we automatically learn about relations of identification, about the nature of kinship, and we are inculcated with various senses of belonging from the local to the national. In Taiwan as elsewhere, practical semantic memory includes learning about separation, loss and death and about such emotion-laden categories as devils and ghosts, both from stories about recent events and from taking part in death rituals.[6]

'Transmission' is a good way of describing this inculcation of social meaning in domestic and more public institutions and occasions. It is not only transmission from generation to generation but also from social into psychic life and then back onto social life through participation and innovation.

The result of the activity of transmission and the capacity or power to transmit is often described as 'memory' or more precisely 'social memory'. I would prefer to call it 'public memory'. *Public memory* is not only a result. It is also a *capacity* like individual psychological memory with equivalent procedures to those of recalling, forgetting and of course censorship. It covers the powers and activities of creating and erasing archives (trees and other landmarks, documents, attic lumber, photograph albums, street architecture, names of places), of commemorating or denigrating or worse negating people or events (inclusion and exclusion from graves, portraits, museums), and of recording and ignoring narratives in chronicles, histories, and myths.

The issue I have begun to highlight here is how public memory intersects with the processes of transmission and recall among individuals who learn and have differential access to its resources and results. Public memory is always hierarchical, an honouring and a denigrating power of authoritative recognition. Narratives that are transmitted habitually or consciously have a ranked or even completely excluded possibility of identification with the public memory presented to the transmitters. Exclusion can give rise to the demand for inclusion, which is to demand a new establishment of public memory. The feeling of such a demand can be long-lasting and itself transmitted as grievance, for instance about an event that was experienced as a personal but also shared harm, and was caused by the same powers that controlled public memory. It is transmitted as a painful feeling of social injustice. Its demands and any resolution of them will be determined by the political and legal culture in which it is transmitted and by the surrounding authorities to which it can appeal. I shall describe one such transmission. But first I want to suggest the range of what a demand for apology could entail in modern political circumstances.

III.   On the demand for apology

An adequate apology is likely to entail some resolution of the shame, humiliation, and sheer negation of worth that an act of injustice created, feelings that have been perpetuated by various means. One starting point has been to see in public apology a new and universal moral propensity to feel guilt and empathy. It has the merit of staying within the discourse of morality that liberal democratic states use to describe themselves. But I want to get behind that to draw on the sources of horror that more personal accounts feed into discourses of injustice. My starting point is therefore a concept not of guilt but of violation, which can be imagined as powerlessness before an authority that treats you as a horrifying object. It is worse than lack of power to withstand negative discrimination, marginalization, imprisonment, torture, and humiliation. It is powerlessness, in which you are invaded by the same repugnance into which you are thrust in the eyes of the authority. The authority has the power both to treat you as repugnant and in the process to make you repugnant. The authority says you are something that threatens and treats you as an invasive pestilence. It inserts and reinforces in you a life-threatening image and propensity for self-hatred.

The finding of a language in which to contain and split off this horror, and then to stop its transmission altogether, to allow oneself to forget it, is what a demand for 'apology' at its most adequate could be asked to accomplish. The public alternative is to try to organize the power of righteous resistance that would expel the life-threatening force, a resistance that assumes its own authority to recognize. A much examined example of this is the Civil Rights movement, its legislative success frustrated by continuing police brutality, its turn to urban riot, and its conjunction with a restoration of slave narratives, Black history, and demands for an apology from the US government. Apology would be a peaceful resolution of such counterviolence. Indeed, pleas for apology and the resulting memorials and statements often include the hope that apology will be a way of overcoming or avoiding violent conflict.

Subjects deprived of citizenship, refugees, and internal exiles or political prisoners are deprived of recognition as 'human' with rights and are therefore open to such humiliation and degradation. One recourse, unfortunately after the event, is the prospect of trials that recognize the lethal injustice they have suffered. Such trials for crimes against humanity have been called cosmopolitan trials because they are not of nations and states, not inter-national. They share the same project of independence from state executive powers as does the judiciary in a democratic state, but they try the actions of states and similar powerful formations, their agents and apologists when they have committed crimes against humanity. The increasing body of precedent and organization of cosmopolitan trials establishes legitimacy for recognizing individual humanity even if, in fact particularly when, that recognition has been denied by any or all states.[7] Cosmopolitan trials can induce or encourage states to recognize what they later accept are cases for apology. So let us consider what apology by the accused state involves.

IV.   The problem of continuity

The claim to having been cast into a position of shame demands recognition of a relationship between the injured party and a state. It was at least initially a very active relationship of violence and indifference to the violations inflicted. Subsequently it continues with at least neglect if not also continuing humiliation. There is therefore a question of who are the responsible actors in this relationship. Who constitutes one party, demanding an apology? Who on the other hand are the targets of this demand? This brings up a peculiarly legal problem of transmission, namely the continuity of the two parties.

Plainly an apology that occurs while humiliation continues would not be sincere. In other words, apology entails a reversal of conduct, from one that humiliates to one that gives respect. But there is an inherent problem in this relationship. The descendants of the victims have to establish that they are suffering current harm and that it has continuity with those who were victims of the original injustice. They also have to establish continuity of responsibility by a current actor or a group and its agency with the actor(s) who committed the original injustice. Yet, before there can be apology and redress, a major change needs to have occurred. The victims need to have become powerful enough to raise the issue. Does that change not imply a decreasing need for redress? Is the claim for apology and redress itself not transformed beyond recognition into a position of political resourcefulness already won? On the other side, that of the state, willingness to recognize injustice must have been brought about by a major change in the agency held responsible for it. Can it then be held responsible for apology and redress? In short, the legal problem opens onto a wider question, which involves the disciplines of historical scholarship.[8]

We can conclude that an adequate apology implies a change of the originating relationship. It must have become a relationship where the victims and the agents are political partners if not equals. But the legal conditions for this transformation demand that the apology be the last act of the old relationship. The important point to be drawn here is that an end point to the relationship is envisaged, where the obligations of the perpetrator have been fulfilled. The hopes that are carried by the prospect of such an end include the possibility of forgetting the relationship of injustice, or rather of being able to put it into a past that can be as easily remembered as forgotten.

V. History, myth and ritual as transmission and recognition

What I have considered so far is the issue of the substantiation and resolution of claims of profound breaches of human justice. Historical scholarship plays a role in the gathering of evidence for a story told in court. History in the sense of a trusted and told story can in part itself resolve the issue of apology by supplying the recognition of worth, such as the worth of being a martyr for the continuing collective identity of the victim group. Such recognition is also perpetuated as a political claim. It thus becomes the basis for a new historical narrative that turns injustice into a foundation myth for a social movement that occasionally becomes political in its demand for wider recognition.

History as myth opens onto a further topic, the interplay of different senses of time and narrative. A founding myth is a perpetual truth, a story of vindication and salvation. A past that is present, it fuses the sequence of events in ordinary history, making the founding event a part of current experience Here the bonds of chronological narrative are dissolved and transcended. Behind, beside and beyond material compensation and redress is the issue of adequate repentance and reparation in a spiritual sense on the part of the perpetrators, carrying with it, ideas of mourning and of being able to forget. There is a question of culture here, in particular of religious, legal and political culture. It will determine whether and how the two transmissions, of suffering and of responsibility, are related. Perpetuations of injustice on one hand and on the other the passing on from one generation to the next of senses of injustice include the practises and symbols of mourning and the worlds of the dead. Religious stories of salvation, for instance, are told or entailed by ritual acts for the expulsion of ghosts or mourning for those long dead but not properly mourned. The telling of such stories and the commissioning of appropriate rituals are in the power of the aggrieved, and do not require the actions of the perpetrating party. On the other hand they may be considered foreign and threatening or backward and superstitious, and subject to ridicule and suppression by the agencies of the state that could be held responsible for the original injustice. So the two kinds of reckoning, juridical-historical on one hand and ritual on the other, become intertwined.

It is my contention that there are in fact three kinds of temporality at work simultaneously. There is the time of mourning and of accommodation of the dead – a time of repeated interventions in both directions across a border between the present and the past, the living and the dead. There is the time of a myth of founding a subject of history, the linear, tragic, grievous but also progressive time of a collective subject, including its transformations. And finally there is the time of the present resolution and dissolution of a serious and debilitating injustice, a utopian vision or a hope that an apologetic and true account of injustice will be a warning and a prevention of its repetition. A politico-juridical settling of obligations is part of the latter. The chronological writing of history and its academic study is implicated in all three. I hope to show this by a case study based in Taiwan.

VI.   28–2 1947, Taiwan, and Professor Lin Tsung-yi

The incident with which I am concerned occurred in 1952. High in the mountainous border region between three townships of Taipei County in Taiwan in the winter of 1952 a large-scale military operation encircled the scattered residents of several hamlets. It was reminiscent of the encirclement campaigns that laid siege to the Communist areas on the mainland in the 1930s during the civil war between the forces of the Nationalist (Guomindang) government and the Communist insurgents. But what occurred in 1952 was after the defeat of the Nationalists on the mainland and their retreat to Taiwan. It took place just under five years after a more famous incident of Nationalist rule in Taiwan. Indeed a few of those rounded up in the 1952 incident had links with the former incident. More to the point, current historians and politicians link the 1952 incident with the earlier and larger incident.

So I will first give a brief account of the earlier incident. In this way I will convey the chronology that is now part of the narrative very many Taiwanese tell of themselves as an island people. I shall rely in large part on a book documenting the 1947 incident and its commemoration, edited by the descendant of one of its victims.

Taiwan had been a colony of Japan since 1895 and was returned to Chinese sovereignty in 1945. The Nationalist government in 1945 installed a government of military command that reminded the Taiwanese of the Japanese viceregal government so much that they called the commander of the Nationalist government the New Viceroy.[9] The governor and the troops sent to the island were brutal and exploitative. This is how the British counsel reported the situation in February 1947: 'the arrival of the mainlanders and their acquisitiveness, corruption and apparent inefficiency, as revealed in the declining standard of living, has bitterly disappointed the Formosans'.[10]

On the last day of February government troops shot one of the people protesting against government agents who the evening before had beaten up a widow selling cigarettes in breach of the government monopoly on tobacco. A crowd gathered and attacked a police station. The date 28 February is now the name given to this incident. But the situation soon escalated. In the days that followed, other crowds attacked those who had come from the mainland with the post-1945 government. The protest grew to the point where Taiwanese took over a number of city governments and their leaders formed a committee that drew up a set of thirty-two demands for settlement of the dispute with the Nationalist government. The governor reluctantly accepted them and promised not to send for troop reinforcements. But on 8 May thirteen thousand troops from the mainland landed and began a concerted attempt to destroy the leadership and intelligentsia of the Taiwanese, the 'intellectual decapitation of the island'.[11] George Kerr, an official of the US consulate highly critical of the silence of his Consul, published eyewitness accounts in English.[12] But in Taiwan nothing could be published until the ending of martial law in 1987.

Professor Lin Tsungyi, the editor of the book I have been employing, is a psychiatrist resident in Canada. He is an exile because he is the son of one of the most prominent victims of the 1947 atrocity. Plainly he is not a victim himself, and would not have been subject to the extreme humiliation that I described earlier. But, following the codes of Chinese family honour, he harbours the bitter feelings and feels the sense of obligation of a son to his father. In memory of his father and out of the experience of his exile he used his considerable prestige in the Taiwan diaspora, as he calls it, to organize a campaign for an apology. He addressed an appeal to the government of Taiwan and in particular to Lee Tenghui, the first Taiwan-born leader of the Nationalist Party who succeeded to the presidency after the death of Chiang Ching-kuo, the son of Generalissimo Chiang Kai-shek. Such an appeal was possible only after a radical change of the Taiwanese regime. After many failed attempts, a letter of December 1990 in which Professor Lin sought what he calls a 'peaceful resolution of the 2–28 Tragedy' finally prompted a response.

The letter presented five objectives. There should be an official commission of respected scholars to investigate and report on the 28 February incident. A monument should be constructed in central Taipei, the biggest city and capital of the island province. The highest government authority should issue an apology and compensate surviving victims. 28 February should be designated a national day of commemoration. And finally, a foundation for the revival and reconstruction of Taiwanese culture should be established. Within five years, the first four had either been realized or were well on the way to completion. The last is a long-term cultural and political project, one spearheaded by the main opposition party, the Democratic Progressive Party, and by Lee Teng-hui's faction of the Nationalist Party (a faction that has since become an entirely separate party). This already gives an indication of the extent of change.

So great a change is ground for questioning the obligation to apologize. In 1990, when the letter was sent, the main government leaders responsible for the massacres were dead. This fact had already been pointed out by an official publication at province level, seeking to stop growing agitation for a full account. Professor Lin overcame the problem of dead perpetrators and of the changed regime by an appeal to rectify the record, a truth accountable to three constituencies: the victims and their families, the people of Taiwan, and the international community. Plainly the second is what dignifies the first, and the third is what recognizes the second. One of his models is the apology and compensation payments made by the governments of the United States of America and Canada to the families of Japanese Americans whose homes and businesses were destroyed and who were imprisoned in camps as potential enemy aliens during the Pacific War.[13] As a standard this model is part of the international community to which he appeals. It must also include the laws and courts to try war crimes and abuses of human rights established after the Second World War. But it is not in their particulars that he addresses them, it is rather as an idealized court that can recognize truth and justice. In effect he is interpellating each one of us as a world citizen. We are expected, as by so many other similar appeals, to be benign judges with the authority to demand that injustice be rectified. We are personifications of a benign superego. In any case, Professor Lin writes that he moved President Lee, who must have had his own similar feelings.

In a speech at the newly built commemorative monument for the victims of 28 February and their families, President Lee declared that 'I, Lee Teng-hui, as Head of State, assume the responsibility of the government for the mistake committed by it, and deeply and sincerely apologize'. He continued with a hope for peace, assuaging its opposite in the hearts of the victims: 'I believe that you, in the generosity of your hearts, will transform resentment into goodwill and harmony, warming the spirit of the whole people.'[14] Apology and the erection of a monument marks an end and a beginning, making the past past. By what he calls 'a purifying of the national spirit and a promoting of personal dignity' his apology should be a 'signpost on the way to our country's new era'.

To understand the political and constitutional ramifications of this stance it is essential to understand that Taiwan is a sovereign state but not one recognized in the global system of nations. Its constitution is still that of the Republic of China, which had been the constitution for the whole of the mainland and Taiwan until the establishment of the People's Republic of China. When the PRC was recognized by most other states and the Security Council of the UN as the representative of China, Taiwan became a government in exile, 'the RoC in Taiwan'. In other words, Lee Tenghui was the President of the RoC. It was in his capacity as head of the same state of the whole of China but in exile that he could accept responsibility in its name for the 1947 massacre. By contrast, no one on the mainland, survivors and descendants of similar atrocities committed by the troops and other agents of the RoC,[15] can possibly make claims on the RoC in Taiwan. They fall under another sovereign state, the People's Republic. My point here is that a radical change of regime breaks the continuity of a relationship of obligation. A division into two sovereign states has effectively broken that relation. I doubt whether the PRC government would apologize for atrocities committed by its predecessor on the mainland.

VII.   The Luku incident

I turn now to the events that took place from December 1952 to March 1953. They could not be spoken of or written about for more than forty years after it occurred. The re-opening of the case forty years later was the object of a similar and connected campaign to the one that produced the 28 February monument and apology. Its entry into the domain of written history and the release of its secrets is the work of academic historians, reporters, and members of the Nationalist Party's main opposition, the (Democratic Progressive Party, Minjin Dang) (DPP).

Taiwan had been insulated from the civil war on the mainland by the fact that it was a Japanese colony. In 1945, when Taiwan was reunited with the mainland, recurrence of civil war between forces of the Nationalist government and of mainly Communist-led forces occurred on the island just as it did on the mainland. Communists in Taiwan were now part of the mainland Chinese Party and their number grew with the disaffection from and opposition to the corrupt and brutal Nationalist government.[16] The remnants of the strongholds held by anti-Nationalist forces were wiped out in the years following the Nationalist retreat to the island in 1949 after its defeat on the mainland by the Communist armies. The years of repression, in which all opposition was liable to be labelled 'Communist' have been called 'white terror' (*baise kongbu*). The same name had already been used to describe the violent suppression of labour organizations and the Communist Party in Shanghai in the late 1920s and early 1930s by the Nationalist government in alliance with the British and French colonial police forces. In Taiwan, the words 'white terror' are now openly used, having started as a whispered description in opposition to the perpetrating government of the Nationalist Party. Acceptance of a period and its name is an important preliminary to retrieving it and the personal stories implicated in it from confusion and secrecy. It gains for them the singular sense of a shared tragedy.[17]

There are court records of the trials of people accused of being the leaders of nine 'communist' bases between 1950 and 1953.[18] The biggest was that of prisoners taken in what has become known as the Luku incident (Luku *shijian*). From interviews and documents it can be said that at some time between 1948 and 1950, some political activists, who had professed an admiration for Communism, moved from being a study group in Taipei city to organize villagers into a rural base under their rule.[19] Only a handful, including one or two from the mainland, had in fact joined the Communist Party. Two members of the study group were from Luku, a mountainous area of scattered hamlets on the border between two townships (Xizhe and Shiding). By 1952 the rest formed a group of about 40 outsiders living in wooden huts that they built alongside the houses of the local residents. The outsiders organized the residents into a collectivity, promising a struggle for a more just and egalitarian government.

On 28 December 1952, some ten thousand government troops and police encircled the hamlets. They detained all residents over the age of 10, demanding identity documents of them and of anyone entering the area. Many were identified and charged with the crime of assisting Communists. Police informants included self-professed Communists who turned themselves over to the Nationalist government. According to surviving witnesses a few of the Luku residents were shot on the spot, and the detained were kept hungry, cramped and tied together. They were beaten into identifying those who had been organizers and into admitting their association with them, even though in most cases they did not understand the language, the accusation or the politics of the labels used.

In total those executed or imprisoned for treason made up most of the adult male population of the cordoned off hamlets.[20] 'Traitor' was stamped on the ID cards and police records of released prisoners. For forty years none were allowed to talk about it except in terms of Communist bandits and treason. Even in October 2001, the words 'communist spies' (*hui tiap*, in Taiwanese) stopped the flow of the story told to my co-researcher, Shih Fanglong, and me by a local coal-miner who had been rounded up in the operation but not imprisoned. Whenever his account referred to the hills above us where the bulk of the jailed men had lived, these words came up. The words were the means by which he kept his distance from involvement in the activities of which 'they' were accused, and at the same time it still literally gave him pause. Another Luku villager, imprisoned for 8 years, had eventually returned after many odd jobs, difficult to get as an ex-prisoner with 'traitor' stamped on his ID card. He told us that he had spoken about his experience immediately upon being released, but only to his children. It could not be mentioned outside the family.[21] Others are known to have said nothing at all to anyone after their release. To have become openly admissible, to have overcome the fear or shame, required the major political shift marked by Lee Tenghui's apology for 28 February in 1995.

Note that the politically suppressed can and do claim for themselves the authorship of the shift in their favour. It is a shift from resentment of the Mainlanders who came between 1945 and 1949, and who were held responsible for the 1947 and subsequent atrocities, as well as being disliked for having privileged access to top government positions. Mainlanders now have to make efforts to be seen as members of a united Taiwanese people. The shift delineates the existence of a distinct and sovereign island people.

As this shift was occurring under President Lee, Lin Zhongxin, a young man from the township of Shiding where the Luku incident had occurred, was just finishing his compulsory military service. In the mid-1980s he worked in the capital city, Taipei. He is the son of one of the main shopkeepers in the small town that is the centre of government and commerce in Shiding Township. As he recounts, he supported and became acquainted with a DPP politician who was eventually elected to the RoC legislature.[22] This man had heard about the Luku incident and was compiling a book of political prisoners' stories. Advised by his politician friend, Lin Zhongxin returned to his home town and began to investigate further, interviewing those who were involved and eventually getting to know all those who had returned from prison and from working in other parts of Taiwan. Eventually Lin became a representative in the township assembly, the only one openly in his electoral literature to declare himself DPP.[23]

He is proud of his investigations and of supplying the information not just to his DPP sponsor but to an historian from the central research academy, Professor Zhang, who in the late 1990s eventually produced the first of two books of interviews and documents on the incident. Lin Zhongxin is particularly proud of overcoming the villagers' fears of speaking about it. From this success, he claims, came some of the thrust for the legislation by which they could be compensated and a memorial to their sufferings built. The legislation to which he referred is a law passed in 1998 encouraging victims and descendants of victims of the

White Terror in Taiwan to tell their stories, dig up their documents of imprisonment, and claim compensation.[24] The law regulates the right to rehabilitation of people suffering injury during the period of martial law. It defines the period of martial law and the limits of rights to compensation.

Compensation to the families of the injured parties of those tried and inappropriately sentenced for sedition as 'bandit spies' varies according to severity of sentence, from death to various lengths of imprisonment. Regulations specify what documentary proof is required. They also name the sources of statutory funds for investigating the martial law trials and to subsidize teaching materials and publications about them. The promulgation of these regulations was dated 12 Feb 1999 – starting a period of two years during which claims must be made (which was later extended). The text of the official commentary and explanation of the law accompanying its promulgation justifies compensation for those who were tried under martial law. 'Under abnormal conditions', it says the 'law was wrongly used'. Therefore the legislature has passed 'regulations to regain justice for people whose rights were abused during the period of martial law'. In sum, the law is necessary to correct a significant defect in the application of the constitution and the law of the RoC. It establishes direct continuity under the constitution of the RoC. Note too that the law is not just for compensation to the victims of the perpetration of injustice. It is also for funds to pay for investigations that set the record straight.

Another level of government, Taipei County, provided further funds for a monument commemorating the victims. The historian Professor Zhang was closely involved with its construction and wrote the memorial text on its plaques. It was inaugurated on 29 December 2000, the anniversary of the beginning of the encirclement campaign of 1952.

There are two plaques on the memorial. The smaller one on the lower level starts by describing the political situation after 1949 as unstable and autocratic. It goes on to give a brief factual summary of the event, but it is set in tones of emotive sympathy. The language is markedly different from that used in the regulations for compensation. 'In the encirclement of the mountainous area of Luku, villagers were detained under suspicion of being members of an armed base of Chinese Communist sympathisers'...'This was the biggest political incident in Taiwan in the 1950s.' 'The villagers were detained in the Vegetarian Hall of Luku, now called the Buddhist temple of Broad Enlightenment (Guangmingsi)' where they were 'beaten into confession or charged on

The Luku Incident Memorial October 2001

the basis of informants' intelligence without any evidence being brought forward'. 'The result was countless wronged souls [of those killed] and suffering in prison. Families were broken, suffering torments of grief.' The last paragraph then states the purpose of the monument. It is 'not only to commemorate those who died unjustly but to learn the lesson from their arbitrary arrest and sentences that human rights were crushed and that we should today join hands to make Taiwan a democracy and a society in which rule of law and fair justice prevail'. It expresses a similar aspiration to the practical utopia that Professor Lin Tsung-yi persuaded President Lee Teng-hui to endorse.

The larger plaque at the upper level amplifies the emotive tone of regret and repair. It explains the symbolism of the monument's design and materials. 'The stainless steel scimitar is the twisted sword of distorted justice, a monument to the silent who had to bear it without being able to speak out.' 'The parallelograms of stone at the base with their angular edges are the scars of the beaten bodies.' 'The steep slopes and surfaces reflect extremes of imbalance and of blind spots, in order to remind us to lower our heads and descend the steps as if walking into an abyss of disaster, and at the same time to lower our heads in memory of the victims.' 'The small pebbles laid into the walls need water to wash them and bring shine to the surface as if bringing out the stone-like grievances of the victims.'

Together, the laws on compensation, the inclusion of the injustice in local school books, and this memorial amount to an apology that could well close the relation between perpetrator and victims. They effect a closure by completing, in aspiration if not yet in fact, the radical change of regime that has made the apology possible in the first place.

VIII.   Remaining ghosts

But the vocabulary for describing the victims has hinted at an entirely different set of institutions. What in the law are designated as people charged incorrectly with rebellion, in the more emotive language of the monument are described as wronged souls. Remember that the Luku memorial is a public and political monument, not a grave.

Shih Fanglong and I met a group of three walkers aged between 60 and 70 who had come up the winding road to visit the monument, which they had seen on TV and in newspapers. They had known about 28 February as children, but not the Luku incident. In their more idiomatic language, spoken in Taiwanese, the wronged souls have become 'good brothers', the euphemism for orphan, hungry souls. 'Because it was not fair, the good brothers seek revenge and haunt bad Nationalist Party members.' 'Now is their time. Now the Nationalist Party has lost power, because of Lee Tenghui. At the time of old Chiang Kaishek, people were too scared to speak about it. Now they can seek justice.' 'The soldiers just shot them and pushed them over. They had no proper burial. So they are good brothers.'

Wronged souls have become vengeful ghosts. We are now dealing with the institutions of burial, mourning and the reproduction of family lines. The omission of proper burial and treatment of the dead as ancestors of a family or of proper care for those who might otherwise have produced a family line takes us into another means and another reckoning of perpetuity, in which the memory of a wrong is transmitted. Most if not all those who were executed or shot will not have had proper burials at the time. They were in a limbo. In Chinese religious practice and discourse they were ghosts (*guishen*) who have not been commemorated properly so that they can become ancestors and transcendent souls. Their survivors and their descendants should feel obliged to carry on that grievance. But of course they can also split it off and ignore it, leaving the souls hungry and forgotten and a matter of concern to others who believe in their injury and consequent mistreatment. That is what the visitors assumed to be the case. In fact, from our interviews with victims' families, we found that all had eventually conducted rites to honour the dead.

Nevertheless, we asked the nun custodian of the new temple of Broad Enlightenment whether the reading of sutras and the burning of candles in her temple included the wronged spirits of the Luku victims and their broken families, particularly in the seventh lunar month festival of alms to orphan souls. She could not have known whether their families had conducted rites for them, and she made no direct reference to them. Instead, her answer was carefully non-committal: 'everyone is invited. If the spirit wants to come, it will.'

The temple is a branch of one of the biggest of the Buddhist foundations that have grown to prominence in Taiwan since the 1970s. It is built on the grounds of the Vegetarian Hall that was the main place for detaining and interrogating the villagers rounded up, as mentioned in the Memorial. For fear of becoming involved in politics, the foundation refused a request to build the monument to the Luku victims where the temple car park is now. But the temple grounds do include an ossuary for the care of the bones of the forgotten dead. It is the only remaining part of the original Vegetarian Hall.

A similar process to the change of regime seems to be at work here. The village and its context of myth and religion have changed. But remnants such as the old ossuary and the stories of vengeful ghosts carry into this change that has made apology and memorial possible a record that recalls a need for at least ritual redress and reparation. This need was acknowledged sincerely but inadequately met by the Compensation Fund. The head of its planning section told us that there was a need for something more than mere money: 'It is something that money cannot deal with. We want to use something that would comfort the spirit, to remedy the injury.'[25] He is a quiet but passionate adherent to the modern Buddhism that has accompanied the rise of Taiwan consciousness. He commissioned another new Buddhist organization to hold a rite of remembrance for the victims of the White Terror, including the families of those who had been wronged in Luku. The ceremony took place in October 2004. But it was aimed entirely at the living, not the salvation of the souls of the dead that ordinary mortuary rituals perform. Its motto and motif, designed by a public relations company, were 'Love and compassion transforming grief into fertile earth' with a picture of cupped hands holding earth out of which springs a shoot. The Vice-President of the DPP government was in attendance. It was certainly recognition of their grief. But it left the families of Luku to their own rituals, in a more local public domain. Taiwan is a mix of secular history and its republican politics, a new Buddhist religion of worldly welfare, and an older local culture of ghosts and rituals, each affecting the other without being integrated.

The uses of history are much greater in the judicial and political processes than they are in the ritual process. The historian's compilation of documents is similar to the making of a case for the award of compensation and at the same time it is a support for and activation of an appeal for the rewriting of a narrative giving priority to certain events. On the other hand, the sense of grievance conveyed by the idea and the rituals of wronged souls enters into the political movement for the rewriting of history.

Experience of the harm suffered and the harm that may be done by ghosts is one institution of public memory. A record of names, such as that supplied by the researches and publications of Professor Zhang, rescued from, in this case, government archives, is another. At the very least it provides the individuation that can turn ghosts into ancestors and also martyrs. But beside such academic and official retrieval, there is another archive for oral and ritual transmission, distinct and independent of the historian's narrative and judicial documents. Perhaps this is now inevitable in a world of narrative modelled on the historiography of nations. Stories told within families have been released by politicians and historians into this universalizing public domain. But the more personal and local public domain of transmission with its own rituals and other devices had already been used by the aggrieved families to perform a recognition of their pain and humiliation, bringing its internal recall into a declarative memory of family stories by social conventions that are far older, like the ossuary in the grounds of the new Buddhist temple. The transformation of the larger public domain has included inventions of new kinds of ceremony and acknowledgement that have released that declarative memory from its former secrecy and shame, still leaving the local and personal domain to its own devices but teaching another possible convention of public transmission.

In the larger public domain, the Luku Incident has become an important event in the rewritten history of Taiwan as the story of an oppressed people. Like all stories of a 'people', in the larger domain it becomes an object of political contestation. The 1952 Luku incident adds to the 28 February incident a question of the socialist ideals of some of its leaders in the issue of the future of the people of Taiwan.[26]

IX.   Conclusion

Of course the Luku incident and the particular politics of Taiwan, as well as the religions and rituals practiced in Taiwan, are distinctive if not singular. But I hope that my description has shown a more general truth, how transmission of personal experience that started as declarative recall can become empathetic recall not only by descendants and intimate friends but also by interested historians and politicians and thus receive recognition that can transform shame into something more like honour. I hope I have also been able to suggest that ritual remedy can be another form of recognition. There is a necessary distinction of process and of effect between the experience of humiliation recalled personally and the declarative memory informed by the semantics of either ritual remedy or the historian's narrative and documentation and the evidence required by a case for compensation. There is also a distinction between domains of public memory, between what I have called a local and a general and universalizing public domain. But I hope that I have shown that these distinctions are mutually effective, either negatively, sealed into censored secrecy or released into a series of acknowledgements. Public apology and monuments constitute a civic ritual of recognition that can assuage the shame of those originally humiliated. They in turn have significant political consequences. In this case, the consequences include the demand that the international community recognize the Taiwanese as an autonomous people whilst simultaneously maintaining peace with the PRC.

10

Remembering and Forgetting the Korean War

From Trauma to Reconciliation

*Roland Bleiker and Young-Ju Hoang**

> Occasionally I hear talk from the dead
> of the Korea of centuries past.
> They usually leave out a few things, I think.
> After all, how could they say everything
> in one brief resurrection?[1]

I. Introduction

For over half a century now, the Korean peninsula has been one of the world's most volatile regions. At regular intervals Cold War tensions risk escalating into a more direct confrontation between the communist North and the capitalist South.[2] The roots of the current conflict are located not only in the externally imposed division of the peninsula, but also, and above all, in the three-year war that devastated the peninsula from 1950 to 1953. More than a million people died as a result of the conflict. The trauma and hatred that the war generated continues to dominate virtually all aspects of politics. Each of the two Korean states has sponsored a historical representation of the war that is geared towards legitimizing its own views while discrediting those of the rival regime. Questions of memory are thus essential to understand both the dynamic of the current conflict and the sources for a more peaceful future. This chapter engages ensuing political challenges by examining the relationship between historical memory, identity and conflict.

The first part of the chapter (sections I to III) analyses how diverging North and South Korean historical interpretations of the Korean War have contributed to the present climate of confrontation and fear.

Central, here, is to understand how historical narratives are intertwined with the antagonistic identity practices that still prevail in Korea's Cold-War political climate. On each side, an unusually strong state emerged and was able to promote a particular ideological vision of politics and society: a vision that constructs the other side of the dividing line as an enemy and a source of fear and instability. A virulent anti-capitalist and anti-imperialist attitude dominates the reclusive North while a more moderate but still pronounced anti-communist discourse prevails in the South. We will be employing the term memory in a broad sense – as a conceptual tool to understand how these juxtaposed antagonistic identities have been manipulated in the context of ideologically tainted attempts to construct narratives of nationhood. The struggle over memory then becomes as much a political as a historical issue.

The second part of the chapter (sections IV to VII) moves into more normative terrains. It explores possibilities for alternative historical approaches that may lead to a more tolerant perception of the arch-enemy on the other side of the thirty-eighth parallel. A sustained diplomatic breakthrough cannot occur without a prior promotion of a culture of reconciliation: a willingness to contemplate forgiveness and accept that after half a century of division North and South Koreans have acquired a different and often incompatible understanding of politics and society. More specifically, the chapter argues that a more tolerant and peaceful future can be constructed only once the notion of a single historical narrative gives way to multiple visions of the past and the future. Reorienting memory is, in this sense, an essential component for the construction of a more peaceful political climate on the peninsula. The key ethical challenge, then, consists of finding dialogical agreements on certain historical 'truth' claims, without necessarily embedding them in a single interpretative modality.

Before beginning we must stress that our task is not to analyse the most recent political events on the peninsula. Instead, we seek to identify broad recurring patterns of conflict and their relationship to historical representations. The type of normative suggestions we derive from this analysis are, likewise, not designed to deliver policy recommendations or concrete answers to specific recent challenges, such as tensions over how to deal with North Korea's nuclear ambitions. Doing so is the task of politicians, diplomats and policy analysts. Our ambition, by contrast, is to identity the type of intellectual mindset with which questions of trauma and memory are most adequately approached. Doing so does, however, entail exploring the pre-conditions necessary for more nuanced political judgments.[3]

II.   Identity, conflict and the state

Reconciliation, JeanPaul Lederach argues, is 'the point of encounter where concerns about both the past and the future can meet'.[4] In Korea, this encounter would need to deal with competing memories of national division and war. The 'facts' are well known, their contentious nature less so: the peninsula became tentatively divided along the thirty-eighth parallel in the context of Soviet–American rivalry at the end of the Second World War. With the creation of two politically and ideologically separate Korean states in 1948, and their subsequent confrontation during the Korean War, this supposedly provisional division became a permanent feature of Northeast Asia. The Korean War claimed the lives of more than a million people and, almost half a century after the events, an estimated ten million individuals are still separated from their families.

The memory of war continues to dominate Korean politics. Antagonistic identity constructs, born out of death, fear and longing for revenge, are continuously used to fuel and legitimize aggressive foreign and repressive domestic policies. Indeed, much of the conflict in Korea is based on identity constructs that portray the opposite side of the divided peninsula not only as an ideological archrival, but also, and perhaps more importantly, as a threatening Other, as something that is inherently evil and thus incompatible with one's own sense of identity.[5] These opposing images are disseminated through a variety of mechanisms, from ideology-based education to a tightly controlled media environment. From a South Korean perspective North Korea became the national other. Anti-communism was far more than a government policy, it penetrated every aspect of South Korea's national consciousness, to the point that it gained, as one commentator puts it, 'a hegemonic hold over civil society'.[6] The situation in the North is comparable, for an anti-imperialist and anti-capitalist discourse prevails in an equally strong manner. 'In order to understand North Korea', one commentator argues, 'one only needs to look at the South, for whatever characterizes the South is denounced and demonized in the North'.[7]

Drawing attention to the juxtaposed identity constructs that dominate Korean politics is not to argue that the state looks the same on both sides of the DMZ. The North is dominated by a highly anachronistic authoritarian regime that is characterized by massive human rights abuses and disastrous economic policies. The South, by contrast, has managed to promote not just remarkable economic development but also a largely successful transition to democracy. Nevertheless, on both sides of the peninsula questions of identity (what it means to be a South or North Korean citizen) have come to be constructed essentially in negative terms, that is, in direct opposition to the arch enemy across the dividing line. It is, of course, not unusual that states use their privileged position to advance particular political objectives. For centuries, states all over the world have promoted, legitimized and protected identity constructs, particularly those essential for the process of nation building. The state provided mythological and institutional frameworks that separated self from other, inside from outside, safe from threatening.[8] But these constructions are particularly fateful in Korea, where the state is unusually dominant, where identities are unusually antagonistic, and where the presence of a large arsenal of weapons on both sides creates a constant danger of a military escalation.

One of the main reasons why these artificially constructed enemy images persist is the almost total state-control over inter-Korean relations. Although the state assumes a very different role in the North than in the South, there are also many parallels. Both Korean states have gone to great lengths to control political and social life within their respective sovereign boundaries. As a result, for the past half a century the Korean Demilitarized Zone has perhaps been the most hermetically sealed border in the world. There is virtually no travel and communication across the thirty eighth parallel, and the few contacts that exist are limited to state-based interactions, such as diplomatic negotiations or meetings of the Military Armistice Commission in the Truce Village of Panmunjom. Neither North nor South Korean people have a realistic idea of how everyday life looks like in the vilified other half. For decades the two regimes have shielded their populations from 'subversive' influences stemming from the other side.

III.   Competing narratives of the Korean War

Not surprisingly, state-control over politics is particularly pronounced when it comes to understandings of the past. Both Korean states have strenuously promoted historical narratives that legitimize the respective political regimes. History is, of course, always as much about the present as it is about the past. At the time an event takes place there is no memory. Historical awareness emerges later and by necessity includes values and interests that have nothing to do with the original occurrence. An event as complex as the Korean War, for instance, cannot possibly be represented in its totality. Remembering the war, then, is as much about forgetting it as it is about remembering it. The mixture of remembering and forgetting is an inherently political process, and this is why the stories we tell about the past are an integral element of the present and play a crucial role in shaping the future.

Nowhere is the process of re-writing history more obvious and more politically consequential than with regard to the Korean War. The most neutral descriptions of the conflict, to the extent that this is possible given the highly emotional issues at stake, hold that 'tension along the thirty-eighth parallel flared up in intermittent military clashes until a full-scale war broke out in June 1950, when North Korea launched a general invasion against South Korea in an attempt to bring all of Korea under its rule'.[9]

The two Korean governments have, however, sponsored much more black-and-white accounts of the war: accounts that put all blame for the conflict on the other side. The respective narratives then became essential elements in the creation of the two separate and diametrically opposed conceptions of nationhood. For instance, Park Chung Hee, South Korea's president during the 1960s and 1970s, argued that 'the north Korean Communists villainously unleashed an unwarranted armed invasion of the south with a view to communising the entire Korean peninsula'.[10] The North, by contrast, blames the South entirely for the initiation of the War. These juxtaposed interpretations are deeply rooted in the respective state mythologies.

The question of who started and was responsible for the war has but one right answer, Bruce Cumings stresses, but it depends on which side of the DMZ one is located.[11] South Korean school textbooks hold that during the late 1940s the North Korean communists tried to topple the southern government by promoting various demonstrations and labour strikes. When these efforts failed the North proposed peace talks, but in fact secretly planned an invasion of the South. Once Kim Il Sung had received Russian and Chinese support for an invasion, he ordered his armies to cross the DMZ on the morning of 25 June 1950, thus starting the war.[12] North Korean school textbooks, by contrast, present the war as a criminal aggression for which the United States government and its South Korean 'puppet regime' are responsible. The respective text stresses that Pyongyang initiated peace talks and tried everything possible to prevent a conflict, but that the South rejected the peace offer and, on the morning of 25 June 1950, crossed the thirty-eighth parallel and marched north.[13] There are similarly incompatible narratives with regard to other aspects of the war, such as its evolution and the reason for the cessation of direct hostilities.

For half a century now both sides have rehearsed their ideologically tainted memories of the war. They have done so *ad infinitum*, while making every effort to shield their populations from the diametrically opposed narrative promoted by the other side. As a result, the respective positions have long passed the stage of being mere ideology and propaganda, even if the corresponding narratives have little or nothing to do with what actually happened during the conflict. One of the most explicit confirmations of how much these two versions of the past diverge, and how they continue to influence societal consciousness, is the fact that most North Korean defectors are 'simply stunned' when they are first confronted with South Korean representations of the war.[14]

IV.   Remembering and forgetting the Korean War

Central to any lasting political solution on the peninsula is the question of how to deal with competing memories of the war, and with how the related narratives have become part of the antagonistic identity practices that have fuelled conflict on the peninsula. The chapter now examines how various small but nevertheless significant activities within South Korea demonstrate how the promotion of a more tolerant historical awareness can contribute to an eventual culture of reconciliation.

While the North usually employs the term '*Choson Haebang Jeonjaeng*' (national liberation war), South Korean history textbooks tend to present the conflict by referring to what is considered its starting date, 25 June 1950. The 1979 version of texbooks thus calls the war the '6.25 incident'. With each subsequent change of textbooks the terminology seems to get more violent: in 1982 it is the '6.25 intrusion' and in 1990 the '6.25 war'.[15] This way of labelling the conflict emphasizes a specific inaugural moment, and thus stresses questions of causality and responsibility. But such questions are highly contentious. Bruce Cumings, in one of the most authoritative and controversial treatments of recent Korean history, argues that the war 'did not begin on 25 June 1950, much special pleading and argument to the contrary'.[16] He points out that intense fighting had already taken place for the nine preceding months. Without denying Kim Il Sung's 'grave responsibility', Cumings presents the war as a complex and interconnected set of events that 'originate[d] in multiple causes, with blame enough to go around for everyone – and blame enough to include Americans who thoughtlessly divided Korea and then re-established the colonial government machinery'.[17] By presenting the conflict as a civil war that emerged gradually, Cumings stresses that questions of causality and responsibility are far too complex to be attributed to a single side. He also believes that historians and politicians must look beyond the issues of origin and causality. People are no longer interested in who started the American Civil War or the Vietnam War, Cumings points out, and he thinks that Koreans will one day 'reconcile, as Americans eventually did, with the wisdom that civil wars have no single authors'.[18] This revisionist position has led to much opposition in South Korea and the West, ranging all the way from factual critiques related to recently released Soviet material[19] to regrets about an 'unappealing ... bias towards the Communists'[20] and unusually hostile accusations of irresponsible scholarship, subjective teleology and pro-North Korea propaganda.[21] But there was not only opposition to Cumings' attempt to move beyond a history and politics of blame. A number of revisionist South Koran historians, such as Choi Jang-jip, Chong Hae-gu and Kim Nam-sik, have also sought to advance representations that defy the entrenched black-and-white logic that constitutes North Korea as the evil other and only cause of the war.[22] The trauma of the Korean War is undoubtedly still too fresh to stop debating and disagreeing over questions of origin and responsibility. But the arguments advanced by Cumings and revisionist South Korean historians get to the heart of what the war is today: a past event, a contentious memory, a site for political struggles.

To move from trauma to reconciliation some aspects of the war have to be 'forgotten'. Nietzsche stresses that the past suffocates the present unless we forget it, and he calls upon people to have the courage to 'break with the past in order to live'.[23] Forgetting, in this sense, does not mean ignoring what happened. Forgetting, after all, is a natural process, an inevitable aspect of remembering; we all do it, whether we want it or not. We cannot possibly remember everything. We cannot give every event the same weight. Our memory of the past is the result of a process through which certain events and interpretations are remembered and prioritized, while others are relegated to secondary importance or forgotten altogether. This is particularly the case with a major event like the Korean War, which is far too complex to be remembered in its totality. The task of historians is to select the few facts, perspectives and interpretations that ought to be remembered. The combination of forgetting and remembering is as inevitable as it is political. Being aware of this inevitability is to explore possibilities for reshaping the past and using this process in the service of creating a better future.[24] Nietzsche is particularly critical of periods during which historical understandings lack critical awareness of this process – situations, say, when powerful rulers fail to gain legitimacy on their own and thus rely on the misappropriation of historical figures and events to justify their form of dominance.[25] Such is undoubtedly the case in contemporary Korea, where history has been geared far more towards supporting particular regimes than towards actually representing what happened in the past.

But South Korea also displays signs of what Nietzsche calls 'critical histories': attempts to challenge the notion of a single historical reality and create the political space in which diverging narratives of the past can compete with each other, perhaps even respect each other despite the differences that divide them. A recent example of a breakthrough in this direction, timid as it may well be, can be found in revisions of history school textbooks. Several generations of history texts have studiously avoided even mentioning the role that northern Communist guerrillas played in the fight against the Japanese colonial occupiers. One of six new secondary school history textbooks, released in 2003, for the first time mentions the existence of communist resistance, in a passage dealing with a 1937 clash between Japanese colonial forces and resistance fighters allegedly led by Kim Il Sung, the future leader of North Korea. The clash, which occupies a central role in North Korea's portrayal of the struggle against Japanese imperialism, is portrayed as follows in the South Korean textbook:

> In June, 1937, the Northeast Anti-Japanese United Army crossed the Yalu river and seized Bocheonbo, south of Hamgyong province ... The Japanese were shocked by the attack and began to aggressively crack down on the Korean national movement. After Korea was liberated from Japan, Kim Il Sung was revered by North Koreas as a leader of Korean independence ... Some academics in South Korea have been critical of North Korea for exaggerating the battle.[26]

This account is undoubtedly far more balanced and less hostile than the overtly ideological representations that had prevailed for decades. A representative of the Ministry of Education called it an attempt to present 'strictly the facts'.[27] That is hardly possible, of course, since history always involves some sort of representation. In addition, the changes are admittedly miniscule and occurred in only one of six new textbooks. But this small change is nevertheless of symbolic importance, for it signals a new willingness, approved by the government, to recognize that the other side of the DMZ may have a different story to tell about what happened during the crucial lead up to the Korean War. Nevertheless, the new and more balanced representation still generated protests from conservative elements of South Korean society. Park Sung Soo, head of the Institute of Documenting Accurate History, warned of succumbing to North Korea's propaganda. He argued that 'the reference to the battle needs to be removed or it may taint the pure minds of youth'.[28]

Other attempts to present a more accurate account of Korea's past met similar and similarly strong opposition. Grinker, for example, presents a highly insightful analysis of a South Korea television feature on the war. The programme, broadcast in 1996, was aimed at elementary-school children. As opposed to 'normal' historical representations, the programme did not portray North Koreans as evil, nor did it clearly blame them for causing the war.[29] It simply sought to present the war as a human and national tragedy. Here too, opposition emerged immediately. Journalists argued that the programme was 'too neutral and objective', that it failed to clearly identify the North as the side that initiated the war. There was also opposition to the relatively detached terms 'northern soldiers' and 'southern soldiers', which were used instead of the usual labels, such as 'northern communists' and the 'invasion of the south'.[30]

The struggle over historical consciousness in South Korea partly reflects generational tensions. The television programme mentioned above was produced by a young Korean who was eager to move beyond the memory of hatred and fear. Opposition to such revisionist history tends to come from the older generation of Koreans, from people who experienced the war and are thus directly marked by the trauma it caused. The very same tension is, to some extent, present within many people themselves. Or so argue Kim Ki-Jung and Park Jae-min, who stress that 'most South Koreans seem to exhibit two contrasting features: a strong Cold War ethos (anti-communist and anti-North Korean sentiment) and a strong desire to overcome such an ethos'.[31]

The generational tensions and disagreements in Korea can be conceptualized helpfully by drawing on Duncan Bell's distinction between memory and myth. He argues that the concept of memory is usually employed in an unhelpfully imprecise manner, as a way simply of referring to collective representations of history.[32] However, such representations can assume multiple, conflicting forms. Consequently, Bell proposes that we limit the concept of memory to the experiences of people who directly witnessed and shared events under consideration. Memory, he argues, is always anchored in common experience, as is the case, for instance, with the older generation of Koreans who had lived through the war. Such memories, he continues, should be distinguished from myths, from the more general processes of generating national (or other) identities by representing the past through media and state-sanctioned discourses, school curricula, art, music and so forth. The latter mode of understanding history is the only way in which many of the younger Koreans have come to 'know' the Korean War. That a certain tension emerges from these different genres of historical representation is thus inevitable.

V. Exchanging narrative memories

Acknowledging the political and inherently contestable dimension of history is one of the most important ways of overcoming the cycle of violence that has dominated Korea for half a century. The memory of pain and death is far too present for a single historical narrative to emerge in the foreseeable future. Given the deeply entrenched antagonisms on the peninsula, there will necessarily be different interpretations of how to understand and represent the war.

Recognizing the existence of historical differences is a crucial element in the effort to promote a culture of reconciliation. Paul Ricoeur stresses that by 'acknowledging that the history of an event involves a conflict of several interpretations and memories, we in turn open up the future'.[33] Linking an ethics of difference with the promotion of a tolerant historical consciousness entails a variety of different dimensions. It necessitates what Richard Kearney calls an 'exchange of narrative memories'. Although writing in the context of Northern Ireland, Kearney's recommendation is just as relevant for Korea, for such exchanges would allow the opposing sides to 'see each other through alter-native eyes'.[34]

North and South need to open up political spaces in which it becomes possible to contemplate the other's memory of the past, even if this memory appears distorted and inherently wrong. Such a level of tolerance is possible only once each side accepts within its own political culture the possibility of multiple pasts, presents and futures. Dipesch Chakrabarty uses the term 'minority histories' and refers to the need to protect various versions of the past, even if they contradict each other and cannot be subsumed under prevailing narrative constructions of the nation.[35] This is precisely why the work of revisionist historians is important. Their interpretations and conclusions may well be contentious, but far more important is the fact that they defy the prevailing black-and-white logic and thus open up spaces for multiple narratives of the past. Promoting and protecting such an ethics of difference is an ongoing and inevitably incomplete process. Consider some of the contradictions that became evident in the above-mentioned work of historians such as Choi Jang-jip and Chong Hae-gu. They may well have overcome the prevailing tendency to abuse history to discredit the North at any cost, but they have done so through a new nationalist narrative that entails its own problems and contradictions. Or so at least believes Henry Em, who argues that these revisionist narratives, although critical in a variety of ways, are still based on the assumption of a 'preexisting subject'. As a result they too run the risk of oppressing and suppressing other identities, for instance those of marginalized societal segments, such as women and Chinese-residents.[36]

The greatest impetus towards a historical awareness that respects difference may not come from historians, and certainly not from politicians, generals and diplomats, but from the realm of the everyday and of popular culture. One highly positive development is that a select number of North Korean films are now screened in the South, as, for instance, at the Pusan International Film Festival.[37] There are also an increasing number of South Korean films that defy the tendency to vilify the North, including such recent releases as *Huk Su Son* (*Last witness*, 2001), *Swiri* (1999) and *Joint Security Area* (or *JSA*, 2000). The domestic and international success of the latter is particularly important, for the film is one of the rare public features that clearly resists perpetuating the entrenched stereo typical image of cold, calculating and evil North Koreans. Instead, *JSA* narrates how a small group of soldiers from both sides develop a friendship, secretly and against all odds. In the end conflict becomes inevitable and the respective soldiers must chose country over friendship. But the film is nevertheless a milestone, for it portrays soldiers on both sides as normal Koreans, with a variety of similar emotions, concerns and interests. This contrasts quite sharply not only with the security discourse that still dominates high politics, but also with a relatively recent James Bond film. Entitled *Die Another Day*, and released in 2002, the film portrays North Koreans in the stereotypical role of evil madmen bent on destroying the world. Not surprisingly, there was considerable public protest against the Cold War antics of 007, not only in the North, but also in the South.[38] While Her Majesty's secret agent, judging the world from neo-imperial London, was clearly uninterested in the necessity of reconciliation on the peninsula, *JSA* has demonstrated, as one commentator puts it, that there is a 'surging demand for films and literary works that can be shared by the two sides to promote understanding and accommodation'.[39] While such works offer possibilities for healing, there exists a certain degree of scepticism about them. Consider, for instance, that *JSA* received a restrictive

'R' rating in South Korea, rather than an 'M', for it was judged that young people would not have the maturity necessary to watch a film that presents North Korea in a favourable light.

The role of humour, literature and theatre is equally important. William Callahan, for example, draws attention to the often-neglected significance of laughter.[40] Choi Chungmoo, likewise, examines how folk theatre, such as the *madang guk*, may overcome stereotypical images of the other. Embedded in a mixture of ritual and carnevalesque communal festival, it is able to challenge the notion of a single narrative of the nation. *Madang guk* can thus be seen as a cultural practice that tolerates a variety of different, overlapping or often even contradictory beliefs and narratives. The promotion of such diversity is all the more significant since folk theatre is actually able to reach and politicize a significant part of the population.[41]

Mikhail Bakhtin's examination of the sixteenth-century French author François Rabelais is perhaps the best-known study that demonstrates the power of such carnevalesque interventions in the public sphere. Rabelais' grotesque and satirical stories were part of a popular culture of laughter – a sub-culture, so to speak, that was deeply subversive, for it opposed, even ridiculed, the seriousness and hypocrisy of the official feudal culture. It mocked the clergy and its rigid Christian rituals. In this sense, Bakhtin stresses, laughter was freedom because it 'celebrated temporary liberation from the prevailing truth and from the established order; it marked the suspension of all hierarchical rank, privileges, norms, and prohibitions'.[42]

This suspension and, in a more general sense, the language of the market place and of carnival, created possibilities for uninhibited speech. Laughter opened up, at least for a short moment, a glimpse of utopian freedom, a life beyond the Christian mythology of death and eternal punishment. Laughter, Bakhtin argues, purifies from dogmatism and pedantry, from fear and intimidation. It shatters the belief that life has a single meaning.[43]

VI. Against relativism and essentialising difference

The promotion of an ethics of difference is hampered by a variety of practical and ethical dilemmas. For one, the experience of history teaching in South Korea shows that tolerance simply takes time to emerge, that entrenched identity practices cannot be transformed over night. Reconciliation is a long and ongoing process. There are also more direct or at least more directly recognizable challenges to an ethics of difference. They have to do with the pitfalls of relativism and with the danger of essentializing difference. The first would lead to a situation where one can no longer judge between good and evil. The second would eventually engender an apartheid society in which differences are not tolerated, but used to confirm and assert a single notion of identity. Neither of these dangers, however, are automatically entailed by an ethics of difference.

If history is to be placed in the service of reconciliation, then it has to go beyond merely acknowledging that the two sides have different notions of the past. Leaving it at that would only entrench existing antagonisms, and thus legitimize or even intensify the existing conflict. Michael Williams and Keith Krause draw attention to this danger, pointing out that in places like Bosnia and Rwanda an awareness of difference led 'not to celebration but destruction'.[44]

An ethics of difference does not essentialize difference, but seeks to create the conditions under which different identities can co-exist.[45] Reconciliation, in this sense, creates commonalties and develops from them the type of understanding, respect and tolerance needed for the articulation of a non-violent relationship between identity and difference. Memory is essential in this process, which would need to start with a search for the lowest common denominator that could possibly unite the diverging historical narratives on the peninsula. Susan Dwyer identifies three stages in the process of reconciliation. The first consists of an effort to find agreement on 'the barest of facts'. The second stage involves an effort to identify a range of different interpretations of the respective events. And the third stage would entail narrowing things down to a limited set of interpretations that the two sides can tolerate.[46] While such a goal of agreeing to disagree seems modest, the path towards it is littered with seemingly insurmountable obstacles. The first hurdle alone is gargantuan, for Dwyer defines agreeing on 'the barest of facts' as finding a clear view on 'who did what to whom and when'.[47] In Korea, these 'bare facts' are, of course, precisely the major point of contention – and the source of trauma and hatred. And even if there were agreement on certain truth claims, promoting them may not necessarily bring more justice. Kwon Hyuk Bom, for instance, warns of problems entailed in searching for common roots between North and South and using them as a basis for reconciliation. The strong masculinism that still dominates both parts of the peninsula promotes identity practices that constitute women as 'kind, gentle and subservient'. Grounding reconciliation in common Confucian values may thus only strengthen the patriarchal social order and lead to further dis-criminations against women.[48]

While finding and developing commonalties between North and South is a major challenge, developing tolerance for the differences that remain may be even more difficult, but also more important in the process of reconciliation. The ethics of difference that is required for such tolerance is often dismissed, for it tends to be associated with a fall into a nihilist abyss. International relations scholars are particularly concerned that subscribing to a post-modern embrace of difference would open up the floodgates to relativistic ravings according to which 'anything goes' and 'any narrative is as valid as another'.[49] Upon closer reading such strong warnings often indicate a fear of not being able to articulate and ground specific value commitments and the political projects that issue from them. But there is no reason why an appreciation of difference would prevent the possibility of judging. If anything, it is an essential precondition for taking informed and adequate decisions. For instance, a historian who opens up possibilities for alternative narratives diminishes the chance of relativism, for s/he increases the range of sources and evidence available and thus 'opposes the manipulation of narratives by ... providing a space for confrontation between opposing testimonies'.[50]

Making choices, drawing lines and defending them are inevitable, par-ticularly in a context like Korea, where interests and perspectives clash. An unconditional acceptance of otherness cannot – and indeed should not – always work in practice. There are moments when the reassertion and imposition of one identity over another becomes desirable, perhaps even a political imperative. But successful and fair solutions to political challenges are more likely to emerge if positions are not dogmatically asserted, but carefully justified through a critical and self-reflective understanding of the tensions between identity and difference.

Advancing an ethics of difference does not therefore necessitate aban-doning the ability to judge, particularly when it comes to questions of responsibility for war and conflict on the Korean peninsula. Gerrit Gong stresses that addressing such questions will be one of the main challenges in a unified Korea.[51] Claus Offe, writing about the task of coming to terms with Germany's divided past, argues likewise that a general amnesty is out of the question.[52] But one must recall at the same time that the institution of amnesty is not to be equated with amnesia. Paul Ricoeur, for instance, stresses that there is a duty to forget as much as there is a duty to remember, for 'the duty to remember is a duty to teach, whereas the duty to forget is a duty to go beyond anger and hatred'.[53] Richard Kearney adds that 'genuine amnesty' is a way of remembering that goes beyond a form of memory dominated by 'the deterministic stranglehold of violent obsession and revenge'.[54] Korea needs such a willingness to forgive in the service of healing and reconciliation: it needs a way out of the cycle of violence and hatred that has dominated interactions on the peninsula for half a century now.

Here too, the role of history is illustrative, not least because it forces us to confront questions of evidence and truth. Not any version of the past can be sustained. Although the content of a historical account is inevitably intertwined with the values espoused by the narrator, a historian cannot simply make up events and interpretations. One of Australia's leading historians, Henry Reynolds, repeatedly stressed this point. He argues that to advance a progressive historical account – an account that does justice to the all too often forgotten or marginalized voices of indigenous peoples – one needs to find agreement on certain historical truth claims. To view history as merely a clash of different interpretations would be to forgo the opportunity to critique the type of colonial historiography that was advanced in the interest of legitimizing domination and empire.[55] Many more postmodern historians would not necessarily disagree. Ricoeur, for instance, seeks to avoid an abuse of memory by grounding it in 'what really happened'.[56] This is, of course, an aspiration that inevitably remains unfulfilled, for history is a form of representation, and a representation is always incomplete and, at least to some extent, distorted. It cannot capture the object it represents as it is, void of perception and perspective.[57] Ricoeur stresses the need to supplement historical memory with documentary and archival evidence. He illustrates this inevitable combination between event and representation, fact and narration, as follows: 'You have to accurately *count* the corpses in the death camps as well as offering vivid narrative *accounts* that people will remember.'[58] Even so-called post-modern historians stress the need for rules of scholarship and verification. Hayden White, for instance, admits that every historical narrative contains a 'desire to moralise' the event it seeks to capture. But to count as 'proper history', White emphasizes, the narrative 'must manifest a proper concern for the judicious handling of evidence, and it must honour the chronological order of the original occurrence of events'.[59] Chakrabarty, likewise, defends the notion of 'minority histories' while rejecting relativist position that may dismiss such accounts as purely personal or arbitrary. He stresses that an alternative memory of the past can only enrich, or be absorbed into the mainstream historical discourse if the following questions can be answered in the affirmative: 'Can the story be told/crafted? And does it allow for a rationally defensible point of view or position from which to tell the story?'[60]

It is not our task here to define which interpretations of the Korean War are factual and defensible, separating them from the many other more ideologically tainted historical appropriations. But some of the highly ideological and hagiographical narratives that make up North Korea's national mythology are unlikely to survive if confronted with rigorous historical testing principles. But the same can be said about aspects of South Korea's historical consciousness as well. A recent example of the need to revise the official memory of the Korean War can be found with regard to the so-called Nogun-ri massacre. For decades citizens of the small village of Nogun-ri had insisted that on a day in late July 1950, American soldiers machinegunned hundreds of civilians under a railroad bridge near the village. But US military officials, as well as the South Korean government, consistently denied that such events ever occurred, arguing that they could find no basis for the allegations. No history text mentioned the incident. Public discussion about the issue only emerged in the late 1990s, when a dozen former US soldiers gave evidence that largely confirmed the claims that Nogun-ri's inhabitants had advanced for decades. After a year-long review, the US army had to admit officially that 'US ground forces fired towards refugees in the vicinity of Nogun-ri during this period ... As a result, an unknown number of refugees were killed or injured'.[61]

VII.   Conclusion

The devastating Korean War has created wounds that still decisively influence politics on the peninsula half a century later. On each side, an unusually strong state emerged and was able to promote a particular ideological vision of politics and society: a vision that constructs the other side of the dividing line as an enemy and a source of fear and instability. A strong anti-communist discourse has acquired a quasi-hegemonic status in the South while an equally strong anti-capitalist and anti-imperialist attitude prevails in the reclusive North.

Much has changed in Korea over the last decades. The North largely remains isolated, authoritarian and plagued by recurrent famines. The South, by contrast, has embarked on a successful path of democratization and economic development. But antagonistic identity constructs continue to dominate the interaction between North and South. This is why questions of memory are essential to understand and deal with the ensuing dilemmas. We have thus used the term memory as a conceptual tool to understand how representations of the Korean War have decisively shaped the political climate on the peninsula. To appreciate the significance of this phenomenon it is important to ask what is remembered, how, why and with what consequences.

A successful reconciliation process in Korea will have to mix the search for justice with the ability to forgive. We have argued that a route from trauma to reconciliation can open up through the promotion of an ethics of difference: a willingness to recognize and deal with the fact that over the last half a century the two divided parts of Korea have developed different and incompatible identities. The promotion of a more tolerant historical consciousness must thus start by creating space for dissent within one's own culture. Some Korean scholars have thus started to argue that both the South and the North must show more tolerance for the other's identity practices, that they must make an effort to view and accept the other as 'the other within oneself'.[62] Such efforts to create space for the 'stranger within' remain very isolated so far. The North still imprisons people even at the slightest hint of dissent. The South has meanwhile adopted a more democratic system, but still shows a stunning inability to accommodate difference and dissent. Dozens of citizens have been imprisoned for decades, for no other crime than their persistent refusal to renounce communist believes and become 'law-abiding' South Koreans. Some of these prisoners of consciousness, which are brandmarked as 'spies' and communist 'sympathizers', were returned to the North in the context of humanitarian exchanges that followed the June 2000 summit.[63] But this gesture hardly changed the more fundamental practice of annihilating difference within South Korea. However, there is also hope, for the increasing democratization of South Korean has generated signs of a more tolerant attitude as well. Among the respective examples are efforts by historians and teachers to promote tolerance for multiple narratives of the past. Although neglected by security experts, such low-key efforts are crucial for developing a culture of reconciliation.

Promoting an ethics of difference as part of a reconciliation process inevitably takes time. Entrenched identities cannot be uprooted over night, nor can the antagonistic political attitudes and practices that are intertwined with these identities. But there are more immediate challenges too, notably by those who fear that an ethics of difference either promotes more conflict or generates a form of relativism that prevents judging and defending particular political projects. Neither fear is justified. If there is a source of tension and conflict on the peninsula, then it is located precisely in the attempt to erase difference and impose one memory of the past, one right way of life for the present, and one vision for the future. This is why the most serious causes of violence today stem not from interactions with difference, but, as William Connolly argues convincingly, from doctrines and movements that suppress it by trying to reinstate a unified faith in one form of identification.[64] Tolerating different coexisting narratives does not prevent making judgements about their content or desirability. Quite to the contrary, adequate decisions about key political and ethical challenges can be taken only once a variety of perspectives, interests and arguments have been taken into account. Repressing difference between them will neither lead to better decisions nor avoid the fact that they are based on certain political and moral values.

11

Remembering to Forget/ Forgetting to Remember

Maja Zehfuss

I. Introduction

War is often conceptualized and legitimated in relation to memory, and it is consequently important to engage the issue of memory in analyses of international politics.[1] This chapter explores aspects of the struggle in Germany over remembering and forgetting the period of 1933 to 1945, and particularly the Second World War, and relates this to the invocation of such memory in debates over the use of force today. Although remembering and forgetting are clearly opposed to each other in debates over memory, and the former valued over the latter, they are inextricably linked: remembering always already entails forgetting and forgetting is possible only where there is remembering in the first place. It is precisely this problematic status of memory that is crucial to the ethico-political question of war.

In 1995 almost 300 'Conservatives and critical Liberals'[2] signed an appeal under the heading '8 May 1945 – Against Forgetting' published in the *Frankfurter Allgemeine Zeitung*, citing the first President of the Federal Republic of Germany Theodor Heuss: 'Basically, this 8 May 1945 remains the most tragic and questionable paradox for everyone of us. Why? Because we were saved and destroyed at the same time.'[3] The advertisement asserted that, in contrast to Heuss's apt characterization, the date of the unconditional surrender of the German Reich to the Allies had increasingly come to be represented as 'liberation' by politicians and the media. This meant, according to the advertisements, that there was a danger of forgetting that this day had marked not only the end of the National Socialist terror regime but also 'the beginning of the terror of expulsion and of new oppression in the east and the beginning of the division of our country'. This was a problem because an 'image of the past that conceals, suppresses or qualifies these truths cannot be the basis for the self-conception of a self-assured nation that we Germans have to become in the European family of peoples in order to rule out comparable catastrophes in future'.[4]

This reasoning could be questioned on a number of levels but here I am interested specifically in one aspect: the rhetoric *against* forgetting and by implication *for* remembering. This concern may be surprising, for on the surface it might appear obvious that we *should* strive to remember, particularly where violence and oppression are concerned. Three reasons for this spring immediately to mind: first, because we have a duty towards the victims, second, because the possibility for reconciliation may be found in acknowledging the past and, finally, of course, so that we may learn from the past. Such arguments are, however, fraught with difficulty. They presume that there is a particular memory we must work towards, that that which must be remembered may be clearly identified, such as the 'truths' referred to in the advertisement campaign. As Klaus Neumann observes in relation particularly to the Holocaust: 'Those who admonish Germans today not to forget seem often to assume that what needs to be remembered is self-evident.'[5]

This chapter explores the ways in which remembering always already entails forgetting, upsetting any simplistic imperative to remember. It starts by highlighting the positive connotation of remembering, taking into account not only commemorations of events that occurred during the Third Reich but also the invocation of memories of the Second World War in political debate in Germany over the use of military force. The chapter then briefly looks at the supposed opposite of remembering – forgetting. The consideration of forgetting reconfirms that remembering is valued, despite Friedrich Nietzsche's intervention in support of forgetting. What may appear as a struggle between remembering and forgetting could rather be construed as one about *how* to remember. The following section pushes this point further and highlights that political debate seems unaware of the implications of memory as a practice and indeed that some forms of political analysis define memory away, even as they seem to engage it. I then explore a memory practice that at the same time reflects upon memory itself: fictional literature. Through a reading of Günter Grass's *Im Krebsgang*, a novella focusing on the expulsion of Germans from the East, I highlight not only the multiplicity of possible memories but also the tensions within them. In conclusion, I argue that remembering and forgetting are inextricably linked, and that recognizing this – something facilitated by reading fiction – is crucial if we are to engage the problem of war as an ethico-political question.

II. Remembering

With their 1995 campaign 'against forgetting' German conservatives caught up with the *Zeitgeist*. In the 1980s *Historikerstreit* (Historians' Dispute) they had been accused of wanting to 'draw a line' under the past, though it is by no means clear that they had actually argued against remembering.[6] The campaign against forgetting, at any rate, implies that remembering is good, even that it is crucial in order to prevent history from repeating itself. It admits that the memory of the horrors of the National-Socialist rule must be kept alive but expresses satisfaction at having set off public debate about the 'crimes of expulsion'.[7] In other words, the rhetoric is one of more memory – not less – and thus it expresses widely held convictions; for, in recent decades, the assertion of the necessity and value of remembering has been extremely powerful in relation to the history of the Third Reich.

In 1985, in his famous speech on the fortieth anniversary of the end of the Second World War in Europe, Federal President Richard von Weizsäcker – urging incidentally that 8 May 1945 should be seen as liberation – cited the cabbalistic saying inscribed at the Yad Vashem memorial: 'Wanting to forget prolongs the exile, and the secret of redemption is remembering.'[8] Von Weizsäcker argued that Germans had to face the truth about their country's past as best they could. The saying – usually cut short into 'the secret of redemption is remembering' – subsequently gained considerable prominence in German discourse on the Third Reich. In Helmut Dubiel's view, it became clear from this reception that von Weizsäcker's discussion had not been differentiated enough. The saying had been 'stripped of its Jewish origin' and strangely referred to 'the possibility of a moral emancipation of the perpetrator through memory of guilt'.[9] Klaus Naumann also criticized that von Weisäcker seemed to be unaware that the cabbala deals with 'the victims of historical injustice', not the perpetrators.[10] Despite these criticisms, the faith in redemption through remembering evidently persisted. Ten years later in Federal President Roman Herzog's speech on the fiftieth anniversary of the bombing of Dresden it took the form of invoking community through recalling the dead.[11] Naumann notes that, in Herzog's speech, 'there is a suggestion of the Christian motive of salvation. A new community constitutes itself in the face of mass death.'[12]

Despite a struggle over the particular form that remembering should take, as indicated by the campaign 'against forgetting', there is a widely shared belief in the value of remembering. Given this commitment to memory, it is perhaps not surprising that the motif of remembering appears not only in relation to commemorations of the Holocaust and the Second World War but also in debates about current politics, particularly when the issues are seen to touch in some way on the 'lessons' of this past. This is the case with respect to questions about the use of military force. At the time of the 1991 Gulf War, Chancellor Helmut Kohl pointed out that Germans of the older generation still remembered the horrors of war and that these 'experiences have been deeply ingrained in the memory of our people as a whole'. Therefore Germans, he argued, empathize in a special way with the suffering of people in war.[13] One might assume that such memories would have biased the Germans against war forever, and this is certainly how the attitude of the FRG and its people was seen for some time. As Michael Schwab-Trapp puts it, at the time of the 1991 Gulf War Germany seemed to be almost 'identical' with the peace movement.[14] However, matters were much less straightforward than it first appeared. The past and war memories were used to argue both for and against German contributions to military operations.[15]

In the *Bundestag* debate on 30 June 1995 about the deployment of troops for the protection and support of the rapid reaction force in Bosnia Foreign Minister Klaus Kinkel contextualized the decision within an understanding of the past. Two aspects are significant here: first, his reference to the Allied 'liberation' of Germany and, second, his reconfirmation of the so-called 'Kohl doctrine'. Kinkel argued that the Germans had a political and moral duty to help in Bosnia, in particular because of their past. He asserted that they had 'forgotten too quickly' that it had been the Allies who, using military force, had liberated the Germans from the Nazi regime and made the new democratic beginning possible.[16] Thus the *Bundeswehr* ought to assist people in distress like the Allies had done. Kinkel here invoked a memory of the outcome of the Second World War as liberation and thereby supported his particular political choice. However, in referring to the Second World War, Kinkel also faced a problem: the 'Kohl doctrine', that is, the idea that, due to the past, no German ground troops could be deployed to the former Yugoslavia. Kinkel affirmed this principle – the decision was not about *ground* troops – but seemed to overturn its spirit.

This was where Kinkel's opponents took their cue. Rudolf Scharping, the leader of the opposition, argued that, though the Germans wanted to support the United Nations in Bosnia-Herzegovina, they did not want to participate in the implementation of this mandate. He represented this as living up to 'a human and political duty towards this part of Europe which had to suffer under the dreadfulness of the Second World War'.[17]

Scharping recalled Kohl's view that German soldiers should not be deployed to the former Yugoslavia because 'the memory of the atrocities in the Second World War could only lead to an escalation of the conflicts and an irresponsible endangering of German soldiers', and warned against changing this policy.[18] Obviously both sides to the argument portrayed the past as pertinent. Although they drew different conclusions, they agreed on the need to remember the past, not merely in the context of commemoration but in that of making policy choices.

Of course, the question of remembering – and indeed of confronting painful memories – is not exclusive to German discourse. Andreas Huyssen notes the 'emergence of memory as a key concern in Western societies', set off by the increasing debate about the Holocaust and the media interest in the fortieth and fiftieth anniversaries of events during the Third Reich.[19] Moreover, the 'recurrence of genocidal politics in Rwanda, Bosnia and Kosovo in the allegedly posthistorical 1990s has kept the Holocaust memory discourse alive'.[20] But Huyssen sees the 'memory boom' as a much wider phenomenon ranging from 'the historicizing restoration of old urban centers', to a 'popular obsession with "self-musealization" by video recorder', to work 'related to genocide, AIDS, slavery, and sexual abuse' to name but a few of his examples.[21]

One may ask why there is such a surge of interest in memory now.[22] One reason is frequently noted: the passing away of those who lived through the Holocaust.[23] Crucially, this 'explanation' already takes as given that we want to and ought to remember, out of respect for the victims, perhaps, or for fear of repeating history. Federal President Herzog certainly asserted a common motivation for remembering when he said that 'One's own history teaches one the best lesson.'[24] As has been noted, Herzog also displayed a belief in redemption through memory. Avishai Margalit observes that the Truth and Reconciliation Commission in South Africa similarly was 'established with the hope that it would bring social catharsis – that the truth about the past will, by being revealed, bring reconciliation'.[25]

Margalit points out, however, that 'memory breathes revenge as often as it breathes reconciliation'.[26] As Ilana R. Bet-El says in relation to the former Yugoslavia, 'Words of the past became weapons of war.'[27] This 'danger' of memory may appear even more acute given the alleged scope for manipulation, though distortion is often by no means necessary to incite a desire for revenge. It is interesting to note that the charge of manipulation implies that there is a 'correct' memory from which such manipulated memories deviate. In the context of the passing away of survivors of the Holocaust, Aleida Assmann identifies a shift from individual to what she calls cultural memory. She sees this as problematic 'because it brings with it the danger of distortion, reduction, instrumentalisation'.[28] She assumes that personal memory and cultural memory are somehow distinct and that the former is not distorted, reduced and instrumentalized. Yet both these assumptions are untenable.[29] Significantly, the fear of manipulation actually seems to suggest not so much that we should liberate ourselves from dangerous memories but indeed that the more we remember the better; for surely those who know more about the past are less easily manipulated. And yet Huyssen, for one, seems unsure about the value of the trend towards more and more remembering: 'Total recall seems to be the goal. Is this an archivist's fantasy gone mad?'[30]

III. Forgetting

Some, then, do not want to be part of this memory-fest, whatever its reasons. Nietzsche is often cited as the great champion of forgetting.[31] He is indeed concerned that the past must not become the 'gravedigger' of the present.[32] Nietzsche's championing of forgetting has to be read in its context: the discussion of the relevance of history to human life in which he suggests that there are three types of history: monumental, antiquarian and critical. The critical attitude towards the past – which calls for the strength to break with and dissolve the past in order to be able to live – becomes necessary from time to time when knowledge of the past threatens to rule over life.[33] Nietzsche asserts that 'Forgetting belongs to all actions: as to the life of everything organic belongs not just light, but also darkness.' Indeed, according to Nietzsche, it is possible to live with hardly any memory but 'it is entirely impossible to live without forgetting altogether'.[34] Nietzsche dismisses here, with characteristic verve, the necessarily positive connotation of remembering. In fact, remembering may wear us down, stop us from action and be generally pernicious. Nietzsche is often read to be saying: Forget![35]

This is interesting in a number of ways but certainly because, inevitably, there is a problem with the instruction to forget: it only serves to remind us and hence we remember. Not surprisingly, it is therefore difficult to find advocates of concrete forgetting in politics. The Conservative historians of the *Historikerstreit*, who are seen to have wanted to 'draw a line' under the past (of the Third Reich), actually seem to suggest that the Germans ought to remember differently, with more positive attachment to the nation. Michael Stürmer, in one of his contributions to the debate, complained that 'Anything is possible in a country without memory.' The search for the 'lost past', he argues, is 'morally legitimate and politically necessary'.[36] If anything, then, he claimed to be advocating more – not less – remembering. Similarly, in the 1997 *Bundestag* debate about the exhibition on *Wehrmacht* crimes, Alfred Dregger of the CDU – who is seen as a key proponent of a view of the *Wehrmacht* that seeks to 'forget' its involvement in atrocities – seems motivated by reminding Germans of the situation of ordinary soldiers in the Second World War, that is by a desire to *remember* the fate of the *Landser* (privates).[37] In sum, those accused of (promoting) forgetting actually regard themselves as (promoting) remembering.

Even the high-profile polemic against the culture of (Holocaust) memory by novelist Martin Walser in his acceptance speech for the 1998 Peace Prize of the German Book Trade, for which he was accused of a 'refusal of memory',[38] does not break with this pattern. Walser said that he closes himself to all ills which he cannot help remove, that he 'had to learn to look away'.[39] Not only that. He asserted that his reaction to the 'unbearable' was proportionate, unavoidable and justified: 'I do not have to bear the unbearable.' He raised this in the context of ills continuously projected by television into his life but developed the argument further in relation to the Germans' attitude to their past: 'Everyone knows our historical burden, the everlasting disgrace, no day on which we are not reproached with it.' He suspects that this 'cruel service of memory' might be part of the illusion that a little bit of exoneration is possible, something he excludes altogether. However, he wants to resist the 'permanent representation of our disgrace', for which he suspects there are instrumental, if worthy, reasons in the present.[40]

For all the controversy that the speech set off,[41] Walser nowhere actually so much as mentions forgetting. He observes that, when confronted with filmic representations of concentration camps, he has 'looked away' at least twenty times. Walser's image, however, is telling. Looking away is always already a looking somewhere else: there is no escape from memory as such. It is also interesting to note that the planned Holocaust memorial that he criticised as a 'monumentalisation' of German disgrace,[42] has also been called a 'Kranzabwurfstelle' (a place to drop wreaths).[43] In other words, official commemoration may actually conceal forgetting: the dropping of wreaths by politicians creates no more than an illusion of remembering. In Assmann's view, symbolic commemoration is closer to forgetting than to active memory work.[44] Memorials and museums, for example on the sites of concentration camps, as spaces of memory may indeed 'obstruct memory'.[45] So the 'memory boom' might be in danger of inadvertently allowing people to forget, as they trust that the memorials take care of the business of remembering.[46]

IV. Remembering and forgetting

Nietzsche's argument seeks to upset a widespread conviction that we must strive to remember. Remembering and forgetting are still opposed in his conceptualization, but now the idea is to value the latter over the former. However, despite accusations that certain groups are forgetting, no one seems to actually embrace forgetting as in some way better or more ethical. In other words, apart from Nietzsche himself perhaps, it is difficult to find any outright advocates of forgetting.[47] Thus Nietzsche's intervention – his overturning of the dichotomy – appears to have failed with respect to the context explored here: the privileging of remembering is fully intact. Yet the distinction between promoters of remembering and promoters of forgetting is not clear, and cannot be. Huyssen hence argues that the issue 'is not whether to forget or to remember, but rather how to remember and how to handle representations of the remembered past'.[48] The argument 'against forgetting', with its implied imperative 'remember!', is a move in the struggle over *how* to remember. Similarly, von Weizsäcker's speech promotes a particular version of memory. His pronouncement, though made from the authority of office, notes the context of struggle.

Von Weizsäcker refers to 'debates about the past'. His call for honesty in the commemoration already implies that this has been in some way lacking. He reiterates several times that 8 May is a 'day of memory' and that it calls for truthfulness.[49] Despite criticisms that von Weizsäcker's truthfulness is itself limited,[50] his argument is important. He refers to the diversity of experiences on 8 May 1945, many of them marked by hopelessness. Yet he concludes: 'And nevertheless what it is today nec-essary to say for us all together became clearer day by day: 8 May was a day of liberation.' This is not to say that the suffering that started on this day should be forgotten, merely related to its reason: the start of the war and the beginning of the Nazi regime. Overall, memory must be kept alive, not least because it is relevant to policy choices today, for example those concerning political asylum and relations to neighbouring coun-tries. Von Weizsäcker sees a 'danger of forgetting' and appeals to his fel-low Germans: 'Let us look truth in the face on today's 8 May as best we can.'[51] Von Weizsäcker opens up the question of the multiplicity of memories when he notes the diversity of experiences at the end of the Second World War. At the same time his speech enacts interpretative authority in arguing that, whatever these experiences, all Germans should now regard 8 May 1945 as a day of liberation, disregarding that this might be difficult for those, for example, who lost their possessions and often their loved ones as a result of flight or expulsion from eastern territories.

Clearly, which memory is appropriate is a controversial issue. At the same time, the past is, however, as we have seen, confidently used as a shared repertoire through which to interpret the present in debates about uses of military force. Despite the continuing struggle over how to properly characterize 8 May 1945 – with the campaign 'against forgetting' forcefully rejecting von Weizsäcker's portrayal of the date as 'liberation' – Foreign Minister Kinkel confidently referred to Allied liberation in his justification of the *Bundeswehr* deployment to Bosnia. This raised no objection, certainly within the *Bundestag* debate. Thus, Kinkel apparently expected people to share his understanding of the outcome of the Second World War as essentially liberating and those who might object to this representation in commemorations of the Second World War accepted – or at least acquiesced in – this interpretation in the context of current policy choices. There seemed to be no awareness that Kinkel is engaging in a memory practice. Political debate deploys memories but it does not engage the problem of memory. This is perhaps not surprising. It is vexing, however, if analysis of politics and memory does the same.

There is now increasing recognition that, as Jan-Werner Müller puts it, 'Memory matters'. Müller asserts that 'there have been almost no studies of the nexus between memory and political power, especially if one defines politics rather narrowly as the output of political institutions'.[52] This claim is interesting chiefly for its exclusionary move: it defines away in one fell swoop all the fascinating work on trauma and memory practices as perhaps quite interesting but essentially not speaking to the real issues of politics.[53] Müller's edited collection is based on the premise that 'memory matters *politically* in ways which we do not yet fully understand' and proposes to 'clarify the relationship between power and memory'. Müller is keen to explore how one is 'to get a handle on a seemingly vague concept such as memory'.[54] This is evidently to be done by making clear distinctions, such as between, first, collective and mass individual memory and, second, both of those on the one hand and the use of historical analogy on the other.[55] Whilst Müller's collection and his own contribution to it certainly raises a number of interesting issues, there seems to be an attempt to define away what is most intriguing about memory. What is particularly interesting for the purposes of this chapter is Müller's claim that one also 'has to distinguish between memory and history'.[56] This seems to me to be a rather more complex issue than is acknowledged. Timothy Snyder's interpretation of this distinction in the volume is certainly peculiar, and particularly relevant: 'Memory cannot be studied as memory, at all. Our recollections are always recollections of something, and unless we have an independent source of knowledge about this something, we can learn nothing about how memory works.'[57] This is an extraordinary argument: somehow memory itself has no political implications or at any rate none that we may have anything interesting to say about unless we can hold it up against what 'an independent source of knowledge' – whatever that may be – tells us. This seems to be the surest recipe for missing the political implications of memory.

V. 'It will never stop'

One of the ways in which we might analyse memory without starting by defining away the problem of memory is by exploring representations of memory that include an element of reflection upon the practice itself, for example, fictional literature. Reading such texts may raise interesting questions about memory. Here I want to explore, in this spirit, a novella about an issue raised in the campaign 'against forgetting': the flight and expulsion of ethnic Germans from the East towards the end of the Second World War. Günter Grass's *Im Krebsgang* (translated as *Crabwalk*) revolves around the sinking on 30 January 1945 of the *Wilhelm Gustloff*. The ship which was carrying several thousand German refugees from the port of Gdingen (now Gdynia) had been torpedoed by a Russian U-boat. The narrator, Paul Pokriefke, and his mother, Tulla, are survivors of the disaster: Paul is born on the day. Tulla has always wanted Paul to tell the world, to bear witness, but Paul has resisted this idea. Konrad, Paul's son, eventually takes up this task, with tragic consequences.

The story is complex; it shifts between different narrative strands. If the events of 30 January 1945 and their memory are read as central, several narrative elements can be seen as grouped around them. First, there is the nexus of information about historical events and figures, such as Wilhelm Gustloff, his murderer David Frankfurter, the U-boat commander Alexander Marinesko, the refugees aboard the ship, the history of the *Wilhelm Gustloff* up to 30 January 1945, and finally the events of that day. To complicate matters this 'information' emerges from the interplay of Konrad's postings on a website in honour of the Nazi Gustloff and Paul's reflections upon them. Second, there is the story about Tulla as the survivor of the disaster. And third, the story in the present of the novella tells of Konrad becoming obsessed with Gustloff and his memory, and eventually murdering a boy his own age. The link between the three is the sinking of the *Gustloff*, though there is a subtle, but significant, shift from the *Gustloff* to Gustloff in the narrative present.

That *Im Krebsgang* is both a contribution to memory and a reflection on it is clear from the first pages. The dedication page reads 'in memoriam' and the text itself starts: 'Why only now?'[58] Paul as a journalist had, after all, written on just about everything else. The book is represented as disrupting an uncomfortable silence – as overcoming forgetting – and the reaction it has provoked appears to confirm this view.[59] Writing about the sinking of the *Wilhelm Gustloff* – a particular event in flight and expulsions of Germans from the East – raises questions. Although Robert G. Moeller forcefully argues that there has been a public memory of the expulsions in the FRG since the 1950s,[60] this topic was considered taboo or at least unpopular later. Grass's story is disrupted throughout to grapple with the issue of how, when and why this story should be told. Clearly, there are no easy answers; the matter is difficult to approach. The narrator finds it difficult to get started. He says that the 'words still have difficulties with me',[61] though this relationship later changes: then he 'is searching for words'.[62] Whether language is in charge of the narrator or *vice versa* in this difficult endeavour, the matter is approached 'crabwise', that is, obliquely rather than directly. There are numerous references to this 'crabwise' approach in the text, most obviously, of course, the title.[63] 'Krebsgang' is the movement of a crab: sideways, obliquely.

In *Im Krebsgang* different attitudes towards the memory of the sinking of the *Gustloff* are represented by different characters. Tulla, the survivor, complains about what 'this Russian' could possibly have been thinking when he attacked the ship. Her understanding of the events has not been changed by historical scholarship on the matter: that the U-boat commander believed the ship to be carrying troops, for example, and that there were not only civilian refugees on board.[64] Tulla is, in Paul's view, stuck in the past, and this is so not merely because she clings on to her East Prussian dialect and has failed, in the narrator's view, to learn the 'lessons of the past'. She is stuck in the past more fundamentally. Paul's jibe that she talks of the past as if all this time had not passed since then indicates this. She says: 'One can't forget something like this. It never stops. I don't only dream about it, how, when it was all over a single cry went up over the water. And all the little children between the ice floes …'.[65] For her, this event is 'out of time', *sui generis* and permanently present. She is not interested in how it might relate to other matters. For her it is a matter primarily of bearing witness.

It is extremely important to Tulla that the story of the *Gustloff* is told, despite – or because of – the failure of both German states to show any interest. As she puts it: 'I only live for this that my son one day will bear witness.'[66] Both Tulla and Paul assert that there has been little engagement with the flight and expulsion of Germans from the East. *Im Krebsgang*, it seems, has become necessary because of this. Paul refers to himself as a 'survivor of a tragedy that has been forgotten by the whole world'.[67] Though he is critical of his mother's harping on about the disaster, he also voices an objection to the lack of remembering. Instead of writing the story, Paul sends Tulla books. One is a documentation of the disaster, 'written quite factually but too disinterestedly', even in Paul's view. Therefore it is no surprise that Tulla rejects this account. She comments: 'All this is not experienced in a way that is personal enough in my view. It doesn't come from the heart!'[68] Tulla's memory is at least in part affective and she does not recognize it in traditional historiography.

As Paul refuses, Tulla hopes that her grandson Konrad will write about the *Gustloff*.[69] Konrad indeed starts a webpage, interestingly dedicated to Gustloff rather than the *Gustloff*. In Konrad's writings on the net, the desire to bear witness on behalf of his grandmother blurs with neo-Nazi thought. He refers to his 'dear grandmother to whom I have sworn, in the name of the *Kameradschaft* Schwerin on her white hair to bear witness to the truth and nothing but the truth: It is the Jewry of the world that wants to chain us Germans to the pillory for all time and eternity ...'.[70] Tulla's memories are not affected by such anti-Semitism. Her stories have here come to be politicized. It is this particular politicization – the return of Nazi ideology – that seems to mark the intended centre of the novella, and that leads to the peculiar tension between the desire to tell the story of the expellees and the desire to escape memory. For Konrad, the matter is political: he shoots another boy in order to commemorate 'the martyr' Gustloff.[71] Bearing witness for the drowned of the *Gustloff*, Tulla's motivation, appears at best secondary. It is unclear how the shooting could have contributed to that aim. After Konrad is sent to jail, Paul goes onto the internet again and finds a website championing his son as a role model. The novella ends with Paul's desperation: 'It does not stop. It will never stop.'[72]

Im Krebsgang enacts a paradox, epitomized in Paul's role as unwilling narrator. On the one hand, it contributes to a fight against forgetting the memories of the expellees' suffering at the end of the Second World War. On the other hand the novella speaks of an urgent desire to escape this memory because of the possibility of right-wing abuse. This tension becomes palpable by reading the dedication page and the last two sentences of the novella together: 'in memoriam' it begins, only to end: 'It does not stop. It will never stop.' Three points are worth noting. First, there are obviously different ways of remembering the sinking of the *Gustloff*. For example, Paul has a much less affective relationship to the events of which, in contrast to Tulla, he has no recollections of his own. Second, each of the different proposed ways of remembering entails a forgetting. Most obviously, Tulla and Konrad 'forget' about German crimes. But Paul, in his desire to overcome such forgetting, in his turn forgets that there may actually have been 'innocent' Germans suffering. This relates to a third point, the relationship of knowledge or truth to memory.

Paul enacts a belief in a straightforward relationship between historical knowledge and memory. The 'taboo' surrounding the sinking of the *Gustloff* is made problematic in Paul's eyes because it creates an opportunity for right-wing manipulation. Paul describes the *Gustloff* as 'a ship, which did not only sink, but which is a legend because [this was] suppressed'.[73] In other words, the disaster of the sinking of the *Gustloff* had become open to abuse, in particular by neo-Nazis, because it had not been appropriately remembered in the first place. So the obvious solution is to provide more information about what happened to the public. Paul puts this view into practice when, throughout the book, he supplements the information he reports from his son's website with further historical detail, in what appears to be an expectation to be able to amend and correct the picture of the past, and indeed to prevent forgetting.

However, problems with Paul's 'neutral' provision of historical information become obvious when he intervenes on his son's webpage. Konrad enthuses about the young girls whose innocence was to be protected from the reach of the Russian beast by taking them on board the ship. This is a reference to the justification of the *Wehrmacht's* continuation of the lost fight on the Eastern front in order to protect German civilians from the barbarity of the Soviet troops.[74] Paul points out that, innocent or not, these girls had been in uniform complete with swastika, had been drilled militarily, and had sworn an oath to the *Führer*.[75] Whilst this information is correct, the intervention is peculiar. Is Paul really implying that it was acceptable – or at least more tolerable – for German women to be raped as long as they were in uniform, drilled and sworn in? Moreover, Paul is hardly providing any new information here; rather he considers information that Konrad does not deny to be particularly pertinent. He is offering not forgotten historical detail – as he seems to suggest – but an alternative, and frankly questionable, interpretation of information already available. Paul's comment thus undermines his own belief that the problem with the memory of the *Gustloff* has been a lack of information.

A further problem with Paul's attempt to amend memory through knowledge is the radical impossibility of knowing and making known everything about the past, the impossibility of representing the past simply 'as it was'. This is something Paul is aware of. In writing a book about the memory of the sinking of the *Gustloff* the story inevitably arrives, at some point, at the sinking itself. Of the mass flight from East Prussia Paul says: 'I cannot describe it. No one can describe that.'[76] However, even whilst asserting this, he is describing it. Though it may be impossible to represent it, it is equally impossible not to do so. Similarly, 'what happened inside the ship cannot be grasped by words.'[77] Paul escapes into describing how a 1950s film represented the situation, which is, of course, despite the claim to the contrary, also a representation of what happened. Thus it is impossible to 'find' and express 'neutral' knowledge that would counteract problematic memories, both because the relationship between knowledge and memory is more complex and because such neutral knowledge about the past is impossible. If this is the case, it seems increasingly unclear what precisely is meant by forgetting.

VI.   Remembering to forget/forgetting to remember

A 'common sense' definition of forgetting might be being 'unable to remember'.[78] However, the issue is far more insidious. Omer Bartov insists, in relation to French memories of the Holocaust, 'that one cannot forget what one does not remember'.[79] In other words, in order to forget, one has to remember in the first place. The same is crucially also true in reverse. In order to remember, one has to forget. Assmann argues that forgetting is necessary for the process of remembering.[80] She claims that what 'is selected for memory is always defined by the edges of forgetting'.[81] Memory without forgetting is impossible. As Jacques Derrida points out, a 'limitless memory would in any event be not memory but infinite self-presence'.[82] This means, however, that any simplistic opposition of remembering versus forgetting, and by implication simply valuing one over the other, is impossible. Derrida and Bernard Stiegler point out, in the context of the politics of the archive: 'The very fact that there is a politics of memory already poses a problem. It is necessary to have memory, we think spontaneously, and memory is better than amnesia.'[83] However, it is, as they suggest, not as simple as that: 'Why is it necessary to have memory, in the end? You are never going to prove that memory is better than nonmemory. What is more, memory includes forgetting. If there is selectivity, it is because there is forgetting.'[84]

Foreign Minister Kinkel's argument in support of a *Bundeswehr* deployment to Bosnia was certainly marked by forgetting. Obviously, he 'left out' what the Conservatives raise in their advertisement campaign, the expulsions of ethnic Germans from the east and the division of Germany, and thus information that may have raised doubts as to whether one could simply say that the Germans had been 'liberated'. More significantly, however, his argument is haunted by another absence. Kinkel refers to the 'Kohl doctrine' without ever spelling out *why* it is that German soldiers should not be deployed to the Balkans. He conspicuously fails to respond to shouts of 'why?' from the opposition.[85] One might expect the opposition to clarify this issue. Scharping indeed refers to 'good reasons' for not participating in the implementation of the United Nations mandate in Bosnia and the 'dreadfulness' of the Second World War. This 'dreadfulness' appears at first only in the passive voice: this 'part of Europe' had to 'suffer under the dreadfulness of the Second World War'.[86] There is no indication as to how this 'dreadfulness' came about. Still, it might be too obvious to say so. Scharping refers a few more times in the abstract to 'the historical situation' and the 'German past' which mean that a deployment of German soldiers to the former Yugoslavia is ill advised.[87] But things become interesting when he does start spelling out why 'the German past is at work in the heads of the Serbian soldiers'. First, there is the issue of propaganda and thus not *per se* of the previously cited German past but its – obviously illegitimate – instrumentalisation by particular Serbian groups. Second, there are particular circumstances of the German actions in Yugoslavia and especially Bosnia that go beyond the generic dreadfulness of the Second World War. As an example Scharping cites the co-operation of the SS leadership with Muslim Bosnians. These Bosnians perpetrated atrocities 'that confused even those who otherwise had little objection against cruelty'.[88] So, in Scharping's representation the problem lies not at all, as one might have expected, with crimes committed by the Germans but with unreasonable propaganda and the Germans' unfortunate association with overzealous and barbarous Bosnians. The Germans *themselves* are not represented as perpetrators in Scharping's argument at all.

Further opposition statements acknowledge German crimes but remain in the abstract. Joschka Fischer asserts that 'memories of a warring

Germany' should not be refreshed anywhere, and particularly not in the former Yugoslavia, but he does provide an explanation.[89] He opposes deployments to areas where 'the Wehrmacht caused havoc in the cruellest way in the Second World War'.[90] Gregor Gysi of the PDS makes a similar point.[91] Still the audience is left to fill in a rather large blank about the way in which the *Wehrmacht* had 'caused havoc'. The outrage over the 1997 exhibition 'War of Extermination: Crimes of the Wehrmacht 1941 to 1944'[92] suggests that the atrocities had been anything but too obvious to mention. So the reconfirmation of the 'Kohl doctrine' revolves around a simultaneous remembering and forgetting. *Wehrmacht* atrocities are remembered in as much as they form the centre of the very doctrine but they are at the same time forgotten: entirely left out in Kinkel's case, curiously defined away in Scharping's and abstracted in Fischer's and Gysi's. So, in some sense, they all 'forget' some of the 'truth' about the past.

The reference to the 'truth' of the past or 'truthfulness' in confronting the past, such as in the campaign 'against forgetting' and in von Weizsäcker's speech, trivializes the problem of memory. If memory is treated as a form of what is generally taken to be 'knowledge' – and thus as in a comparative relationship with history – it can only ever turn out to be a lesser form of it. In this way of thinking, history necessarily trumps memory: 'History [...] can at least sometimes awaken us from the nightmare of memory'.[93] Yet the concern about the relationship between memory and history is the wrong question to ask. Of course, memory is very unreliable as a form of knowledge. As we have seen, emotions are important and, what is more, forgetting is an inevitable part of remembering. Forgetting is not simply the opposite of remembering. Remembering is structurally dependent on forgetting, is always already marked by forgetting. This means that the idea of getting memory to conform more closely to 'truth' is not only a narrow concern but one doomed to fail. Quite apart from the radical impossibility of 'true' knowledge about the past, this simply ignores the inextricable relationship of remembering and forgetting.

The problem with Kinkel's argument is not that his memory of the Second World War entails a forgetting. Little is gained by just demonstrating forgetting; for this is inevitable. The issue is that this forgetting is obscured by an understanding of memory that renders it as telling the truth about the past. Such an understanding plays on the power of the 'we remember'. What is more, the supposed 'knowledge' about the past is presented as an answer to an ethico-political question in the present: we know what is right because we remember. Whether or not German troops should be deployed to the Balkans is certainly an issue that calls on memories but there is something distinctly disturbing about *answering* it through memory. It is crucial to reflect on what is going on here, and therefore to explore memory in politics. Memory as a political practice does not exist apart from its invocation, representation, performance and therefore it changes even as we examine it. Some may worry that 'memory' is too vague a phenomenon to be included in political analysis but it is indeed this very 'vagueness' that must be recognized.

It would be no mean feat to disturb the confidence of those asserting not only the need to remember but their certainty as to *how*. The confident use of memory as knowledge to fix the problem of military intervention obscures the ethico-political problem. Reflection on memory is powerful precisely because it undermines certainty. How we should remember is a significant ethico-political question, particularly when memories are deployed in political debate. It is a question that cannot be answered within the category of 'knowledge' alone, but one that requires a decision precisely because the matter goes beyond the concerns of knowledge.[94] In as much as the imperative to remember is an expression of a desire to *know* it fails to appreciate this. The problem of 'unwelcome' memories – such as of the suffering of German expellees – cannot be solved through an appeal to knowledge either. Such an attempt rather represents a category error and one that would obscure what is important here: the inevitable tension between different experiences of and perspectives on these events, the impossibility of arriving at a representation that does justice to everyone. This impossibility might be vexing to some, but it is at the same time what keeps open the space for politics.[95]

It is in this context that the 'crabwise' approach of fiction to the issue of memory is important. Unlike official acts of commemoration which necessarily seek to paper over struggles about memory in a bid to invent community, literature can bear the tension. Volker Hage observes that the 'many-voiced access to the tragedy gives Grass the possibility of addressing aspects beyond the politically correct'.[96] However, it is not just that literature may present a multiplicity of positions without necessarily judging between them. By stressing the fictionality of what might appear as information – the reflexivity about the act of representation – literature disturbs our faith in knowing and thereby keeps open the question of memory. By refusing an answer as to what constitutes appropriate memory it places us where we should be – and inevitably always are – with respect to difficult memories. When we have all available information but still know that we do not know we are most open to the need of an ethico-political decision. Recognizing that we are confronted with the need for such a decision, and that we will be over and over again, would be an important step in repoliticizing matters that, certainly in Germany, have been dealt with in ritualistic and closed but eminently 'acceptable' ways, that is, in ways that apparently solve and thereby always already forget about the ethico-political questions involved.

Notes

1 Introduction: Memory, Trauma and World Politics

1. Walter Benjamin, 'A Berlin Chronicle' in Benjamin, *One Way Street, and Other Writings*, trans. Edmund Jephcott & Kingsley Shorter (London: NLB, 1970), p. 314.
2. Lewis Carroll, 'Through the Looking Glass' in *The Complete Illustrated Works of Lewis Carroll* [1872] (London: Chancellor Press, 1982), p. 171.
3. Andreas Huyssen, 'Present Pasts: Media, Politics, Amnesia', *Public Culture*, 12 (2000), 26.
4. Winter, 'Notes on the memory boom', p. 54. See also Jeffrey K. Olick and Joyce Robbins, 'Social Memory Studies: From "Collective Memory" to the Historical Sociology of Mnemonic Practices', *Annual Review of Sociology*, 24 (1998), 105–41; Jan-Werner Müller, 'Introduction: The Power of Memory, the Memory of Power and the Power over Memory' in Müller (ed.), *Memory and Power in Post-war Europe: Studies in the Presence of the Past* (Cambridge: Cambridge University Press, 2002), pp. 1–39; Andreas Huyssen, *Present Pasts: Urban Palimpsests and the Politics of Memory* (Stanford: Stanford University Press, 2003); and Allan Megill, 'History, Memory, Identity', *History of the Human Sciences*, 11 (1998), 37–62.
5. Müller, 'Introduction', pp. 28–31; and Victor Roudometof, 'Beyond Commemoration: The Politics of Collective Memory', *Journal of Political and Military Sociology*, 32 (2004), 3–4.
6. Avishai Margalit, *The Ethics of Memory* (Cambridge, MA.: Harvard University Press, 2003), p. 14. Italics in original.
7. Yuen Foong Khong, *Analogies at War: Korea, Munich, Dien Bien Phu, and the Vietnam Decisions of 1965* (Princeton, NJ: Princeton University Press, 1992); Richard Neustadt and Ernest May, *Thinking in Time: The Uses of History for Decision-Makers* (New York: Free Press, 1986); Robert Jervis, *Perception and Misperception in International Politics* (Princeton, NJ: Princeton University Press, 1976). See also Anne Norton, *95 Theses on Politics, Culture and Method* (London: Yale University Press, 2004), Thesis 11.
8. Assmann, *Moses the Egyptian: The Memory of Egypt in Western Monotheism* (Cambridge, MA.: Harvard University Press, 1997), p. 9. See also the discussion in Tzvetan Todorov, *Hope and Memory*, trans. David Bellow (London: Atlantic, 2003), chs. 3, 4 and 5.
9. Megill, 'History, Memory, Identity'.
10. This process is explored, in historical context, in Reinhart Koselleck, *Futures Past: On the Semantics of Historical Time*, trans. Keith Tribe (Cambridge, MA: MIT Press, 1985).
11. Jeffrey K. Olick, 'Collective Memory: The Two Cultures', *Sociological Theory*, 17 (1999), 338.
12. See Müller (ed.), *Memory and Power in Post-war Europe*; and Claudio Fogu, Richard Ned Lebow, and Wulf Kansteiner (eds), *The Politics of Memory in*

Postwar Europe (Durham, NC.: Duke University Press, 2005). For a set of regional cases, see Victor Roudometof, *Collective Memory, National Identity and Ethnic Conflict: Greece, Bulgaria & the Macedonian Question* (Westport, CT.: Praeger, 2002). For a less Euro-centric focus, see Jeffrey K. Olick (ed.), *States of Memory: Continuities, Conflicts, and Transformations in National Perspective* (Durham, NC.: Duke University Press, 2003).

13. Olick and Demetriou, 'From Theodicy to *Ressentiment*: Trauma and the Ages of Compensation', p. 75.

14. For the use of the term 'identification' rather than the more multivalent 'identity' see Rogers Brubaker and Frederick Cooper, 'Beyond Identity', *Theory and Society*, 29 (2000), 1–47; and Brubaker, *Ethnicity Without Groups* (Cambridge, MA.: Harvard University Press, 2004). See also his exchange with Craig Calhoun in *Ethnicities*, 3 (2003), 531–68. 'Identity' of course has a history: see Philip Gleason, 'Identifying Identity: A Semantic History', *Journal of American History*, 69 (1983), 910–31.

15. Note, however, that the connection between memory and identity (both on an individual and collective level) may well be an invention of the modern age, a contingent rather than a necessary relation, as Bartelson argues in his chapter: Bartelson, 'We Could Remember it for you Wholesale', pp. 34–8.

16. Allan Young, *The Harmony of Illusions: Inventing Post-Traumatic Stress Disorder* (Princeton, NJ: Princeton University Press, 1995), p. 221. The relationship between memory and identity is, though, far from straightforward. See, for example, Mary Warncock, *Memory* (London: Faber & Faber, 1987); and Christoph Hoerl and Teresa McCormack (eds), *Time and Memory: Issues in Philosophy and Psychology* (Oxford: Oxford University Press, 2001). On the gendered aspects of memory see the special edition ('gender and cultural memory') of *Signs: Journal of Women in Culture and Society*, 28 (2002).

17. For general accounts of social memory, see, Maurice Halbwachs, *On Collective Memory*, trans. Lewis A. Coser (Chicago, IL: University of Chicago Press, 1992 [1925]); Paul Connerton, *How Societies Remember* (Cambridge: Cambridge University Press, 1989); James Fentress and Chris Wickham, *Social Memory* (Oxford: Blackwell, 1992); Eviatar Zerubavel, *Time Maps: Collective Memory and the Shape of the Past* (Chicago, IL: University of Chicago Press, 2003); and Susannah Radstone (ed.), *Memory and Methodology* (Oxford: Berg, 2000).

18. The phrase is from Benedict Anderson, *Imagined Communities: Reflections on the Origin and Spread of Nationalism* (London: Verso, 1983).

19. Smith, 'Memory and Modernity: Reflections on Ernest Gellner's Theory of Nationalism', *Nations and Nationalism*, 2 (1996), 383.

20 Winter, 'Notes on the memory boom', p. 55.

21. Maier, 'A Surfeit of Memory? Reflections on History, Melancholy, and Denial', *History & Memory*, 5 (1993), 147.

22. Megill, 'History, Memory, Identity', 40 and 42.

23. Taylor, *Sources of the Self: The Making of the Modern Identity* (Cambridge: Cambridge University Press, 1989).

24. Mary Kaldor, *New and Old Wars: Organized Violence in a Global Era* (Cambridge: Polity, 1999). On how memory can be manipulated by 'political entrepreneurs' to generate conflict, see Charles Tilly, *The Politics of Collective Violence* (Cambridge: Cambridge University Press, 2003).

25. Larry Ray, 'Mourning, Melancholia, and Violence'. See also Julie Mertus, *Kosovo: How Myths and Truths Started a War* (Berkeley, CA: University of California Press, 1999); Ilana Bet-El, 'Unimagined Communities: The Power of Memory and the Conflict in the Former Yugoslavia' in Müller (ed.), *Memory and Power in Post-war Europe*, pp. 206–23; Maria Todorova (ed.), *Balkan Identities: Nation and Memory* (London: Hurst, 2004); and the special edition ('Memory, Identity and War') of *Rethinking History*, 6 (2002).
26. *Oxford English Dictionary.*
27. Olick, 'Collective Memory', 344. See also Piotr Sztompka, 'Cultural Trauma', *European Journal of Social Theory*, 3 (2000), 449–67; and Wolfgang Schivelbusch. See also Piotr *The Culture of Defeat: On National Trauma, Mourning, and Recovery*, trans. Jefferson Chase (New York: Metropolitan Books, 2003); and Frank R. Ankersmit, 'Trauma and Suffering: A Forgotten Source of Western Historical Consciousness' in Jörn Rüsen (ed.), *Western Historical Thinking: An Intercultural Debate* (Oxford: Berghahn, 2001), pp. 72–84.
28. Caruth, *Unclaimed Experience: Trauma, Narrative, and History* (London: Johns Hopkins University Press, 1996); and Caruth, 'Introduction: Trauma and Experience' in Caruth (ed.), *Trauma: Explorations in Memory* (Baltimore, MD: The Johns Hopkins University Press, 1995). For a powerful critique of Caruth, see Ruth Leys, *Trauma: A Genealogy* (Chicago, IL: University of Chicago Press, 2000), ch. 8, and Wulf Kansteiner, 'Genealogy of a Category Mistake: A Critical Intellectual History of the Cultural Trauma Metaphor', *Rethinking History*, 8 (2004), 193–221.
29. Alexander, 'Towards a Theory of Cultural Trauma' in Alexander, Ron Eyerman, Bernhard Giesen, Neil J. Smelser, and Piotr Sztompka, *Cultural Trauma and Collective Identity* (Berkeley, CA: University of California Press, 2004), p. 1, and the essays therein. Emphasis added. See also Ron Eyerman, *Cultural Trauma: Slavery and the Formation of African American Identity* (Cambridge: Cambridge University Press, 2001).
30. Alexander, 'Towards a Theory of Cultural Trauma', pp. 8 and 10 (emphasis added); and Alexander, 'On the Social Construction of Moral Universals: The "Holocaust" from War Crime to Trauma Drama', *European Journal of Social Theory*, 5 (2002), 5–85. On the formation of 'African American' identity from the trauma drama of slavery, see also Ron Eyerman, 'The Past in the Present: Culture and the Transmission of Memory', *Acta Sociologica*, 47 (2004), 159–69.
31. Smelser, 'Epilogue: September 11, 2001, as Cultural Trauma' in Alexander et al., *Cultural Trauma and Collective Identity*, pp. 264 and 266.
32. Sztompka, 'Cultural Trauma', 450 and 457.
33. Améry, *At the Minds Limits*, quoted in Edkins, *Trauma and the Memory of Politics*, p. 8. On Améry see also the discussion in Olick and Demetriou, 'From Theodicy to *Ressentiment*', pp. 84–7.
34. Sebald, 'Against the Irreversible: On Jean Améry' in his, *On the Natural History of Destruction*, trans. Anthea Bell (Harmondsworth: Penguin, 2004), p. 154.
35. Richard McNally, *Remembering Trauma* (Cambridge, MA: Harvard University Press, 2003).
36. Kansteiner, 'Finding Meaning in Memory: A Methodological Critique of Collective Memory Studies', *History and Theory*, 41 (2002), 187. For some

other criticisms, many of them persuasive, see also Kansteiner, 'Genealogy of a Category Mistake'.

37. Leys, *Trauma*, pp. 298–99 and 2.
38. Bourke, 'When the Torture Becomes Humdrum', *Times Higher Educational Supplement*, February 10 (2006), p. 19.
39. Edkins, 'Remembering Relationality'. On 9/11 as a 'collective Freudian trauma' see James Der Derian, '*In Terrorem*: Before and After 9/11' in Ken Booth and Tim Dunne (eds), *Worlds in Collision: Terror and the Future of Global Order* (London: Palgrave, 2002), p. 106.
40. Fierke, 'Bewitched by the Past: Social Memory, Trauma, and International Relations', p. 132. Italics in original.
41. See, for example, Edkins, *Trauma and the Memory of Politics*; Maja Zehfuss, 'Forget September 11', *Third World Quarterly*, 24 (2003), 513–28; Roland Bleiker, 'Pablo Neruda and the Struggle for Political Memory', *Third World Quarterly*, 20 (1999), 1129–42; and David Campbell, 'Atrocity, Memory, Photography: Imagining the Concentration Camps of Bosnia', I and II, *Journal of Human Rights*, 1 (2002), 1–33 and 143–72.
42. Mill, *Considerations on Representative Government*, in Mill, *On Liberty, and Other Essays*, ed. John Gray (Oxford: Oxford University Press, 1991), p. 427; and Tocqueville, quoted in Jennifer Pitts, *A Turn to Empire: The Rise of Imperial Liberalism in Britain and France* (Princeton, NJ: Princeton University Press, 2005), p. 193.
43. Renan, 'What is a Nation?' reprinted in Geoff Eley and Ronald Grigor Suny (eds), *Becoming National: A Reader* (Oxford: Oxford University Press, 1996), pp. 45–6.
44. Burke, 'Speech on Opening of Impeachment', 15 February 1788, *Writings and Speeches of Edmund Burke, Vol. VI: India*, ed. P. J. Marshall (Oxford: Oxford University Press, 1991), pp. 316–17.
45. Peter J. Katzenstein (ed.), *Cultures of National Security: Norms and Identity in World Politics* (New York: Columbia University Press, 1996); Friedrich Kratochwil and Yosef Lapid (eds), *The Return of Culture and Identity in IR Theory* (London: Lynne Rienner, 1996); and Alexander Wendt, *Social Theory of International Politics* (Cambridge: Cambridge University Press, 1999).
46. Cruz, 'Identity and Persuasion: How Nations Remember their Pasts and Make their Futures', *World Politics*, 52 (2000), 310. As Rogers Smith argues, all 'political people's' require 'constitutive stories' that characterise the distinctive features of that people: Smith, 'Citizenship and the Politics of People-building', *Citizenship Studies*, 5 (2001), 73–96. See also Smith, *Stories of Peoplehood: The Politics and Morals of Political Membership* (Cambridge: Cambridge University Press, 2004).
47. Lebow, *The Tragic Vision of Politics: Ethics, Interests, and Orders* (Cambridge: Cambridge University Press, 2004), ch. 8. Lebow also stresses the importance of memory for identity: 'The Memory of Politics in Postwar Europe' in Fogu, Lebow, and Kansteiner (ed.), *The Memory of Politics in Postwar Europe*. See also Norton, *95 Theses*, Thesis 31.
48. Anne Deighton, 'The Past in the Present: British Imperial Memories and the European Question' in Müller (ed.), *Memory and Power in Post-war Europe*, pp. 100–21; and Andrew Gamble, *Between Europe and America: The Future of British Politics* (London: Palgrave, 2003), ch. 4. This has led repeatedly to

Britain over-estimating its global influence; see, for example, John Kampfner, *Blair's Wars: A Liberal Imperialist in Action* (London: Free Press, 2003).

49. Alison Brysk, Craig Parsons, and Wayne Sandholtz, 'After Empire: National Identity and the Post-Colonial Family of Nations', *European Journal of International Relations*, 8 (2002), 267–305.

50. Jeffery Herf, *Divided Memory: The Nazi Past in the Two Germanys* (Cambridge, MA: Harvard University Press, 1997); Geoff Eley, 'The Unease of History: Settling Accounts with the East German Past', *History Workshop Journal*, 57 (2004), 175–201.

51. See Herf, *Divided Memory*; Siobhan Kattago, *Ambiguous Memory: The Nazi Past and German National Identity* (London: Praeger, 2001); Jeffrey K. Olick, *In the House of the Hangman: The Agonies of German Defeat, 1943–1949* (Chicago, IL: University of Chicago Press, 2005); Alon Confino and Peter Fritzsche (eds), *The Work of Memory: New Directions in the Study of German Society and Culture* (Urbana, IL: University of Illinois Press, 2002); Klaus Neumann, *Shifting Memories: The Nazi Past in the New Germany* (Ann Arbor: The University of Michigan Press, 2000); and 'Special Double Issue: Histories and Memories of Twentieth Century Germany', *History & Memory*, 17 (2005).

52. Herf, 'Traditions of Memory and Belonging: The Holocaust and the Germans since 1945' in Ulf Hedetoft and Mette Hjort (eds), *The Postnational Self: Belonging and Identity* (Minneapolis, MN: University of Minnesota Press, 2002), p. 276; and also, Wulf Kansteiner, 'Nazis, Viewers and Statistics: Television History, Television Audience Research and Collective Memory in West Germany', *Journal of Contemporary History*, 39 (2004), 575–98.

53. W. G. Sebald, *On the Natural History of Destruction*; Mark Mazower, *The Dark Continent: Europe's Twentieth Century* (Harmondsworth: Penguin, 1998), p. 220; and Antony Beevor, *Berlin: The Downfall, 1945* (London: Viking, 1992).

54. Eley, 'The Unease of History', 175.

55. Olick, 'The Guilt of Nations?' *Ethics and International Affairs*, 17 (2003), 114.

56. See Zehfuss, 'Remembering to Forget/Forgetting to Remember'; Andrei Markovits and Simon Reich, *The German Predicament: Memory and Power in the New Europe* (Ithaca, NY: Cornell University Press, 1997); and Thomas Berger, 'The Power of Memory and Memories of Power: The Cultural Parameters of German Foreign Policy-Making since 1945' in Müller, *Memory and Power in Post-war Europe*, pp. 76–100.

57. Robert Schulzinger, 'Memory and Understanding U.S. Foreign Relations' in Michael Hogan and Thomas Paterson (eds), *Explaining the History of American Foreign Relations*, 2nd ed. (Cambridge: Cambridge University Press, 2004), p. 352.

58. Jerry Lembcke, *The Spitting Image: Myth, Memory, and the Legacy of Vietnam* (New York: NYU Press, 1998); Fred Turner, *Echoes of Combat: The Vietnam War in American Memory* (New York: Anchor, 1996); and Walter L. Hixon, *Historical Memory and Representations of the Vietnam War* (New York: Garland, 2000).

59. Arthur G. Neal, *National Trauma and Collective Memory: Extraordinary Events in the American Century*, 2nd ed. (M. E. Sharpe, 2005), chs. 4 and 11; and especially Emily Rosenberg, *A Date Which Will Live: Pearl Harbor in American Memory* (Durham, NC.: Duke University Press, 2003), ch. 10.

60. George W. Bush, Speech to the Air Force Academy, 2 June 2004 [http://www.whitehouse.gov/news/releases/2004/06/20040602.html]. See also

his speech to the Army War College, 24 May 2004 [http://www.whitehouse. gov/news/releases/2004/05/20040524-10.html]; Sidney Blumenthal, 'Bush Takes Refuge in History' *The Guardian*, 3 June 2004, 25; and, Tom Brokaw, *The Greatest Generation* (New York: Random House, 1998).

61. Ferguson, 'This Vietnam Generation of Americans has not Learnt the Lessons of History', *The Daily Telegraph*, 10 April 2004, 19.

62. See Ferguson, *Empire: How Britain Made the Modern World* (London: Allen Lane, 2003); and *Colossus: The Price of American Empire* (Harmondsworth: Penguin, 2004). Cf. Frederick Cooper, 'Empires Multiplied', *Comparative Studies in Society and History*, 46 (2004), 247–72; and Jon Wilson, 'Niall Ferguson's Imperial Passion', *History Workshop Journal*, 56 (2003), 175–83.

63. Bush, speech to commemorate VJ Day, Coronado, California, 30 August 2005 [http://www.whitehouse.gov/news/releases/2005/08/20050830-1.html].   For an autobiographical attempt to remind people of the horrors of serving in the allied forces in the Second World War, see Paul Fussell, *The Boys' Crusade: American GI's in Europe: Chaos and Fear in World War Two* (London: Weidenfeld, 2004).

64. Cruz, 'Identity and Persuasion'.

65. Liisa Malkki, *Purity and Exile: Violence, Memory, and National Cosmology among Hutu Refugees in Tanzania* (Chicago, IL: University of Chicago Press, 1995); Jeannette Marie Mageo, *Cultural Memory: Reconfiguring History and Identity in the Postcolonial Pacific* (Honolulu, HI: University of Hawai'i Press, 2001); and Richard Werbner (ed.), *Memory and the Postcolony: African Anthropology and the Critique of Power* (London: Zed, 1998).

66. Wulf Kansteiner argues that studies of collective memory frequently make implicit assumptions about cultural homogeneity: 'Finding meaning in Memory'. See also Winter and Sivan, 'Setting the Framework' in Sivan and Winter, *War and Remembrance in the Twentieth Century*, pp. 6–40.

67. Jenny Edkins, 'The Rush to Memory and the Rhetoric of War', *Journal of Political and Military Sociology*, 32 (2004), 232.

68. Liam Kennedy, 'Remembering September 11: Photography as Cultural Diplomacy', *International Affairs*, 79 (2003), 315–26. On 'securitization' as a response to trauma, see Jenny Edkins, 'Forget Trauma? Responses to September 11', *International Relations*, 16 (2002), esp. 249–51.

69. Edkins, 'The Rush to Memory and the Rhetoric of War'; and Rosenberg, *A Date Which Will Live*, ch. 10.

70. Edkins, 'Forget Trauma?'

71. The phrase is from Ira Katznelson, *Desolation and Enlightenment: Political Knowledge after Total War, Totalitarianism, and the Holocaust* (New York: Columbia University Press, 2003). On European responses, see Tony Judt, *Postwar: A History of Europe Since 1945* (Harmondsworth: Penguin, 2005).

72. On European identity, see Iver Neumann, *Uses of the Other: The 'East' in European Identity Formation* (Minneapolis, MN: University of Minnesota Press, 1999); Michael Bruter, *Citizens of Europe? The Emergence of a Mass European Identity* (Basingstoke: Palgrave, 2005); Thomas Risse, 'A European Identity? Europeanization and the Evolution of Nation-State Identities' in Maria Green Cowles, James Caporaso and Thomas Risse (eds), *Transforming Europe: Europeanization and Domestic Change* (Ithaca, NY: Cornell University Press, 2001), pp. 198–216; and Bo Stråth, 'A European Identity: To the Historical Limits of a Concept', *European Journal of Social Theory*, 5 (2002), 387–401.

73. Levy and Sznaider, 'Memory Unbound: The Holocaust and the Formation of Cosmopolitan Memory', *European Journal of Social Theory*, 5 (2002), 102. See also, Ilana Bet El, 'Unimagined Communities'.

74. Klaus Eder and Willfried Spohn (eds), *Collective Memory and European Identity: The Effects of Integration and Enlargement* (Aldershot: Ashgate, 2005), 208.

75. Judt, 'The Past is Another Country: Myth and Memory in Post-war Europe' in Müller (ed.), *Memory and Power in Post-war Europe*, pp. 182–3.

76. Wendt, 'A Comment on Held' in Ian Shapiro and Casiano Hacker-Cordón (eds), *Democracy's Edges* (Cambridge: Cambridge University Press, 1999), p. 130. He cites Chris Shore, 'Transcending the Nation State? The European Commission and the (Re)-Discovery of Europe', *Journal of Historical Sociology*, 9 (1996), 473–96. Wendt remains skeptical about this, however.

77. Jeffrey C. Alexander, 'On the Social Construction of Moral Universals', 6, 8 and 32. It has become, he argues in Durkheimean language, a 'sacred evil, set apart from ordinary evil things' (27) and therefore capable of transcending its context(s).

78. Levy and Sznaider, 'Memory Unbound', 98. See also Levy and Sznaider, *The Holocaust and Memory in a Global Age* (Philadelphia, PA: Temple University Press, 2005).

79. Indeed Alexander, despite the boldness of his title, repeatedly stresses that he is talking about the 'West', and even here he seems mainly to mean Europe and North America. Alexander, 'On the Social Construction of Moral Universals', 58.

80. Paul Hirst and Grahame Thompson, *Globalisation in Question: The International Economy and the Possibilities of Governance* (Cambridge: Polity, 1995); Justin Rosenberg, *The Follies of Globalisation Theory: Polemical Essays* (London: Verso, 2000); and Duncan S. A. Bell, 'Globalisation and History: Reflections on Temporality', *International Affairs*, 79 (2003), 801–15.

81. Smith, *Nations and Nationalism in a Global Era* (Cambridge: Polity, 1995), p. 24; see also Smith, *Myths and Memories of the Nation* (Oxford: Oxford University Press, 1999), pp. 225–53. For a challenge to Smith, see Ray, 'Mourning, Melancholia, and Violence'.

82. Walzer, *Thick and Thin: Moral Argument at Home and Abroad* (Indiana, IN: University of Notre Dame Press, 1994), p. 8. Italics in original. See also, Margalit, *The Ethics of Memory*. Cf. Gil Eyal, 'Identity and Trauma: Two Forms of the Will to Memory', *History & Memory*, 16 (2004), 5–36.

83. Kaldor, *New and Old Wars*.

84. Omer Bartov, 'Intellectuals on Auschwitz: Memory, History and Truth', *History & Memory*, 5 (1993), 94.

85. Müller, 'Introduction', p. 26. See also, Joshua Foa Dienstag, ' "The Pozsgay Affair": Historical Memory and Political Legitimacy', *History & Memory*, 8 (1996), 51–65.

86. Richard J. Evans, 'Redesigning the Past: History in Political Transitions', *Journal of Contemporary History*, 38 (2003), 5.

87. Alexandra Barahona De Brito, Carmen Gonzalez Enriquez, and Paloma Aguilar (eds), *The Politics of Memory: Transitional Justice in Democratizing Societies* (Oxford: Oxford University Press, 2001); and Anne Sa'adah, *Germany's Second Chance: Trust, Justice, and Democraticization* (Cambridge, MA.: Harvard University Press, 1998).

88. Kutz, 'Justice in Reparations: The Cost of Memory and the Value of Talk', *Philosophy & Public Affairs*, 32 (2004), 283.

89. See John R. Gills (ed.), *Commemorations: The Politics of National Identity* (Princeton, NJ: Princeton University Press, 1994); T. G. Ashplant, Graham Dawson, and Michael Roper (eds), *The Politics of War Memory and Commemoration* (London: Routledge, 2000); George Mosse, *Fallen Soldiers: Reshaping the Memory of the World Wars* (Oxford: Oxford University Press, 1990); Sivan and Winter (eds), *War and Remembrance in the Twentieth Century*; and Edkins, *Trauma and the Memory of Politics*.

90. Bleiker and Hoang, 'Remembering and Forgetting the Korean War', p. 204. An alternative account can be found in Susan Dwyer, 'Reconciliation for Realists' *Ethics and International Affairs*, 13 (1999), 81–99.

91. Meskell, 'Trauma Culture', p. 160.

92. See, for example, Hannah Arendt, *Eichmann in Jerusalem: A Report on the Banality of Evil* (London: Faber & Faber, 1963); Richard Golsan (ed.), *Memory, the Holocaust, and French Justice: The Bousquet and Touvier Affairs* (London: University Press of New England, 1996); and Donald Bloxham, *Genocide on Trial: War Crimes Trials and the Formation of Holocaust History and Memory* (Oxford: Oxford University Press, 2001). See also Martha Minow, *Between Vengeance and Forgiveness: Facing History After Genocide and Mass Violence* (Princeton: Princeton University Press, 1998).

93. David Hirsh, *Law Against Genocide: Cosmopolitan Trials* (London: Cavendish Press, 2003); Mark Osiel, *Mass Atrocity, Collective Memory, and the Law* (London: Transaction, 1997); Rachel Kerr, *The International Criminal Tribunal for the Former Yugoslavia: An Exercise in Law, Politics and Diplomacy* (Oxford: Oxford University Press, 2004).

94. Richard Wilson, *The Politics of Truth and Reconciliation in South Africa: Legitimizing the Post-Apartheid State* (Cambridge: Cambridge University Press, 2001); Charles Villa-Vicencio and Wilhelm Verwoerd (eds), *Looking Back, Reaching Forward: Reflections on the Truth and Reconciliation Commission of South Africa* (London: Zed Books, 2000); and, for the final document, *Truth and Reconciliation Commission of South Africa Report* (London: Macmillan, 1999).

95. Evans, 'History, Memory, and the Law: The Historian as Expert Witness', *History and Theory*, 41 (2002), 326–45; and Evans, *Telling Lies about Hitler: History, the Holocaust and the David Irving Trial* (London: Verso, 2002).

96. Rousso, *The Haunting Past: History, Memory, and Justice in Contemporary France*, trans. Ralph Schoolcraft (Philadelphia, PA: University of Pennsylvania Press, 2002).

97. Charles Maier, *The Unmasterable Past: History, the Holocaust, and German National Identity* (Cambridge, MA.: Harvard University Press, 1988).

98. Habermas, *The New Conservatism: Cultural Criticism and the Historians' Debate*, trans. Shierry Weber Nicholsen (Cambridge: Polity, 1994); and Habermas, *A Berlin Republic: Writings on Germany*, trans. Steven Rendall (Cambridge: Polity, 1997).

99. Alexander, 'On the Social Construction of Moral Universals', 45.

100. For a sceptical riposte, see W. James Booth, 'Communities of Memory: On Identity, Memory, and Debt', *American Political Science Review*, 93 (1999), 249–63.

101. Booth, 'The Unforgotten: Memories of Justice', *American Political Science Review*, 95 (2001), 779 and 787.
102. Margalit, *The Ethics of Memory*, p. 8.
103. For criticism of his position, see Richard Bernstein, 'The Culture of Memory', *History & Theory*, 43 (2004), 165–78; and Duncan Bell, 'Agonistic Democracy and the Politics of the Past: Reflections on the Ethics of Memory', unpublished paper, University of Cambridge, July 2005. For a complex phenomenological investigation into different understandings of the past, see Paul Ricoeur, *Memory, History, Forgetting* (Chicago, IL: University of Chicago Press, 2004).
104. Nietzsche, 'On the Uses and Disadvantages of History for Life' [1873] in his *Untimely Meditations*, ed. Daniel Breazeale (Cambridge: Cambridge University Press, 1997), p. 62. 'Thus: it is possible to live almost without memory, and to live happily moreover ... but it is altogether impossible to *live* at all without forgetting' (p. 62). Italics in original. See also, Marc Augé, *Oblivion*, trans. Marjolijn de Jager (Minneapolis: University of Minnesota Press, 2004).
105. Ricoeur, *Memory, History, Forgetting*.
106. Zehfuss, 'Remembering to Forget/Forgetting to Remember', section 3.
107. Zehfuss, 'Forget September 11'.
108. See, respectively, Winter, 'Notes on the Memory Boom'; Megill, 'History, Memory, Identity', 38–43; and Todorov, *Hope and Memory*, p. 159.
109. Alon Confino, 'Collective Memory and Cultural History: Problems of Method', *American Historical Review*, 102 (1995), 1387.
110. Todorov, *Hope and Memory*, p. 159.
111. Maier, 'A Surfeit of Memory?' pp. 137 and 141: this leads to 'a wallowing in bathetic memory' (p. 150). For strong criticisms of this position, see Bartov, 'Intellectuals on Auschwitz'.
112. Maier, 'Consigning the Twentieth Century to History: Alternative Narratives of the Modern Era', *American Historical Review*, 105 (2000), 807–31.
113. Maier, 'Consigning the Twentieth Century to History', 828.
114. See Huyssen, *Present Pasts*. For criticisms of the belief in the novelty of the 'collapse of time and space', see Duncan S. A. Bell, 'Dissolving Distance: Technology, Space, and Empire in British Political Thought, c.1770–1900', *The Journal of Modern History*, 77 (2005), 523–63.
115. Noah Gedi and Yigal Elman, 'Collective Memory – What is it?' *History & Memory*, 8 (1996), 30–50.
116. Hynes, 'Personal Narratives and Commemoration' in Winter and Sivan (eds), *War and Remembrance in the Twentieth Century*, p. 206. Italics in original. As he argues, in relation to the emotionally powerful commemorative iconography of the First World War, 'no pile of bricks and stones can cause us to remember what we have not seen' (p. 206). See also Susan Sontag, *Regarding the Pain of Others* (London: Penguin, 2004), pp. 76–7.
117. Bell, 'Mythscapes: Memory, Mythology, and National Identity', *British Journal of Sociology*, 54 (2002), 63–81; and for a fuller elaboration, Bell, 'Agonistic Democracy and the Politics of the Past'.
118. Klein, 'On the Emergence of *Memory* in Historical Discourse', *Representations*, 69 (2000), 128.

119. Pocock, 'The Politics of History: The Subaltern and the Subversive', *Journal of Political Philosophy*, 6 (1998), 229. See also Renan, 'What is a Nation?' 145.
120. Klein, 'On the Emergence of *Memory* in Historical Discourse', 45.
121. Ian Hacking, *Rewriting the Soul: Multiple Personality and the Sciences of Memory* (Princeton, NJ: Princeton University Press, 1995), p. 260.
122. Spiegel, 'Memory and History: Liturgical Time and Historical Time', *History & Theory*, 41 (2002), 156. See also, Barbara Misztal, 'The Sacralization of Memory', *European Journal of Social Theory*, 7 (2004), 67–85. Todorov also notes the dangers of mnemonic sanctification, and stresses the countervailing 'sacreligious' nature of historical practice. Todorov, *Hope and Memory*, pp. 169–74 and 200–1.
123. Michel De Certeau, *The Writing of History*, trans. Tom Conley (New York: Columbia University Press, 1988).
124. Klein, 'On the Emergence of *Memory* in Historical Discourse', 141 and 142–43.
125. Edkins, *Trauma and the Memory of Politics*; and 'Remembering Relationality'. See Giorgio Agamben, *Homo Sacer: Sovereign Power and Bare Life*, trans. Daniel Heller-Roazen (Stanford, CA: Stanford University Press, 1998).
126. Landsberg, *Prosthetic Memory: The Transformation of American Remembrance in an Age of Mass Culture* (New York: Columbia University Press, 2004).
127. Winter, 'Notes on the Memory Boom', p. 56.

2   We Could Remember It for You Wholesale: Myths, Monuments and the Constitution of National Memories

* I would like to thank Duncan Bell, Anders Berg-Sørensen, Henrik Enroth, Mikkel Vedby Rasmussen, Vibeke Schou Tjalve, Tomas Tranæus, Trine Villumsen and Ole Wæver for valuable comments on earlier drafts of this chapter.

1. See Heather Rae, *State Identities and the Homogenisation of Peoples* (Cambridge: Cambridge University Press, 2002), pp. 1–54.
2. Recent studies include M. Lane Bruner, *Strategies of Remembrance: The Rhetorical Dimensions of National Identity Construction* (Columbia, MO: University of South Carolina Press, 2002), pp. 1–11; and Rogers M. Smith, *Stories of Peoplehood: The Politics and Morals of Political Membership* (Cambridge: Cambridge University Press, 2002).
3. James Clifford, 'On Ethnographic Self-Fashioning: Conrad and Malinowski' in Thomas C. Heller, Morton Sisna, and David E. Wellbery (eds), *Reconstructing Individualism: Autonomy, Individuality, and the Self in Western Thought* (Stanford, CA: Stanford University Press, 1986), pp. 140–62.
4. Cf. Paul Veyne, *Did the Greeks Believe in their Myths?* (Chicago, IL: University of Chicago Press, 1988); and also William H. Sewell, 'The Concept(s) of Culture', in Victoria E. Bonnell and Lynn Hunt (eds), *Beyond the Cultural Turn* (Berkeley, CA: University of California Press, 1999), pp. 35–61.
5. John Locke, *An Essay Concerning Human Understanding* [1689] (London: Dent, 1976), p. 163.
6. Locke, *Essay*, p. 171.
7. David Hume, *A Treatise of Human Nature* [1739–40] (London: Longmans, Green & Co., 1874), pp. 534 and 541–3.

8. See also Paul Verhoeven's adaptation of this story in the movie *Total Recall* (TriStar/Carolco, 1990), starring Arnold Swarzenegger as Doug Quail.

9. Compare Martin Hollis, 'Of Masks and Men' in Michael Carrithers, Steven Collins & Steven Lukes (eds), *The Category of the Person: Anthropology, Philosophy, History* (Cambridge: Cambridge University Press, 1985), pp. 217–33; and T. L. S. Sprigge, 'Personal and Impersonal Identity', *Mind*, 385 (1988), 29–49.

10. Friedrich Nietzsche, 'On the Uses and Disadvantages of History for Life' [1874] in his *Untimely Meditations* (Cambridge: Cambridge University Press, 1983), p. 62.

11. Maurice Halbwachs, *On Collective Memory* [1940–8] (Chicago: University of Chicago Press, 1992), p. 38. For a more recent defense of the view that our representations are socially conditioned, see Mary Douglas, *How Institutions Think* (Syracuse, NY: Syracuse University Press, 1986).

12. For an analysis of the relationship between personal and collective memory, see Paul Ricoeur, *Memory, History, Forgetting* (Chicago, IL: University of Chicago Press, 2004), pp. 93–132.

13. For an interesting overview, see Jeffrey K. Olick and Joyce Robbins, 'Social Memory Studies: From "Collective Memory" to the Historical Sociology of Mnemonic Practices', *Annual Review of Sociology*, 24 (1998), 105–40.

14. See Janet Coleman, *Ancient and Medieval Memories* (Cambridge: Cambridge University Press, 1993).

15. See Mary Carruthers, *The Book of Memory: A Study of Memory in Medieval Culture* (Cambridge, MA: Cambridge University Press, 1990).

16. See for example Frances Yates, *The Art of Memory* (Chicago, IL: University of Chicago Press, 1966).

17. Pierre Nora, 'Introduction', in Pierre Nora, *Rethinking France: Les Lieux de Mémoire, Vol. 1, The State* (Cambridge, MA: Harvard University Press, 2001), pp. vii–xxii.

18. Jonathan Boyarin, 'Space, Time and the Politics of Memory' in Jonathan Boyarin (ed.), *Remapping Memory: The Politics of Timespace* (Minneapolis, MN: University of Minnesota Press, 1994), pp. 1–37.

19. Patricia Springborg, 'Global Identity: Cosmopolitan Localism', paper presented at IPSA, Seoul, 17–21 August, 1997, 4. Quoted with kind permission from the author.

20. Anthony Pagden, *Lords of all the World: Ideologies of Empire in Spain, Britain and France, c.1500–1850* (New Haven, CT: Yale University Press, 1995).

21. Jens Bartelson, *A Genealogy of Sovereignty* (Cambridge: Cambridge University Press, 1995), ch. 4; and Coleman, *Ancient and Medieval Memories*, pp. 541–62.

22. Francesco Petrarca, 'Letter to Cola di Rienzo and the Roman People' (Variae 48, Horatorio) in Petrarch, *The Revolution of Cola di Rienzo* (New York, NY: Italica Press, 1996), pp. 10–36. See also Coleman, *Ancient and Medieval Memories*, p. 558.

23. See Ernst Kantorowicz, 'Pro Patria Mori' in Medieval Political Thought', *American Historical Review*, 56 (1951), 472–92; and Liah Greenfeld, *Nationalism: Five Roads to Modernity* (Cambridge, MA: Harvard University Press, 1992).

24. George H. Mead, *Mind, Self, and Society* [1934] (Chicago, IL: The University of Chicago Press, 1962), p. 202. I am grateful to Benjamin Herborth for having drawn my attention to this passage.

25. For a brief analysis of the rhetorical content of *Os Lusíadas*, see Richard Helgerson, *Forms of Nationhood: The Elizabethan Writing of England* (Chicago, IL: The University of Chicago Press, 1992), pp. 149–63.
26. Luís Vaz de Camões, *The Lusiads* (Hammondsworth: Penguin, 1952), p. 42.
27. Camões, *Lusiads*, p. 131.
28. XVI, 18–19.
29. Camões, *Lusiads*, p. 134.
30. Giambattista Vico, *The New Science* [1746] (Ithaca: Cornell University Press, 1976), pp. 102–3.
31. See Helder Macedo, 'The Rhetoric of Prophecy in Portuguese Renaissance Literature', *Portuguese Studies*, 19 (2003), 9–18.
32. Addison, 'Frozen Voices', *Tatler*, No. 254, 23, November 1710, adapted from *The Voyages and Adventures of Fernand Mendez Pinto*, translated into English by H. Cogan 1653 [facsimile by Dawsons of Pall Mall, London, 1969], p. 1. I am grateful to my friends in Lisbon for this gift.
33. *The Voyages and Adventures of Fernand Mendez Pinto*, preface, folio A.
34. *The Voyages and Adventures of Fernand Mendez Pinto*, pp. 21–3.
35. Damião de Góis, *Lisbon in the Renaissance: A New Translation of the Urbis Olisiponis Descriptio by Jefferey S. Ruth* (New York, NY: Italica Press, 1996). For an analysis, see Elisabeth Feist Hirsch, 'The Discoveries and the Humanists', in John Parker ed., *Merchants and Scholars: Essays in the History of Exploration and Trade* (Minneapolis, MN: The University of Minnesota Press, 1965), pp. 33–46.
36. See for example Armando Cortesão, *The History of Portuguese Cartography* (Coimbra: Junta de Investigações do Ultramar, 1969–71), Vol. I; Thomas S. Kuhn, *The Copernican Revolution* (Cambridge, MA: Harvard University Press, 1957), p. 124; and Thomas Goldstein, 'The Renaissance Concept of the Earth and its Influence upon Copernicus', *Terræ Incognitæ*, 4 (1972), 19–51.
37. John M. Headley, 'The Sixteenth-Century Venetian Celebration of the Earth's Total Habitability: The Issue of the Fully Habitable World for Renaissance Europe', *Journal of World History*, 8 (1997), 9.
38. Frank Lestringant, *Mapping the Renaissance World: The Geographical Imagination in the Age of Discovery* (Cambridge: Polity Press, 1994), p. 23. See also David Turnbull, 'Cartography and Science in Early Modern Europe: Mapping the Construction of Knowledge Spaces', *Imago Mundi*, 48 (1996), 5–24; and Mark Neocleous, 'Off the Map: On Violence and Cartography', *European Journal of Social Theory*, 6 (2003), 409–25.
39. For a different interpretation, see Joan-Pau Rubiés, 'The Oriental Voices of Mendes Pinto, or the Traveller as Ethnologist in Portuguese India', *Portuguese Studies*, 10 (1994), 24–43.
40. The de-legitimization of pilgrimage was largely the responsibility of Erasmus and Montaigne. See C. R. Thompson, *The Colloquies of Erasmus* (Chicago, IL: Chicago University Press, 1965); and Wes Williams, ' "Rubbing up against Others": Montaigne on Pilgrimage', in Jas Elsner and Joan-Pau Rubiés, *Voyages & Visions: Towards a Cultural History of Travel* (London: Reaktion Books, 1999), pp. 101–23.
41. *The Voyages and Adventures of Fernand Mendez Pinto*, p. 309.
42. *The Voyages and Adventures of Fernand Mendez Pinto*, pp. 311–12.
43. *The Voyages and Adventures of Fernand Mendez Pinto*, p. 314.
44. See for example Góis, *Lisbon in the Renaissance*, pp. 10–12.

45. William Congreve, *Love for Love* [1695] (London: Macmillan, 1967), II:5: 'Fernando Mendez Pinto was but a type of thee, thou liar of the first magnitude'.
46. Compare Tzvetan Todorov, *The Conquest of America: The Question of the Other* (New York, NY: Harper & Row, 1992); and Anthony Pagden, *European Encounters with the New World* (New Haven, CT: Yale University Press, 1993), pp. 17–49.
47. Helgerson, *Forms of Nationhood*, pp. 107–47.
48. Springborg, 'Global Identity', 16.
49. Michael Drayton, *Poly-Olbion, or a Chorographicall Description of the Tracts, Riuers, Mountaines, Forests, and other parts of this Renowned Isle of Great Britaine*, in *The Works of Michael Drayton*, ed. William Hebel (Oxford: Basil Blackwell, 1933), IV. Quoted in Springborg, 'Global Identity', 29.
50. Sir William Davenant, *Proposition for the Advancement of Moralities* (London, 1651), p. 249. Quoted in Springborg, 'Global Identity', 30.
51. Yates, *The Art of Memory*, pp. 310–54.
52. John Selden, 'Illustrations', in *The Works of Michael Drayton*, IV, p. 15.
53. Emmanuel de Sieyès, *What is the Third Estate?* [1789] (London: Pall Mall Press, 1963), p. 124; Istvan Hont 'The Permanent Crisis of a Divided Mankind: The Contemporary Crisis of the Nation-State in Historical Perspective' in *Political Studies*, special issue, 1994, 166–231; Robert Wokler, 'The Enlightenment and the French Revolutionary Birth Pangs of Modernity', in Johan Heilbron, Lars Magnusson, and Björn Wittrock (eds), *The Rise of the Social Sciences and the Formation of Modernity* (Dordrecht: Kluwer, 1998), pp. 22–40; and Lucien Jaume, 'Citizen and State under the French Revolution', in Bo Stråth & Quentin Skinner (eds), *States and Citizens: History, Theory, Prospects* (Cambridge: Cambridge University Press, 2003), 131–44.
54. Choay, *L'Allegorie du Patrimoine* (Paris: Seuil, 1992); and Arrhenius, *The Fragile Monument: On Conservation and Modernity* (Stockholm: Royal Institute of Technology, 2003).
55. Thordis Arrhenius, *The Fragile Monument*, p. 10.
56. Arrhenius, *The Fragile Monument*, p. 52.
57. Arrhenius, *The Fragile Monument*, pp. 53 and 55–6.
58. Choay, *L'Allegorie du Patrimoine*, pp. 80–90.
59. Arrhenius, *The Fragile Monument*, p. 60.
60. Stanley J. Idzerda, 'Iconoclasm During the French Revolution', *American Historical Review*, 60 (1954), 13–26. Quoted in Arrhenius, *The Fragile Monument*, p. 68.
61. Arrhenius, *The Fragile Monument*, p. 69.
62. Arrhenius, *The Fragile Monument*, p. 71.
63. Reinhart Koselleck, 'Historical criteria of the modern concept of revolution' in *Futures Past: On the Semantics of Historical Time* (Cambridge, MA: MIT Press, 1985), pp. 39–54; and Robert Wokler, 'Contextualizing Hegel's Phenomenology of the French Revolution and the Terror', *Political Theory*, 26 (1998), 33–55.
64. Immanuel Kant, 'Idea for a Universal History with a Cosmopolitan Purpose' [1784] in *Kant: Political Writings*, ed. Hans Reiss (Cambridge: Cambridge University Press, 1990), p. 46.

65. Georg W. F. Hegel, *Lectures on the Philosophy of World History* [1837] (Cambridge: Cambridge University Press, 1975), p. 65.

66. Leopold von Ranke, *The Great Powers* in *Leopold Ranke: The Formative Years*, ed. Theodore H. von Laue (Princeton, NJ: Princeton University Press, 1950), pp. 181 and 215.

67. Jens Bartelson, *The Critique of the State* (Cambridge: Cambridge University Press, 2001), ch. 2.

68. Nietzsche, 'On the Uses and Disadvantages of History for Life', p. 68.

69. Marcel Mauss, 'A Category of the Human Mind: The Notion of Person; the Notion of Self' [1938] in Carrithers et al., *The Category of the Person*, p. 22.

70. Ulrich Beck, 'The Cosmopolitan Perspective: Sociology in the Second Age of Modernity' in Steven Vertovec & Robin Cohen (eds), *Conceiving Cosmopolitanism: Theory, Context, and Practice* (Oxford: Oxford University Press, 2002), pp. 61–85.

3 Notes on the Memory Boom: War, Remembrance and the Uses of the Past

1. See, for example, Charles Maier, *The Unmasterable Past: History, Holocaust, and German National Identity* (Cambridge, MA.: Harvard University Press, 1988).

2. *Les Lieux de Mémoire*, sous la direction de Pierre Nora, 7 vols. (Paris: Gallimard, 1984–1992).

3. Joyce, *Portrait of the Artist as a Young Man* (London: The Egoist Ltd., 1916), p. 253.

4. Frances Yates, *The Art of Memory* (London: Routledge, 1966). See also, Jonathan D. Spence, *The Memory Palace of Matteo Ricci* (New York, NY: Viking, 1984).

5. I am grateful to Jan Assmann for allowing me to read the draft of his forthcoming work, written with Aleida Assmann, on cultural memory, where he makes this and many other points from which I have learned.

6. Charles Maier, 'A Surfeit of Memory? Reflections on History, Melancholy and Denial', *History & Memory*, 5 (1993), 136–51.

7. *Bergson: Biographie*, begun by Philippe Soulez and completed by Frederic Worms (Paris: Flammarion, 1997).

8. E.H. Gombrich, *Aby Warburg: An Intellectual Biography* (Oxford: Phaidon, 1970).

9. Richard Slobodin, *W.H.R. Rivers: Pioneer Anthropologist, Psychiatrist of The Ghost Road* (Stroud: Sutton, 1997).

10. George D. Painter, *Marcel Proust: A Biography* (London: Penguin, 1990).

11. Annette Becker, *Maurice Halbwachs* (Paris: Noesis, 2003).

12. Halbwachs, *Les Cadres Sociaux de la Mémoire* (Paris: F. Alcan, 1925).

13. Halbwachs, *On Collective Memory*, trans. Lewis A. Coser (Chicago, IL: University of Chicago Press, 1992). For recent elaborations, see, Iwona Irwin-Zarecki, *Frames of Remembrance: The Dynamics of Collective Memory* (New Brunswick, NJ: Transaction, 1994); and Peter Burke, 'History as Social Memory' in Thomas Butler (ed.), *Memory: History, Culture and the Mind* (Oxford: Basil Blackwell, 1990), pp. 97–113.

14. Maurice Agulhon, 'La Statumanie au xixè Siècle', *Le Romantisme*, 30 (1981), 20–30.

15. Eric Hobsbawm and Terence Ranger (eds.), *The Invention of Tradition* (Cambridge: Cambridge University Press, 1983).
16. Cannadine, 'The Context, Performance and Meaning of Ritual: The British Monarchy and the Invention of Tradition, c.1820–1977' in Hobsbawm and Ranger (eds), *The Invention of Tradition*, p. 125ff.
17. Renan, *Qu'est-ce qu'une Nation? Conférence Faite en Sorbonne, le 11 mars 1882* (Paris: Calmann Lévy, 1882), p. 28.
18. Jeanne Beausoleil, 'La Collection Albert Kahn' in *Autochromes 1901/1928* (Paris: Tresors de la photographie, 1978); and Jeanne Beausoleil and Pascal Ory (eds), *Albert Kahn 1860–1940: Realites d'une Utopie* (Boulogne-Billancourt: Musee Albert Kahn – Departement des Hauts-de-Seine, 1995).
19. Benito M. Vergara, *Displaying Filipinos: Photography and Colonialism in Early 20th Century Philippines* (Quezon City: University of the Philippines Press, 1995).
20. Madeleine Rébérioux, 'La Mur des Fédérées' in Nora, *Les Lieux de Mémoire*, II, pp. 220–62.
21. Maurice Agulhon, *Marianne au Combat: L'Imagerie et la Symbolique Républicaines de 1789 à 1880* (Paris: Flammarion, 1979).
22. Jay Winter, *Sites of Memory, Sites of Mourning: The Great War in European Cultural History* (Cambridge: Cambridge University Press, 1995).
23. Pieter Lagrou, *The Legacy of Nazi Occupation: Patriotic Memory and National Recovery in Western Europe, 1945–1965* (Cambridge: Cambridge University Press, 1999).
24. Frederic D. Homer, *Primo Levi and the Politics of Survival* (Columbia: University of Missouri Press, 2001), and, Myriam Anissimov, *Primo Levi: Tragedy of an Optimist*, trans. Steve Cox (London: Aurum, 1998).
25. Wieviorka, *L'Ère du Témoin* (Paris: Plon, 1998); see also her essay 'From Survivor to Witness: Voices from the Shoah' in Jay Winter and Emmanuel Sivan (eds), *War and Remembrance in the Twentieth Century* (Cambridge: Cambridge University Press, 1999), pp. 101–29.
26. Primo Levi, *Le Devoir de Mémoire*, p. 75.
27. *The Sorrow and the Pity: A Film*, trans. Mireille Johnston (New York: Outerbridge & Lazard, 1972). See also Henry Rousso, *The Vichy Syndrome: History and Memory in France since 1944*, trans. Arthur Goldhammer (Cambridge, MA: Harvard University Press, 1991).
28. Eric Conan and Henry Rousso, *Vichy: An Ever-Present Past*, trans. Nathan Bracher (Hanover: University Press of New England, 1998).
29. On Grossman, see *Le Livre Noir: Sur L'extermination Scelerate des Juifs par les Envahisseurs Fascistes Allemands dans les Regions Provisoirement Occupees de l'URSS et dans les Camps D'extermination en Pologne Pendant la Guerre de 1941–1945, Textes et Temoignages*, edited by Ilya Ehrenbourg and Vassili Grossman, traduits du russe par Yves Gauthier, *et al.* (Arles: Actes Sud, 1995).
30. See Jay Winter, 'Remembrance and Redemption: A Social Interpretation of War Memorials', *Harvard Design Magazine*, 9 (1999), 71–7.
31. See, Lyotard, *La Condition Postmoderne: Rapport sur le Savoir* (Paris: Editions de Minuit, 1979); Levinas, *God, Death, and Time*, trans. Bettina Bergo (Stanford: Stanford University Press, 2000); and, John Felstiner, *Paul Celan: Poet, Survivor, Jew* (New Haven, CT: Yale University Press, 2001).
32. Max Horkheimer and Theodor W. Adorno, *Dialectic of Enlightenment*, trans. John Cumming (New York, NY: Continuum, 1972).

33. Maier, 'Consigning the Twentieth Century to History: Alternative Narratives of the Modern Era', *American Historical Review*, 105 (2000), 807–831.
34. Communication from Nora, in an exchange and debate between us on 'History and Memory' at the Centre de l'histoire sociale du vingtième siècle, Paris, March 1999.
35. Gustavo Perez Firmat, *Life on the Hyphen: The Cuban-American Way* (Austin, TX: University of Texas Press, 1994).
36. See Allen Megill, 'History, Memory, Identity', *History of the Human Sciences*, 11 (1998), 37–62; and Jeffrey K. Olick and Joyce Robbins, 'Social Memory Studies: From "Collective Memory" to the Historical Sociology of Mnemonic Practices', *American Review of Sociology*, 24 (1998), 105–40.
37. Peter Novick, *The Holocaust in American Life* (Boston MA: Houghton Mifflin, 1999).
38. See Marita Sturken, *Tangled Memories: The Vietnam War, the AIDS Epidemic, and the Politics of Remembering* (Berkeley, CA: University of California Press, 1997).
39. Dolores Hayden, 'The Japanese-American Monument in Los Angeles' in Winter and Sivan (eds), *War and Remembrance in the Twentieth Century*, pp. 142–60.
40. Doris Sommer, *Proceed with Caution, when Engaged by Minority Writing in the Americas* (Cambridge, MA: Harvard University Press, 1999), p. 115.
41. Werner Sollors, from the introduction to Gweneviere Fabre and Ropbert O'Meally (eds), *History and Memory in African-American Culture* (Oxford: Oxford University Press, 1994), pp. 7–8.
42. OECD, *Educational Statistics Yearbook, Vol. 1: International Tables* (Paris: OECD, 1974) Table 7, p. 20; *Eurostat Yearbook 98/99; A Statistical Eye on Europe 1987–1997* (Brussels: European Community, 1999), Table 12, p. 123.
43. On *'patrimoine'*, see Pierre Nora (ed.), *Science et Conscience du Patrimoine: Entretiens du Patrimoine, Théâtre National de Chaillot, Paris, 28, 29 et 30 Novembre 1994* (Paris: Fayard, 1997).
44. Milward, 'Bad Memories', *The Times Literary Supplement*, 14 April (2000), p. 8.
45. Nora (ed.), *Essais d'ego-histoire* (Paris: Gallimard, 1987).
46. Pat Barker, *Regeneration* (New York, NY: Viking, 1991); *The Eye in the Door* (New York: Viking, 1993); *The Ghost Road* (New York, NY: Viking, 1995).
47. Barker, *Another World* (London: Viking, 1998).
48. Sebastian Faulks, *Charlotte Gray* (London: Hutchinson, 1998).
49. Dominick LaCapra, *History and Memory after Auschwitz* (Ithaca, NY: Cornell University Press, 1998), p. 8.
50. Laurence J. Kirmayer, 'Landscapes of Memory: Trauma, Narrative, and Dissociation' in Paul Antze and Michael Lambek (eds), *Tense Past: Cultural Essays in Trauma and Memory* (London: Routledge, 1996), pp. 173–98.
51. See Allen Young, *The Harmony of Illusions* (Princeton, NJ: Princeton University Press, 1995); and Steve Southwick's work, cited in Winter and Sivan (eds), *War and Remembrance*, p. 15n. On this exciting field see Daniel Schachter (ed.), *Memory Distortion: How Minds, Brains and Societies Reconstruct the Past* (Cambridge, MA: Harvard University Press, 1995).
52. Edkins, *Trauma and the memory of Politics* (Cambridge: Cambridge University Press, 2003), p. 230.

4 From Theodicy to *Ressentiment*: Trauma and the Ages of Compensation

1. Hannah Arendt, *On Revolution* (New York, NY: Penguin, 1963), pp. 70–71.
2. Frank R. Ankersmit, 'Trauma and Suffering: A Forgotten Source of Western Historical Consciousness' in Jörn Rüsen (ed.), *Western Historical Thinking: An Intercultural Debate* (New York, NY: Berghahn, 2002), p. 76.
3. Ulrich Beck, *Risk Society: Toward a New Modernity* (Newbury Park, CA.: Sage, 1992), p. 21.
4. Paul Lerner and Mark S. Micale, 'Trauma, Psychiatry and History: A Conceptual and Historiographical Introduction' in Lerner and Micale (eds), *Traumatic Pasts: History, Psychiatry, and Trauma in the Modern Age, 1870–1930* (Cambridge: Cambridge University Press, 2001), p. 6.
5. Wolfgang Schivelbusch, *The Railway Journey: The Industrialization of Time and Space in the 19th Century* (Berkeley, CA: University of California Press, 1986), p. 134.
6. Wolfgang Schäffner, 'Event, Series, Trauma: The Probabilistic Revolution of the Mind in the Late Nineteenth and Early Twentieth Centuries' in Micale and Lerner (eds), *Traumatic Pasts*, p. 82.
7. In this context, it is important to point out both that the Francophone *'ressentiment'* is a relatively more common expression in German, and that it carries overtones of bitterness that exceeds that of resentment in English, which sometimes seems fleeting and petty. Friedrich Nietzsche, *On the Genealogy of Morality*, ed. Keith Ansell–Pearson and Carol Diethe (Cambridge: Cambridge University Press, 1994).
8. Max Weber, *The Sociology of Religion* (Boston, MA: Beacon, 1963), p. 107.
9. Nietzsche, *On the Genealogy of Morality*, p. 21.
10. Friedrich Nietzsche, *Thus Spoke Zarathustra*, in *The Portable Nietzsche*, ed. Walter Kaufman (New York NY: Viking, 1954), p. 251.
11. See the discussion of Wendy Brown below.
12. Weber, *Sociology of Religion*, p. 106.
13. Weber, *Sociology of Religion*, p. 97.
14. Svend Ranulf, *Moral Indignation and Middle Class Psychology* (New York, NY: Schocken Books, 1964 [1938]), p. 1.
15. Max Scheler, *Ressentiment* (Milwaukee, WI: Marquetter University Press, 1998).
16. Scheler, *Ressentiment*, pp. 29ff.
17. Scheler, *Ressentiment*, p. 93.
18. Scheler, *Ressentiment*, p. 99.
19. In all likelihood, Scheler's essay was so well known in Arendt's circle that the connections were obvious. Because Arendt's reputation today far outweighs Scheler's, that connection is no longer so obvious even to close readers.
20. Arendt, *On Revolution*, p. 22.
21. Arendt, *On Revolution*, p. 86.
22. Arendt, *On Revolution*, p. 88.
23. Nietzsche, *On the Genealogy of Morality*, p. 45; Arendt, *On Revolution*, p. 89.
24. Here we think again of the work of Ulrich Beck.
25. Wendy Brown, *States of Injury: Power and Freedom in Late Modernity* (Princeton, NJ: Princeton University Press, 1995), pp. 66–7.

26. For a trenchant critique of Brown, see Lawrie Balfour, 'Reparations After Identity Politics', *Political Theory*, 33 (2005), pp. 786–811.
27. Paul Ricoeur, *Memory, History, Forgetting* (Chicago, IL: University of Chicago Press, 2004).
28. Jean Améry, *At the Minds Limits* (New York, NY: Schocken, 1986), pp. 68–9.
29. Primo Levi, *The Drowned and the Saved* (New York, NY: Vintage, 1989), p. 136.
30. Améry, *At the Mind's Limits*, p. 69.
31. Améry, *At the Mind's Limits*, p. 69.
32. Améry, *At the Mind's Limits*, p. 81.
33. Améry, *At the Mind's Limits*, p. 72.
34. Améry, *At the Mind's Limits*, p. 70.
35. Emmanuel Levinas, 'Useless Suffering' in Mark Larrimore (ed.), *The Problem of Evil: A Reader* (Oxford: Blackwell, 2001), p. 376
36. Levinas, 'Useless Suffering', pp. 376–7.
37. Brown, *States of Injury*, p. 68.
38. Emile Durkheim, *The Division of Labor in Society* (New York, NY: Free Press, 1997).
39. On the sociology of commensuration, see Wendy N. Espeland and Mitchell C. Stevens, 'Commensuration as a Social Process', *Annual Review of Sociology*, 24 (1998), pp. 313–43.
40. Durkheim, *Division of Labor*.
41. Schivelbusch, *The Railway Journey*, p. 159.
42. Reinhardt Koselleck, *Futures Past: On the Semantics of Historical Time* (Cambridge, MA: MIT Press, 1985), pp. 8–9.
43. Lutz Niethammer, *Posthistoire: Has History Come to an End?* (London: Verso, 1992), pp. 135–6.
44. Benedict Anderson, *Imagined Communities: Reflections on the Origin and Spread of Nationalism* (London: Verso, 1991).
45. Ankersmit, 'Trauma and Suffering', p. 79.
46. Odo Marquard, *Farewell to Matters of Principle: Philosophical Studies* (New York, NY: Oxford University Press, 1989), pp. 31 & 41.
47. In this regard, John Torpey's important new book on reparations, which attributes the rise of reparations to the decline of effective faith in the future, is clearly within the Arendtian paradigm, though applying it to the present in perspicuous ways. John Torpey, *Making Whole What has Been Smashed: On Reparations Politics* (Cambridge, MA: Harvard University Press, 2006).

5 Remembering Relationality: Trauma Time and Politics

1. Toni Morrison, 'The Dead of September 11' in Judith Greenberg (ed.), *Trauma at Home: After 9/11* (Lincoln, NE: University of Nebraska Press, 2003), pp. 1–2. Original emphasis.
2. The chapter draws in part on an invited lecture given at the University of Newcastle on 18 May 2004 and organised by the Postcolonial Research Group, the School of English Literature, Language and Linguistics and the Newcastle Institute for the Arts, Social Sciences and Humanities.
3. For an excellent discussion of the centrality of dust and its materiality to history and memory, see Carolyn Steedman, *Dust* (Manchester, NH: Manchester University Press, 2001).

4. Jacques Derrida, *The Gift of Death*, trans. David Wills (Chicago, IL: University of Chicago Press, 1995).

5. In the siege of the school in Beslan, which was in the news as this chapter was being completed, we find again, as in the case of 11 September 2001, that leaders such as Presidents Putin and Bush stand to benefit in electoral terms from traumatic incidents, while those caught up in them face nothing but death or bereavement. In Beslan the narrative Putin wished to tell was strongly contested by those more closely involved; see, for example, Mary Dejevsky, 'Russian Media Condemns Siege "Cover Up" ', *The Independent* (London), 7 September 2004. In the case of 9.11, such criticism was less frequently heard and the dead were more successfully co-opted as heroes in tales of sacrifice, although the challenge still circulated in the form of so-called conspiracy theories.

6. See, for example, Paul Antze and Michael Lambek (eds), *Tense Past: Cultural Essays in Trauma and Memory* (New York, NY: Routledge, 1996); Mieke Bal, Jonathan Crewe, and Leo Spitzer (eds), *Acts of Memory: Cultural Recall in the Present* (Hanover, NH: Dartmouth College, 1999); Cathy Caruth (ed.), *Trauma: Explorations in Memory* (Baltimore: The Johns Hopkins University Press, 1995); Peter Gray and Oliver Kendrick (eds), *The Memory of Catastrophe* (Manchester: Manchester University Press, 2004); Michael S. Roth and Charles G. Salas (eds), *Disturbing Remains: Memory, History and Crisis in the Twentieth Century* (Los Angeles: The Getty Research Institute, 2001); Marita Sturken, *Tangled Memories: The Vietnam War, the Aids Epidemic, and the Politics of Remembering* (Berkeley: University of California Press, 1997); and, Richard Werbner, *Memory and the Postcolony: African Anthropology and the Critique of Power* (London: Zed Books, 1998).

7. Priscilla B. Hayner, *Unspeakable Truths: Confronting State Terror and Atrocity* (New York: Routledge, 2001); Liisa H. Malkki, *Purity and Exile: Violence, Memory and National Cosmology Among Hutu Refugees in Tanzania* (Chicago, IL: University of Chicago Press, 1995); Charles Villa-Vicencio and Wilhelm Verwoerd (eds), *Looking Back, Reaching Forward: Reflections on the Truth and Reconciliation Commission of South Africa* (Cape Town: University of Cape Town Press, 2000); and, Richard Wilson, *The Politics of Truth and Reconciliation in South Africa: Legitimizing the Post-Apartheid State* (Cambridge: Cambridge University Press, 2001).

8. George L. Mosse, *Fallen Soldiers: Reshaping the Memory of the World Wars* (Oxford: Oxford University Press, 1990); James Tatum, *The Mourner's Song: War and Remembrance from the Iliad to Vietnam* (Chicago, IL: University of Chicago Press, 2003); Jay Winter, *Sites of Memory, Sites of Mourning: The Great War in European Cultural History* (Cambridge MA: Cambridge University Press, 1995); Jay Winter and Emmanuel Sivan (eds), *War and Remembrance in the Twentieth Century* (Cambridge: Cambridge University Press, 1999); and, Michael J. Hogan (ed.), *Hiroshima in History and Memory* (Cambridge: Cambridge University Press, 1996).

9. Among many others see, for example, Lawrence L. Langer, *Holocaust Testimonies: The Ruins of Memory* (New Haven, CT: Yale University Press, 1991); Peter Novick, *The Holocaust and Collective Memory: The American Experience* (London: Bloomsbury, 1999); and, James E. Young, *The Texture of Memory: Holocaust Memorials and Meaning* (New Haven, CT: Yale University Press, 1993).

10. Examples include Jeffrey Alexander et al. *Cultural Trauma and Collective Identity* (Berkeley: University of California Press, 2004); Ron Eyerman, *Cultural Trauma: Slavery and the Formation of African American Identity* (Cambridge: Cambridge University Press, 2001); John R. Gilles (ed.), *Commemorations: The Politics of National Identity* (Princeton NJ: Princeton University Press, 1994); Ian McBride, *History and Memory in Modern Ireland* (Cambridge: Cambridge University Press, 2001); Caroline Wiedmer, *The Claims of Memory: Representations of the Holocaust in Contemporary Germany and France* (Ithaca, NY: Cornell University Press, 1999).

11. Jan-Werner Muller (ed.), *Memory and Power in Post-War Europe* (Cambridge: Cambridge University Press, 2002). See also Maja Zehfuss' analysis of the influence of memory in debates about German re-militarization in *Constructivism in International Relations: The Politics of Reality* (Cambridge: Cambridge University Press, 2002).

12. Patrick West, *Conspicuous Compassion: Why Sometimes it Really is Cruel to be Kind* (London: Civitas: Institute for the Study of Civil Society, 2004).

13. See, for example, the contribution by Jay Winter and the discussion of the 'limits of memory' in Duncan Bell's introduction.

14. A fuller version of some of the argument presented here is to be found in Jenny Edkins, *Trauma and the Memory of Politics* (Cambridge: Cambridge University Press, 2003).

15. Benedict Anderson, *Imagined Communities: Reflections on the Origin and Spread of Nationalism*, rev. ed. (London: Verso, 1991).

16. As well as Edkins, *Trauma and the Memory of Politics*, see 'Forget Trauma? Responses to September 11', *International Relations*, 16 (2002), 243–56; 'The Rush to Memory and the Rhetoric of War', *Journal of Political and Military Sociology*, 31 (2003), 231–51; and 'Ground Zero: Reflections on Trauma, Indistinction and Response', *Journal for Cultural Research*, 8 (2004), 247–70.

17. See, for example, Fierke's contribution to this volume.

18. Jacques Lacan, *Écrits: A Selection*, trans. Alan Sheridan (London: Routledge, 1980). For a good introduction to Lacan see Slavoj Zizek, *Enjoy your Symptom: Jacques Lacan in Hollywood and out* (New York: Routledge, 1992); and *Looking Awry: An Introduction to Jacques Lacan through Popular Culture* (Cambridge, MA: MIT Press, 1991). See also Bruce Fink, *A Clinical Introduction to Lacanian Psychoanalysis: Theory and Technique* (Cambridge, MA: Harvard University Press, 1997); and Yannis Stavrakakis, *Lacan and the Political* (London: Routledge, 1999).

19. Jacques Lacan, 'The Mirror Stage as Formative of the Function of the I', trans. Alan Sheridan, *Écrits*, pp. 1–7.

20. Often written in such work with a capital letter, as 'the Real'.

21. Slavoj Zizek, *The Sublime Object of Ideology* (London: Verso, 1989). For the notion of antagonism, see also Ernesto Laclau and Chantal Mouffe, *Hegemony and Socialist Strategy: Towards a Radical Democratic Politics* (London: Verso, 1985).

22. Jenny Edkins, *Poststructuralism and International Relations: Bringing the Political back in* (Boulder, CO: Lynne Rienner, 1999), p. 100.

23. Jacques Derrida, 'Force of Law: The "Mystical Foundation of Authority" ' in David Gray Carlson, Drucilla Cornell and Michel Rosenfeld (eds), *Deconstruction and the Possibility of Justice* (New York, NY: Routledge, 1992), pp. 3–67.

24. Zizek, *Enjoy your Symptom*, p. 103.
25. Lacan, *Ecrits*, p. 86; and Edkins, *Poststructuralism and International Relations*, p. 102.
26. Zizek, *The Indivisible Remainder: An Essay on Schelling and Related Matters* (London: Verso, 1996), pp. 132–36.
27. Cathy Caruth, *Unclaimed Experience: Trauma, Narrative, and History* (Baltimore, MD: Johns Hopkins University Press, 1996).
28. Cathy Caruth, 'Recapturing the Past: Introduction', in Caruth (ed.), *Trauma: Explorations in Memory*, p. 153.
29. Edkins, 'The Rush to Memory and the Rhetoric of War'.
30. Edkins, *Trauma and the Memory of Politics*, p. 95; the time of the state is similar to Benjamin's 'empty, homogeneous time'; see Walter Benjamin, *Illuminations*, trans. Harry Zohn (London: Fontana, 1968/1992), p. 252.
31. Edkins, 'The Rush to Memory and the Rhetoric of War'.
32. For a more extended discussion of this distinction see Jenny Edkins, *Poststructuralism and International Relations*.
33. Edkins, *Trauma and the Memory of Politics*, p. 4.
34. Isabel A. Moore, 'Speak You Also: Encircling Trauma', *Journal of Cultural Research*, 9 (2005), pp. 87-99. (Paper presented at the Aberystwyth-Lancaster Graduate Colloquium, University of Wales Aberystwyth, 2 May 2004.) The notion of abandonment here is interesting in relation to Giorgio Agamben's discussion of the sovereign ban, Giorgio Agamben. *Homo Sacer: Sovereign Power and Bare Life*, trans. Daniel Heller-Roazen (Stanford, CA: Stanford University Press, 1998).
35. Kai Erikson, *A New Species of Trouble: The Human Experience of Modern Disasters* (New York, NY: W. W. Norton, 1994); and, Eyerman, *Cultural Trauma*.
36. Judith Butler, *Precarious Life: The Powers of Mourning and Violence* (London: Verso, 2004).
37. Morrison, 'The Dead of September 11'.
38. Mark Wigley, 'Insecurity by Design' in Michael Sorkin and Sharon Zukin (eds), *After the World Trade Centre: Rethinking New York City* (New York, NY: Routledge, 2002), pp. 69–85.
39. For a fuller discussion, see Edkins, 'Ground Zero'.
40. Giorgio Agamben, *Remnants of Auschwitz: The Witness and the Archive*, trans. Daniel Heller-Roazen (New York, NY: Zone Books, 1999).
41. Agamben draws closely on Primo Levi's writings on the camp: Primo Levi, *The Drowned and the Saved*, trans. Raymond Rosenthal (London: Abacus, 1989); and, *If This is a Man and the Truce*, trans. Stuart Woolf (London: Abacus, 1979).
42. Michel Foucault, 'The Subject and Power' in *Michel Foucault: Power*, ed. James D. Faubion (New York, NY: The New Press, 1994), III, pp. 326–48; see also Foucault. 'Two Lectures' trans. Leo Marshall Colin Gordon, John Mepham and Kate Soper in Colin Gordon (ed.), *Power/Knowledge: Selected Interviews and Other Writings, 1972-1977* (Brighton: Harvester, 1980). For a fuller discussion of this point, see Edkins and Pin-Fat, 'Through the Wire: Relations of Power and Relations of Violence', *Millennium: Journal of International Studies*, 34 (2005), 1–26.
43. This argument is developed more fully in Edkins and Pin-Fat, 'Through the Wire'.

44. Not forgetting trauma, or, in other words, remembering the openness of the traumatic event, rather than seeking to tell the story in narrative form, can be seen in terms of a refusal of distinctions and the assumption of bare or naked life. The latter is close as well to the Lacanian notion of traversing the fantasy or acknowledging the fantasy structure of what we call social reality.
45. This example is taken from Edkins, 'Rush to Memory and the Rhetoric of War'.
46. Artists Network of Refuse and Resist, 'Our Grief is Not a Cry for War', Artists Performance, 2001. URL: http://www.refuseandresist.org/newresistance/ 092301grief.html
47. Although as we have already seen, there is no such thing as the present.
48. Erin Manning, 'Beyond Accommodation: National Space and Recalcitrant Bodies', *Alternatives*, 25 (2000), 51–74; and, Anne Michaels, *Fugitive Pieces* (New York, NY: Vintage International, 1996).
49. The photograph is fascinating because it is a dispatch from this very aporetic space, and the emphasis on the taking of photographs after 11 September 2001 has been read in these terms Marianne Hirsch, 'I Took Pictures: September 2001 and Beyond' in Greenberg (ed.), *Trauma at Home*, pp. 69–86.
50. Jacques Derrida, *Politics of Friendship*, trans. George Collins (London: Verso, 1997).
51. Toni Morrison, 'The Dead of September 11', pp. 1–2.
52. Derrida, *The Gift of Death*, p. 41.
53. Morrison, 'The Dead of September 11', p. 1.

6   Bewitched by the Past: Social Memory, Trauma and International Relations

1. John P. Wilson, 'The Historical Evolution of PTSD Diagnostic Criteria: From Freud to DSM–IV', *Journal of Traumatic Stress*, 7 (1994), p. 687.
2. Recent work in IR focusing on trauma in war includes Jenny Edkins, *Trauma and the Memory of Politics* (Cambridge: Cambridge University Press, 2003); Michael Humphrey, *The Politics of Atrocity and Reconciliation: From Terror to Trauma* (London: Routledge, 2002) and K. M. Fierke, 'Whereof We Can Speak, Thereof We Must Not be Silent: Trauma, Political Solipsism and War', *Review of International Studies* 30 (2005), pp. 471–91. See also Patrick Bracken and Celia Petty, *Rethinking the Trauma of War* (London: Free Association Press, 1998).
3. Novick, *The Holocaust and Collective Memory* (London: Bloomsbury, 1999), p. 4.
4. Jacques Bouveresse, *Wittgenstein Reads Freud: The Myth of the Unconscious* (Princeton, NJ: Princeton University Press, 1995), p. 9. See also Brian McGuinness, 'Freud and Wittgenstein' in Brian McGuinness (ed.), *Wittgenstein and his Times* (Oxford: Blackwell, 1981), p. 42, 43.
5. Axel Honneth, *The Fragmented World of the Social: Essays in Social and Political Philosophy* (Albany, NY: State University of New York Press, 1995).
6. See Wittgenstein, *Philosophical Investigations*, para. 122. For a discussion of his use of perspicuous presentation, see Brian R. Clack, *Wittgenstein, Frazer and Religion* (Basingstoke: Macmillan, 1999), pp. 53–74, and James C. Edwards, *Ethics Without Philosophy: Wittgenstein and the Moral Life* (Tampa: University Presses of Florida, 1982), pp. 142–43.
7. Ludwig Wittgenstein, *Culture and Value*, edited by G.H. von Wright, trans. Peter Winch (Oxford: Blackwell, 1978), p. 16. On Wittgenstein and psychoanalysis,

see John M. Heaton, *Wittgenstein and Psychoanalysis* (Cambridge: Icon Books, 2000).

8. Bouveresse, *Wittgenstein Reads Freud*, p. 24.
9. Bouveresse, *Wittgenstein Reads Freud*, p. 129.
10. Bouveresse, *Wittgenstein Reads Freud*, p. 25.
11. Martha Minow, *Breaking the Cycles of Hatred: Memory, Law and Repair* (Princeton, NJ: Princeton University Press, 2002).
12. While Freud was never explicit about the narrative character of the analytic experience, later writers have pointed to its significance, showing how the psychoanalytic dialogue seeks to uncover the analysands efforts to maintain a kind of narrative discontinuity. Paul Connerton, *How Societies Remember* (Cambridge: Cambridge University Press, 1989), p. 26.
13. This is captured in Freud's concept of *Nachtraglichkeit* or deferred action, in which trauma is constituted by the relationship between two events or experiences. Ruth Leys, *Trauma: A Genealogy* (Chicago IL: University of Chicago Press, 2000), p. 20.
14. Ian Hacking, *Rewriting the Soul: Multiple Personality and the Sciences of Memory* (Princeton, NJ: Princeton University Press, 1995), p. 254.
15. Wittgenstein, *Philosophical Investigations*, para. 109.
16. Wittgenstein's critique of Freud was similar to the critique he made of his own early work in the *Tractatus-Logicus Philosophicus* (London: Routledge and Kegan Paul, [1922] 1974).
17. Leys, *Trauma*, p. 7.
18. Jeffrey Prager, *Presenting the Past: Psychoanalysis and the Sociology of Misremembering* (Cambridge, MA.: Harvard University Press, 1998), p. 134.
19. See the analysis of Bessel van der Kolk and Cathy Caruth in Leys, *Trauma*, p. 266.
20. Connerton, *How Societies Remember*, p. 25. The tendency of the traumatised to replay the past, is a theme in the literature of trauma studies: see Allen Young, *Harmony of Illusions: Inventing Post-Traumatic Stress Disorder* (Princeton: Princeton University Press, 1997); and, specifically as they relate to politics, Edkins, *Trauma and the Memory of Politics*; and, Rena Moses-Hrushovski, *Grief and Grievance: The Assassination of Yitzak Rabin* (London: Minerva Press, 2000).
21. Adrian Forty and Susanne Kuchler, *The Art of Forgetting* (Oxford: Berg, 1999), p. 5.
22. Connerton, *How Societies Remember*, p. 23.
23. Vaclav Havel, 'History of a Public Enemy', *New York Review of Books*, vol. 37, no. 9, 31 May 1990, p. 43.
24. See Connerton's discussion of Michael Oakschott, *How Societies Remember*, p. 30.
25. James M. Glass, *Private Terror/Public Life: Psychosis and the Politics of Community* (Ithaca, NY: Cornell University Press, 1989).
26. Glass, *Private Terror/Public Life*, p. 80.
27. Glass, *private Terror/Public Life*, p. 82.
28. There is evidence of transgenerational transmission of trauma between Holocaust survivors and their children. The latter have a greater propensity for PTSD. See, for instance, Rachel Yehuda, James Schmeidler, Milton Wainberg, Karen Binder-Brynes and Tamar Duvdevani, 'Vulnerability to Polsttraumatic Stress Disorder in Adult Offspring of Holocaust Survivors,' *American Journal of Psychiatry*, 155 (1998), pp. 1163–71.

29. Philip Cushman, *Constructing the Self: Constructing America* (Reading, MA: Addison-Wesley, 1995).
30. Cushman, *Constructing the Self*, p. 302.
31. Cushman, *Constructing the Self*, p. 343.
32. Moses-Hrushovski, *Grief and Grievance*, p. xv.
33. Fentress and Wickham, *Social Memories* (Oxford: Blackwell, 1992), p. 4.
34. Fentress and Wickham, *Social Memories*, pp. 50–51.
35. See, for example, K. M. Fierke, 'The Liberation of Kosovo: Emotion and the Ritual Re-Enactment of Wa'r, *Focaal: European Journal of Anthropology*, 39 (2002), pp. 93–116.
36. Idith Zertal, *Israel's Holocaust and the Politics of Nationhood* (Cambridge: Cambridge University Press, 2005).
37. This was reflected in the Nazi's and Nazi Collaborators (Punishment) Law 1950, which gave the Jewish state a framework for bringing a handful of 'collaborators' among the survivors of the Holocaust to justice. Prior to 1961, all of those brought to trial under the law, with one minor exception, were new immigrants who, upon arrival in Israel, were recognized by other survivors and reported to the police. The law did not make a clear distinction between Nazi criminals and Nazi victims defined as collaborators. It also did not address the role of the Jewish Council and Jewish community leaders prior to deportation or within the ghettos and camps (Zertal, *Israel's Holocaust*, pp. 60–75).
38. Zertal, *Israel's Holocaust*, p. 95.
39. Zertal, *Israel's Holocaust*, p. 100. This thinking also seeped into academic sources, such as the *Encyclopedia of the Holocaust*, completed in the 1980s, where the Mufti were depicted as one of the great designers and perpetrators of the Final Solution. Peter Novoick, *The Holocaust in American Life*, 1999, p. 158.
40. Zertal, *Israel's Holocaust*, p. 111. 'The Eichmann Trial – A Warning Against Absence of Defence Force', *Davar*, 29 May 1961; and Y. Simhoni, 'The Eichmann Trial's Conclusions: Security is the Key to our Existence', *Davar*, 11 May 1961.
41. David Ben-Gurion, broadcast for Independence Day, reproduced in *Davar*, 22 May 1961.
42. Fierke, 'Whereof We Can Speak, Thereof We Must Not be Silent'; Omer Bartov, *Mirrors of Destruction: War, Genocide and Modern Identity* (Oxford: Oxford University Press, 2000).
43. Zertal, *Israel's Holocaust*, p. 122.
44. Shlaim, *The Iron Wall: Israel and the Arab World* (New York, NY: Penguin Books, 2000).
45. Shlaim, *The Iron Wall*, p. 238.
46. On the other side, revisionists pointed out that the intransigence of Israel shares a large responsibility for political deadlock, and saw the situation as one of *yesh breira*, or real political choices with respect to the Arabs.
47. Shlaim, *The Iron Wall*, p. 40.
48. Zahava Solomon, 'From Denial to Recognition: Attitudes Toward Holocaust Survivors from World War II to the Present', *Journal of Traumatic Stress*, 8 (1995), p. 219.
49. Shlaim, *The Iron Wall*, 423.
50. The Israeli state can be understood and was in fact justified in these very Hobbesian terms. Jews in the diaspora, left to themselves in the state of

nature, were subject to conditions where life was 'nasty, brutish, and short'. The only hope was to create a state that could provide protection. In the creation of the state, the problem of isolation and the need for self defense, i.e. the security dilemma became a collective problem.

51. As cited in Novick, *The Holocaust and Collective Memory*, p. 4.
52. Connerton, *How Societies Remember*, p. 38.
53. For an in-depth discussion of denial see Stanley Cohen, *States of Denial: Knowing About Atrocities and Suffering* (Oxford: Polity, 2002).
54. Muller-Fahrenholz, 'Deep Remembering – The Art of Forgiveness' in Jorg Calliess (ed.), *Agenda for Peace: Reconciliation* (Loccum: Evangelishe Akademie Loccum, 1998), p. 227.
55. Merridale, *Night of Stone: Death and Memory in Twentieth Century Russia* (New York, NY: Penguin Books, 2000).
56. Vaclev Havel, et al., *The Power of the Powerless: Citizens Against the State in Central-Eastern Europe*, ed. John Keane (New York, NY: M.E. Sharpe, 1985).
57. Adam Michnik, 'What We Want to Do and What We Can Do', *Telos*, 47 (1981), pp. 70–1.
58. Wittgenstein, *Philosophical Investigations*, para. 109.

7 Mourning, Melancholia and Violence

* This chapter is an elaboration of the discussion in William Outhwaite and Larry Ray, *Social Theory and Postcommunism* (Oxford: Blackwell, 2005), pp. 176–96.

1. Prager, *Presenting the Past: Psychoanalysis and Sociology of Misremembering*, p. 1.
2. Bauman, *Modernity and the Holocaust* (Cambridge: Polity, 1999), pp. 12–18.
3. Elias, *The Germans: Power Struggles and the Development of Habitus in the Nineteenth and Twentieth Centuries*, trans. Eric Dunning and Stephen Mennell (Oxford: Polity, 1996).
4. Eric Dunning and Stephen Mennell, 'Elias on Germany, Nazism and the Holocaust: On the Balance Between "Civilizing" and "Decivilizing" Trends in the Social Development of Western Europe', *British Journal of Sociology*, 49 (1998), 339–57.
5. De Swaan, *Human Societies: An Introduction*, trans. Beverley Jackson (Cambridge: Polity Press, 2001).
6. Daniel Goldhagen, *Hitler's Willing Executioners* (London: Little, Brown, 1996).
7. J. Murer, 'The Clash Within: Intrapsychically Created Enemies and Their Roles in Ethnonationalist Conflict' in Kenton Worcester, Sally Avery Bermanzohn, and Mark Ungar (eds), *Violence and Politics: Globalization's Paradox* (London: Routledge, 2002), pp. 209–25.
8. Sabrina Ramet, *Social Currents in Eastern Europe: The Sources and Making of the Great Transformation* (London: Duke University Press, 1991). There is some dispute whether 'genocide' is the right term to apply to 'ethnic cleansing' in Kosovo. But Martin Shaw points out that 'Genocide does not always involve the slaughter of the majority, let alone the entirety, of the "enemy" group. This is because perpetrators can often achieve the destruction of a group through relatively limited killings, accompanied by other measures'. Shaw, *War and Genocide: Organized Killing in Modern Society* (Cambridge: Polity, 2003), p. 37.
9. Kristeva, *Etrangers à Nous-Mêmes* (Paris: Gallimard, 1997), p. 1.

10. Gergen, 'Mind, Text and Society' in Ulric Neisser and Robyn Fivush (eds), *The Remembering Self: Construction and Accuracy in the Self-Narrative* (Cambridge: Cambridge University Press, 1994), pp. 74–104; and Scott Lash, *Another Modernity* (Cambridge: Polity, 1999), p. 296.

11. Anthony Elliott, *Critical Visions: New Directions in Social Theory* (Oxford: Rowman and Littlefield, 2003), p. 178.

12. Barbara Misztal, *Theories of Social Remembering* (Maidenhead: Open University Press, 2003), p. 196.

13. Misztal, *Theories of Social Remembering*, p. 204.

14. Larry Ray, *Theorizing Classical Sociology* (Buckingham: Open University Press, 1999).

15. Jeffrey K. Olick and Joyce Robbins, 'Social Memory Studies: From "Collective Memory" to the Historical Sociology of Mnemonic Practices', *Annual Review of Sociology*, 24 (1998), 105–41.

16. Ozouf, *Festivals of the French Revolution* (London: Harvard University Press, 1988).

17. Lynn Hunt, 'The Sacred and the French Revolution' in Jeffrey Alexander (ed.), *Durkheimian Sociology: Cultural Studies* (Cambridge: Cambridge University Press, 1988), pp. 25–43.

18. Elizabeth Hallam and Jenny Hockey, *Death, Memory and Material Culture* (Oxford: Berg, 2001), p. 77.

19. Benedict Anderson, *Imagined Communities: Reflections on the Origin and Spread of Nationalism* (London: Verso, 1993).

20. M. Bakhtin, 'Forms of Time and the Chronotype in the Novel' in Michael Holquist (ed.), *The Dialogic Imagination: Four Essays* (Austin, TX: University of Texas Press, 1981), pp. 41–83.

21. Michael Billig, *Banal Nationalism* (London: Sage, 1997).

22. Anthony Smith, 'Towards a Global Culture?' in Mike Featherstone (ed.), *Global Culture, Nationalism, Globalization and Modernity* (London: Sage, 1990), pp. 171–91.

23. Smith, 'LSE Centennial Lecture: The Resurgence of Nationalism? Myth and Memory in the Renewal of Nations', *British Journal of Sociology*, 47 (1996), 575–98.

24. Homi Bhabha, 'DissemiNation: Time, Narrative and the Margins of the Modern Nation' in Bhabha (ed.), *Nation and Narration* (London: Routledge, 1995), p. 297.

25. Sławomir Kapralski, 'Identity Building and the Holocaust: Roma Political Nationalism', *Nationalities Papers*, 25 (1997), 269–83.

26. Mike Featherstone, 'Archiving Cultures', *British Journal of Sociology*, 51 (2000), 161–84.

27. Misztal, *Theories of Social Remembering*, p. 19.

28. Kapralski, 'Battlefields of Memory Landscape and Identity in Polish–Jewish Relations', *History & Memory*, 13 (2001), 35–58.

29. J. Kugelmass, 'The Rites of the Tribe: The Meaning of Poland for American Jewish Tourists' in *YIVO Annual 21* (Illinois: Northwestern University Press and the YIVO Institute for Jewish Research, 1993), p. 419.

30. Misztal, *Theories of Social Remembering*, pp. 121–2.

31. Emma Klein, *The Battle for Auschwitz: Catholic–Jewish Relations under Strain* (London: Vallentine Mitchell, 2001).

32. Similarly, the Romany Holocaust, previously 'forgotten' in European history, is subject to remembrance and the search to document witness from survivors. See Kapralski, 'Battlefields of Memory'.
33. Paul Virilio and Sylvère Lotringer, *Pure War*, trans. Mark Polizzotti (New York, NY: Semiotexte, 1997), p. 5.
34. N. Frijda, 'Commemoration' in James Pennebaker, Dario Paez, Bernard Rimé (eds), *Collective Memory of Political Events: Social Psychological Perspectives* (Mahwah, NJ: Lawrence Erlbaum, 1997), pp. 103–27.
35. Walter Benjamin, 'The Story Teller' in *Illuminations* (London: Fontana, 1997), pp. 83–109.
36. Lowenthal, 'Age and Artefact: Dilemmas of Appreciation' in D. W. Meinig (ed.), *The Interpretation of Ordinary Landscapes: Geographical Essays* (Oxford: Oxford University Press, 1979), p. 104.
37. Winter, 'Forms of Kinship and Remembrance in the Aftermath of the Great War' in Winter and Emmanuel Sivan (eds), *War and Remembrance in the Twentieth Century* (Cambridge: Cambridge University Press, 1999), pp. 40–61.
38. Thomas Laqueur, 'Memory and Naming in the Great War' in John Gillis, *Commemorations: The Politics of National Identity* (Princeton, NJ: Princeton University Press, 1994), pp. 150–76.
39. Lloyd, *Battlefield Tourism: Pilgrimage and Commemoration of the Great War in Britain, Australia and Canada, 1919–1939* (Oxford: Berg, 1998), pp. 100–1.
40. M. Heffernan, 'Forever England: The Western Front and the Politics of Remembrance in Britain', *Ecumene*, 2 (1995), 293–323.
41. Sigmund Freud, 'Mourning and Melancholia' in the *Standard Edition*, ed. J. Strachey (London: The Hogarth Press and Institute of Psychoanalysis, 1953–74), 14, pp. 243–58.
42. D. Paez, N. Basabe, and J. L. and Gonzalez, 'Social Processes and Collective Memory' in Pennebaker, Pacz, and Rimé (eds), *Collective Memory of Political Events*, p. 153.
43. Paul Connerton, *How Societies Remember* (Cambridge: Cambridge University Press, 1989), p. 10.
44. Lury, *Prosthetic Culture: Photography, Memory and Identity* (London: Sage, 1998).
45. As Lury notes: *Prosthetic Culture*, p. 12.
46. Rubie Watson, *Memory, History and Opposition under State Socialism* (Santa Fe: Schools of American Research Press, 1994), p. 18.
47. Ian Hacking, 'Memoro-Politics and the Soul', *History of the Human Sciences*, 7 (1994), 29–53.
48. Alford, 'Freud and Violence' in Anthony Elliott (ed.), *Freud 2000* (Cambridge: Polity, 1998), p. 71ff.
49. Skultans, *Testament of Lives: Narrative and Memory in Post-Soviet Latvia* (London: Routledge, 1998).
50. Skultans, *Testament of Lives*, p. 18.
51. Skultans, *Testament of Lives*, p. 22.
52. Habermas, *The Theory of Communicative Action: Lifeworld and System: A Critique of Functionalist Reason* (Cambridge: Polity, 1989), II, pp. 335–7.
53. Emile Durkheim, *Elementary Forms of the Religious Life* (London: Allen and Unwin, 1976), p. 371ff.
54. Connerton, *How Societies Remember*, p. 64.

55. Durkheim, *Elementary Forms of the Religious Life*, p. 404ff.
56. West, *Black Lamb and Grey Falcon: A Journey Through Yugoslavia* (London: Macmillan, 1982), p. 835.
57. Kaplan, *Balkan Ghosts: A Journey Through History* (London: Macmillan, 1993), p. 38.
58. Serbian Academy of Arts and Sciences, 1986.
59. Ramet, *Social Currents in Eastern Europe*, p. 185.
60. Anderson, *Imagined Communities*.
61. Misha Glenny, *The Balkans, 1804–1999: Nationalism, War and the Great Powers* (London: Granta Books, 1999), pp. 11–12.
62. See the 'Serbian Network' website: http://www.srpska-mreza.com/
63. Serbia Information News 1/3/99.
64. Wolfgang Hoepken, 'War, Memory and Education in a Fragmented Society: The Case of Yugoslavia', *East European Politics and Society*, 13 (1999), 190–227.
65. P. M. Hayden, 'Recounting the Dead' in Watson (ed.), *Memory, History and Opposition*, p. 172.
66. René Girard, *Violence and the Sacred*, trans. Patrick Gregory (Baltimore, MD: John Hopkins University Press, 1977).
67. Rogers Brubaker, 'National Minorities, Nationalizing States and External National Homelands in the New Europe', *Daedalus* (Spring 1995), 107–32.
68. A further example of this is the way that in medieval Europe Easter rituals often spilled over into antisemitic violence. Although the Easter passion is a representation of a sacrifice, the pathos invoked incited actual killing in 'revenge'. See Robert Wistrich, *Antisemitism: The Longest Hatred* (London: Mandarin 1992).
69. R. J. Kosker, 'Building Pasts: Historic Preservation and Identity in Twentieth Century Germany' in Gillis (ed.), *Commemorations*, pp. 215–38.
70. For opposing 'sides' see Srpska Mreza http://www.srpska-mreza.com/ and http://www.kosova.com/

8   Trauma Culture: Remembering and Forgetting in the New South Africa

1. Andreas Huyssen, *Present Pasts: Palimpsests and the Politics of Memory* (Stanford, CA: Stanford University Press, 2003), p. 2.
2. Huyssen, *Present Pasts*, pp. 8–9.
3. Meskell, 'Negative Heritage and Past Mastering in Archaeology', *Anthropological Quarterly*, 75 (2002), 557–74.
4. Antjie Krog, *Country of My Skull: Guilt, Sorrow, and the Limits of Forgiveness in the New South Africa* (New York, NY: Three Rivers Press, 1998), p. 32.
5. Mahmood Mamdani, *Citizen and Subject: Contemporary Africa and the Legacy of Late Colonialism* (Princeton, NJ: Princeton University Press, 1996).
6. Huyssen, *Present Pasts*, p. 10.
7. Carli Coetzee and Sarah Nuttall, 'Introduction' in Nuttall and Coetzee (eds), *Negotiating the Past: The Making of Memory in South Africa* (Cape Town: Oxford University Press, 1998), p. 13; and David Pearce and Lynn Meskell, 'Archaeology After Apartheid: The Status of Archaeology in the New South Africa', unpublished manuscript.
8. This approach follows Paulla Ebron, *Performing Africa* (Princeton, NJ: Princeton University Press, 2002), p. 105.

9. Benedict Anderson, *Imagined Communities* (London: Verso, 1983).
10. Ann Cvetkovich, *An Archive of Feelings: Trauma, Sexuality, and Lesbian Public Cultures* (Durham, CT: Duke University Press, 2003), p. 7.
11. Cvetkovich, *An Archive of Feelings*, pp. 7–8.
12. Huyssen, *Present Pasts*, p. 9.
13. Pearce and Meskell, 'Archaeology after Apartheid'.
14. Tony Binns and Etienne Nel, 'Tourism as a Local Development Strategy in South Africa', *The Geographical Journal*, 168 (2002), 235–44.
15. Cvetkovich, *An Archive of feelings*, p. 36.
16. Najubalo Ndebele, 'Game Lodges and Leisured Colonialists' in Hilton Judin and Ivan Vladislavić (eds), *Blank_Architecture, Apartheid and After* (Rotterdam: NAi Publishers, 1998), p. 10.
17. Cvetkovich, *An Archive of Feelings*, p. 12.
18. Ebron, *Performing Africa*, p. 105.
19. Ingrid De Kok, 'Cracked Heirlooms: Memory on Exhibition' in Nuttall and Coetzee (eds), *Negotiating the Past*, p. 57.
20. De Kok, 'Cracked Heirlooms', p. 57.
21. Leslie Wits, *Apartheid's Festival: Contesting South Africa's National Pasts* (Bloomington, IN: Indiana University Press, 2003).
22. See also, Ciraj Rassool and Leslie Witz, 'The 1952 Jan Van Riebeeck Tercentenary Festival: Constructing and Contesting Public National History in South Africa', *Journal of African History*, 34 (1993), 447–68.
23. Bunn, 'Whited Sepulchers: On the Reluctance of Monuments' in Judin and Vladislavić (eds.), *Blank_Architecture*, p. 4.
24. Bunn, 'Whited Sepulchers'.
25. Elizabeth Delmont, 'The Voortrekker Monument: Monolith to Myth', *South African Historical Journal*, 29 (1993), 86.
26. Bunn, 'Whited Sepulchers'.
27. See, Saul Dubow, *Scientific Racism in Modern South Africa* (Cambridge: Cambridge University Press, 1995); Martin Hall, 'The Burden of Tribalism: The Social Context of Southern African Iron Age Studies', *American Antiquity*, 49 (1984), 455–67; and Hall, 'The Archaeology of Colonial Settlement in Southern Africa', *Annual Review of Anthropology*, 22 (1993), 177–200.
28. Dubow, *Scientific Racism in Modern South Africa*; Martin Hall, 'Archaeology Under Apartheid', *Archaeology*, 41 (1998), 62–64; Hall, 'Social Archaeology and the Theaters of Memory', *Journal of Social Archaeology*, 1 (2001), 50–61; Nick Shepherd, 'Disciplining Archaeology: The Invention of South African Prehistory, 1923–1953', *KRONOS/ Kronos: Journal of Cape History*, 28 (2002), 127–45; Shepherd, 'The Politics of Archaeology in Africa', *Annual Review of Anthropology*, 31 (2002), 189–209; and Shepherd, 'State of the Discipline: Science, Culture and Identity in South African Archaeology, 1870–2003', *Journal of Southern African Studies*, 29 (2003), 823–44.
29. See here Mamdani, *Citizen and Subject*.
30. John Lees Smail, *Monuments and Trails of the Voortrekkers* (Cape Town: Howard Timmins, 1968).
31. Smail, *Monuments and Trails of the Voortrekkers*.
32. Bunn, 'Whited Sepulchers'.
33. See also, Anne McClintock, *Imperial Leather: Race, Gender, and Sexuality in the Colonial Contest* (New York NY: Routledge, 1995).

34. http://www.restinations.co.za/history.asp
35. See, for example, Paul Connerton, *How Societies Remember* (Cambridge: Cambridge University Press, 1989); and Maurice Halbwachs, *On Collective Memory* (New York, NY: Harper & Row, 1980).
36. Hedi Grunebaum and Yasir Henri, 'Where the Mountain Meets its Shadow: A Conversation on Memory, Identity, and Fragmented Belonging in Present-Day South Africa' in Bö Strath and Ron Robin (eds), *Homelands: Poetic Power and the Politics of Space* (Brussels: P.I.E. Lang, forthcoming).
37. http://www.dacpm.org.za/Wecat-Tour/wecat.htm
38. G. Warren-Brown, 'Soldier Henry Comes Home', *Leadership*, December/January (2000), 95.
39. Ciraj Rassool, 'The Rise of Heritage and the Reconstitution of History in South Africa', *Kronos: Journal of Cape History*, 26 (2000), 17.
40. Lazarus Kgalema, *Symbols of Hope: Monuments as Symbols of Remembrance and Peace in the Process of Reconciliation* (Johannesburg: Centre for the Study of Violence and Reconciliation, 2000), p. 19.
41. Patricia Davidson, 'Museums and the Reshaping of Memory' in Nuttall and Coetzee (eds), *Negotiating the Past*, p. 145.
42. Davidson, 'Museums and the Reshaping of Memory'.
43. Lucille Davie, 'The Powerful Apartheid Museum', City of Johannesburg Official Website: 9, April 2003. http://www.joburg.org.za/november/ apartheid.stm
44. Davie, 'The Powerful Apartheid Museum'.
45. Nicholas Kotch, 'Museum Honors Youth Slain in Apartheid Uprising', *Philadelphia Enquirer*, 17 June 2002.
46. Kgalema, *Symbols of Hope*, p. 9.
47. Geoffry Blundell, 'Presenting South Africa's Rock Art Sites' in J. Deacon (ed.), *Monuments and Sites: South Africa* (Sri Lanka: International Council on Monuments and Sites, 1996), pp. 71–80; Blundell, 'Rand, Rock Art and Resources: Tourism and Our Indigenous Heritage', *CSD Bulletin*, 4 (1998), 15–16; Blundell, *The Unseen Landscape: A Journey to Game Pass Shelter (Guide Booklet)* (Johannesburg: Rock Art Research Institute, 2002); Blundell and B. Smith, ' "A Bushman is not Forever": Negative Heritage and the San of Southern Africa', paper presented at the World Archaeology Congress, Washington DC, 2003.
48. David Morris, 'Rock Art as Source and Resource: Research and Responsibility Towards Education, Heritage and Tourism', paper presented at the *Biannual Conference of the South African Historical Society*, 2003.
49. Carli Coetzee, 'Krotoa Remembered: A Mother of Unity, A Mother of Sorrows' in Nuttall and Coetzee (eds), *Negotiating the Past*, pp. 112–19; Davidson, 'Museums and the Reshaping of Memory'; and De Kok, 'Cracked Heirlooms'.
50. Ebron, *Performing Africa*, p. 105.
51. Nuttal and Coetzee, 'Introduction' in Nuttal and Coetzee (eds), *Negotiating the Past*, p. 14.
52. Huyssen, *Present Pasts*, p. 8.
53. Rassool, 'The Rise of Heritage and the Reconstitution of History in South Africa', 1.
54. André Brink, 'Stories of History: Reimagining the Past in Post–Apartheid Narrative' in Nuttall and Coetzee (eds), *Negotiating the Past*, p. 32.
55. De Kok, 'Cracked Heirlooms', pp. 60 and 71.
56. Mamdani, *Citizen and Subject*, p. 5.

9 Memorials to Injustice

1. Anderson, *Imagined Communities: Reflections on the Origin and Spread of Nationalism* (London: Verso, 1991), ch. 4.

2. When in 1882 Ernest Renan made his famous remark that forgetting is a necessary condition for the creation of a nation, he also noted that the work of historians is dangerous for the principle of nationality. This is because enquiry 'brings to light deeds of violence which took place at the origin of all political formations, even of those whose consequences have been altogether beneficial. Unity is always effected by means of brutality ...' ('What is a nation?', trans. Martin Thom, in Homi Bhabha (ed.) *Nation and Narration* (London: Routledge, 2000), p. 11). A few sentences later, he asserts that amnesia is effective despite the work of historians: 'every French citizen has to have forgotten the massacre of Saint Bartholomew [1572, of the Huguenots] or the massacres that took place in the Midi in the thirteenth century'.

3. I would extend Renan's point about original brutality by noting that a nation's formation normally entails the attempted destruction or expulsion of whole categories of population – cultural, religious, linguistic, national or class. Historical enquiry prompts or itself satisfies calls for their adequate recognition in turn.

4. Antonio Damasio, *The Feeling of What Happens: Body, Emotion and the Making of Consciousness* (London: Vintage, 2000), pp. 216–23.

5. Steven Rose, *The Making of Memory: From Molecules to Mind* (London: Vintage, 2003), pp. 137–8.

6. Charles Stafford, *Separation and Reunion in Modern China* (Cambridge: Cambridge University Press, 2000).

7. David Hirsh, *Law Against Genocide: Cosmopolitan Trials* (London: Cavendish Press, 2003), makes a good case for the sheer existence of cosmopolitan justice, even though it has come into existence and must be constrained within the limits of legitimation for the most powerful democracies.

8. For instance, there is the case of the US Congress, the institution that passed slavery laws and so is held responsible for apology and reparation for that injustice. History enters a contentious issue of whether the American Civil War was fought by the North for the sake of the Union or for the liberation of slaves. If not for the liberation of slaves, then its being fought and won, and Abraham Lincoln's second inaugural address on the rightness of going to war cannot constitute an apology and one is still required.

9. Siau-fong Lee, 'Chiang Kai-shek & the 2–28 incident: who should be held accountable?' in Lin Tsung-yi (ed.), *An Introduction to the 2–28 Tragedy in Taiwan: for world citizens* (Taipei: Taiwan Renaissance Foundation Press, 1998). It is obvious from the title and publisher how a book such as this explicitly mobilises historical scholarship for the construction of a new history bearing a new identity, and places both before a readership imagined as a tribunal of world citizens.

10. Quoted in Michael Hoare, 'British Foreign Office policy and the "2–28" events of 1947' in Lin (ed.), *An Introduction to the 2–28 Tragedy in Taiwan*, p. 226.

11. Murray Rubinstein, 'Christianity and Democratisation in Taiwan' in Philip Clart and Charles Jones (eds), *Religion in Modern Taiwan* (Honolulu, HI: University of Hawai'i Press, 2003), p. 215.

12. George Kerr, *Formosa Betrayed* (London: Eyre and Spottiswoode, 1966). The Taiwanese and Nationalist President, Lee Teng-hui, who presided over the loosening of his Party's grip on the media and political organisation from 1988 and continued as elected president from 1996 to 2000, set up a commission to investigate 2:28 in 1991. Its report, released in 1992, estimates the number slaughtered was 20,000 out of a total Taiwanese population of about 6 million.

13. 'A Letter to President Lee' in Lin Tsung-yi (ed.), *An Introduction to the 2:28 Tragedy in Taiwan*, pp. 273–4.

14. 'The Presidential Address of Apology' in Lin Tsung-yi (ed.), *An Introduction to the 2:28 Tragedy in Taiwan*, p. 280.

15. For instance the massacres of students and union protesters in Shanghai from 1927 to 1937.

16. Harry J. Lamley points out that Taiwan's very small Communist party was a branch of the Japanese Communist party according to the direction of Comintern until it was dissolved in 1932. Lamley, 'Taiwan under Japanese rule, 1895–1945: the vicissitudes of colonialism' in M. Rubinstein (ed.), *Taiwan: A New History* (London: M.E. Sharpe, 1999), p. 256 (fn 154).

17. On the mainland the categorisation of the whole decade 1966–76 as the Wen'ge (Cultural Revolution) did the same. Ruby S. Watson, 'Making secret histories: memory and mourning in post-Mao China' in Watson (ed.), *Memory, History, and Opposition under State Socialism* (Santa Fe: School of American Research Press, 1994), ch. 4.

18. Zhang Yanxian and Gao Shuyuan, *Luku Shijian Yanjiu Diaocha (A Research Investigation of the Luku Incident)* (Taipei: County Cultural Centre, 1998), p. 11.

19. They included a writer, Lü Heruo whose works have recently been republished and positively reassessed. In 1945 he had been one of the founders of a youth corps to help maintain order during the chaos immediately following the end of the war. The corps was named Sanminzhuyi Qingniantuan after the principle ideas of the founder of the Chinese republican movement, Song Zhongshan (Sun Yatsen), whose heritage was claimed by the Nationalist Party, then the Party of government. But Chen Yi, the governor it sent to Taiwan, disbanded the corps for being too independent and leftwing and Lü was named the bandit Lü (Lü Fei) and fled to Luku where he died, some say from a snake's bite but his remains have not been found to ascertain the cause of his death. Thanks to Lin Peiyin, a doctoral student at the School of Oriental and African Studies, for this information.

20. Altogether 142 men were jailed, and of these 35 were executed (Zhang Yanxian and Gao Shuyuan, *Luku Shijian Yanjiu Diaocha*, table 2, pp. 30–31). In the upper hamlets of Luku this eliminated most of the male population.

21. He and other villagers were imprisoned for the crime of rebellion (*pan luan*).

22. Interview, 26 October 2001.

23. He took me and Yu Chien, a Taiwanese colleague, around the sites of the incident and had copied for me his folder of the court record of the trial of people arrested in the incident and copies of articles which had by then been published about it.

24. Its text is reprinted in Zhang Yanxian and Chen Fenghua, *Luku Shijian: Hancunde kuqi (The Luku Incident: Lament of a Wintry Village)* (Taipei: County Cultural Bureau, 2000), pp. 386–98. The 1998 law must be taken together with a previous law passed in 1995 and it was itself amended in 2000.

25. Interview, 5 October 2004.
26. Feuchtwang, 'An unsafe distance' in Charles Stafford (ed.), *Living with separation: anthropological accounts* (London: Routledge, 2003), p. 91.

10 Remembering and Forgetting the Korean War: From Trauma to Reconciliation

* This chapter draws in part upon research we conducted for a project on history teaching and reconciliation, directed by Lili Cole at the Carnegie Council on Ethics and International Affairs. Some of the theoretical issues are also explored in Roland Bleiker, *Divided Korea: Toward a Culture of Reconciliation* (Minneapolis MN: University of Minnesota Press, 2005).

1. Ko Un, 'Discipline and after', trans. Brother Anthony of Taize and Young-Moo Kim in *The Sound of My Waves* (Seoul: DapGae Books, 1996), p. 73.
2. For reasons of accessibility we am employing the somewhat colloquial terms South Korea and North Korea, rather than the official names of the respective states: Republic of Korea and Democratic People's Republic of Korea.
3. On the notion of indirect policy relevance see Stephen K. White, *Sustaining Affirmation: The Strengths of Weak Ontology in Political Theory* (Princeton, NJ: Princeton University Press, 2000), pp. 11–12.
4. John Paul Lederach, *Building Peace: Sustainable Reconciliation in Divided Societies* (Washington D.C.: United States Institute of Peace Press, 1997), p. 27.
5. See Roy Richard Grinker, *Korea and its Futures: Unification and the Unfinished War* (London: Macmillan, 1998).
6. Choi Jang Jip, 'Political Cleavages in South Korea' in Hagen Ko (ed.), *State and Society in Contemporary Korea* (Ithaca, NY: Cornell University Press, 1993), p. 23.
7. Park Han, 'North Korean Perceptions of Self and Others: Implications for Policy Choices', *Pacific Affairs*, 73 (2000), 504. For an excellent analysis see Dennis Hart, 'Creating the National Other: Opposing Images of Nationalism in South and North Korean Education', *Korean Studies*, 23 (1999), 69–93.
8. See Benedict Anderson, *Imagined Communities: Reflections on the Origin and Spread of Nationalism* (London: Verso, 1983).
9. Ch'oe Yong-ho et al (eds.), *Sources of Korean Tradition: Volume II: From the Sixteenth to the Twentieth Centuries* (New York, NY: Columbia University Press, 2000), p. 369.
10. Park Chung Hee, 'Three Basic Principles for Peaceful Unification' in *Towards Peaceful Unification: Selected Speeches and Interviews by Park Chung Hee* (Seoul: Kwongmyong Publishing Company, 1976), p. 110.
11. Bruce Cumings, *Korea's Place in the Sun: A Modern History* (New York, NY: W.W. Norton, 1997), p. 125.
12. *Gugsa* [Korean History], Gugsa Pyunchan Ouiwonhoe and Il Jong Doseo Youngu Gaebal Ouiwonhoe [National Institute of Korean History and the Commission for Developing Textbooks] (Seoul: Taehan Koykwaseo, 1996/2001), p. 199.
13. Hong-Su Gang and Yi-jun Jang, *Euidaehan Suryoung Kim Il Sung Wonsunim Hyugmyoungsa* [The Great Leader General Kim Il Sung's revolutionary history] (Pyongyang: Gyoruk Doseo Chulpanasa, 1995/1999), pp. 120 and 127.

14. Oh Kongdan and Ralph C Hassig, *North Korea Through the Looking Glass* (Washington D.C: Brookings Institution Press, 2000), p. 30.
15. Chung Tae-hon, 'Godunghakkyo Kuksa Kyokwaseo ui Gunhyundaesa Naeyong Bunseck' ['A Contextual Analysis of Modern History Taught in Korean High School History Books'], in *Sachong*, 45 (1996), 201–29.
16. Cumings, *Korea's Place in the Sun*, p. 238. For his detailed treatment of the subject see Bruce Cumings, *The Origins of the Korean War: Liberation and the Emergence of Separate Regimes* (Princeton, NJ: Princeton, University Press, 1981); and *Origins of the Korean War: The Roaring of the Cataract* (Princeton, NJ: Princeton University Press, 1990).
17. Cumings, *Korea's Place in the Sun*, p. 238.
18. Cumings, *Korea's Place in the Sun*, p. 265.
19. In particular, Cumings' claim that an escalation of border clashes along the thirty-eighth parallel led to the war has been challenged. Recently released Soviet documents indicate that plans for a Northern invasion of the South existed well before June 1950 and were approved by Stalin. Kim Younghoo, 'International Dimensions of the Korean War', *Korea Journal*, 38 (1998), 134; and Moon Chung-in, *Arms Control on the Korean Peninsula* (Seoul: Yonsei University Press, 1996), p. 50.
20. Allan R. Millett, 'The Korean War: A 50-year Critical Historiography', *The Journal of Strategic Studies*, 24 (2001), 190.
21. Jun Sang-in, 'A Pro-North Korean and Anti-American Interpretation of Modern Korean History', *Korea and World Affairs*, 23 (1999), 262–7.
22. See Henry H. Em, 'Overcoming Korea's Division: Narrative Strategies in Recent South Korean Historiography', *Positions*, 1 (1993), 450–85.
23. Friedrich Nietzsche, 'Vom Nutzen und Nachteil der Historie für das Leben' in *Unzeitgemässe Betrachtungen* (Frankfurt: Insel Taschenbuch, 1981), p. 118.
24. Nietzsche, 'Vom Nutzen und Nachteil der Historie für das Leben', p. 100.
25. Nietzsche, 'Vom Nutzen und Nachteil der Historie für das Leben', pp. 106–7 and 111.
26. Cited in Choi Hae Won, 'Seoul's Textbook Détente: Revised History Reader Reflects South's Waning Fear of the North', *Wall Street Journal*, 14 January 2003.
27. Ku Nan Hee, cited in Choi, 'Seoul's Textbook Détente'.
28. Park Sung Soo, cited in Choi, 'Seoul's Textbook Détente'; and, Chong Hyunmuk Chong, 'Battle of Bocheonbo in our Textbook?' *Joongang Ilbo*, 7.8.2002.
29. Grinker, *Korea and its Futures*, pp. 128 and 130–32.
30. Grinker, *Korea and its Futures*, pp. 132–4.
31. Kim Ki-Jung and Park Jae-min, 'Paradox of Dismantling the Cold War Structure' in Moon et al., *Ending the Cold War in Korea*, p. 320.
32. Duncan S. A. Bell, 'Mythscapes: Memory, Mythology and National Identity', *British Journal of Sociology*, 54 (2003), 63–81.
33. Paul Ricoeur, 'Imagination, Testimony and Trust: A Dialogue with Paul Ricoeur' in R. Kearney and M. Dooley (eds), *Questioning Ethics: Contemporary Debates in Philosophy* (London: Routledge, 1999), p. 13.
34. Richard Kearney, 'Narrative and the Ethics of Remembrance' in Kearney and Dooley (eds), *Questioning Ethics*, pp. 26–7.
35. Dipesh Chakrabarty, *Provincializing Europe: Postcolonial Thought and Historical Difference* (Princeton, NJ: Princeton University Press, 2000), p. 97.

36. Em, 'Overcoming Korea's Division', pp. 452 and 479–80.
37. See http://piff.org (accessed October 2003).
38. See James Brooke, 'The Power of Film: A Bond that United Koreans', *New York Times*, 2.2.2003, A4. The James Bond film is, of course, part of a long tradition of stereotypical representations of Korea, perhaps best exemplified by the popular US television series M*A*S*H. First aired on US television between 1972 and 1983, M*A*S*H was set during the Korean War. Very few Koreans actually appeared on the show, however, and those who did were represented in highly paternalistic and orientalist ways. Although the series was in no way intended to represent the war, its mere popularity inevitably influenced American perceptions of Korea. This was particularly fateful since it was aired a time when, as one commentator puts it, 'the American news media was not making any great efforts to explain the background and reasons for events in Korea'. Most correspondents, for instance, covered Korea from Tokyo, Beijing or Hong Kong and drew much of their information from secondary sources. See Craig S. Coleman, *American Images of Korea: Korea and Koreans as Portrayed in Books, Magazines, Television, News Media, and Film* (Seoul: Hollym, 2000), p. 160.
39. Jeon Woo-Taek, 'Promoting National Harmony in a Unified Korea', unpublished paper presented at Yonsei University, 21.12.2001, 3–7.
40. William A. Callahan, 'Laughter, Critical Theory and Korea' in Han Sang-Jin (ed.), *Habermas and the Korean Debate* (Seoul: Seoul National University Press, 1998), pp. 445–71.
41. Choi Chungmoo, 'The Discourse of Decolonization and Popular Memory: South Korea', *Positions*, 1, (1993), 92–5. See also Mikhail Bakhtin, *Rabelais and his World*, trans. H. Iswolsky (Cambridge, MA: MIT Press, 1968); and Michel Foucault, 'Of Other Spaces', *Diacritics*, 16 (1986), 22–7.
42. Bakhtin, *Rabelais and his World*, p. 10; François Rabelais, *The Histories of Gargantua and Pantagruel*, trans. J.M. Cohen (Harmondsworth: Penguin Books, 1966).
43. Bakhtin, *Rabelais and his World*, p. 123.
44. Keith Krause and Michael C. Williams, 'Preface' to Krause and Williams (eds), *Critical Security Studies* (Minneapolis, MN.: University of Minnesota Press, 1997), p. xv.
45. See, for instance, Emmanuel Levinas, *Time and the Other*, trans. R. Cohen (Pittsburgh: Duquesne University Press, 1987); *Totality and Infinity*, trans. A. Lingis (Pittsburgh, PA: Duquesne University Press, 1969). For applications to the international realm see Michael J. Shapiro, *Violent Cartographies: Mapping Cultures of War* (Minneapolis, MN: University of Minnesota Press, 1997); and David Campbell, *National Deconstruction: Violence, Identity and Justice in Bosnia* (Minneapolis MN: University of Minnesota Press, 1998).
46. Susan Dwyer, 'Reconciliation for Realists', *Ethics and International Affairs*, 13, (1999), 89.
47. Dwyer, 'Reconciliation for Realists', 89.
48. See Sheila Miyoshi Jager, 'Women, Resistance and the Divided Nation: The Romantic Rhetoric of Korean Reunification', *The Journal of Asian Studies*, 55 (1996), 3–21; Kwon Hyuk Bom, 'Tongil kyoyuk-aiso talbundan shimin kyoyuk-uro – pyonghwa, inkwon kuriko chai-ai kongjon [From unification

education to post-division popular education], http://dragon.taejon.ac.kr/~kwonhb/papers/postuni.htm; Kwon Hyuk Bom, *Symposium – Jongsan Huidam hu Hanbando-ai Tongil Kwajon* [*Symposium – The Process of Unification on the Korean Peninsula after the Summit*], proceedings, June 2001, http://dragon.taejon.ac.kr/~kwonhb/papers/buddalec.htm

49. Øyvind Østerud, 'Antinomies of Postmodernism in International Studies', *Journal of Peace Research*, 33 (1996), 386.

50. Ricoeur, 'Imagination, Testimony and Trust', 15.

51. Gerrit W. Gong, 'A Clash of Histories' in Gerrit W. Gong (ed.), *Memory and History in East and Southeast Asia: Issues of Identity in International Relations* (Washington, D C: Center for Strategic and International Studies, 2001), p. 30.

52. Claus Offe, *Der Tunnel am Ende des Lichts: Erkundungen der Politischen Transformation im Neuen Osten* (Frankfurt: Campus Verlag, 1994), p. 188.

53. Paul Ricoeur, 'Memory and Forgetting' in Kearney and Dooley (eds), *Questioning Ethics*, p. 11.

54. Kearney, 'Narrative and the Ethics of Remembrance', p. 27.

55. Henry Reynolds, *Why Weren't we Told? A Personal Search for the Truth about our History* (Ringwood, Vic: Viking, 1999).

56. Ricoeur, 'Imagination, Testimony and Trust', 12.

57. See F.R. Ankersmit, *Aesthetic Politics: Political Philosophy Beyond Fact and Value* (Stanford, CA: Stanford University Press, 1996).

58. Ricoeur, 'Imagination, Testimony and Trust', p. 15.

59. Hayden White, *The Content of the Form: Narrative Discourse and Historical Representation* (Baltimore, MD: The Johns Hopkins University Press, 1987), pp. 4 and 14.

60. Chakrabarty, *Provincializing Europe*, p. 98.

61. 'Statement of Mutual Understanding Between the United States and the Republic of Korea on the No Gun Ri Investigations', January 2001. http/www.defenselink.mil/news/Jan2001. See also 'G.I.'s Tell of a U.S. Massacre in Korean War', *New York Times*, 30 Septmber 1999; Choe Sang-hun et.al, 'American Veterans Speak out on Massacre During Korean War', *Korea Herald*, 1 October 1999; Elizabeth Becker, 'Army Admits G.I.'s in Korea Killed Civilians at No Gun Ri', *New York Times*, 12 January 2001; and for a more detailed analysis, Bruce Cumings, 'Occurrence at Nogun-ri Bridge: An Inquiry into the History and Memory of a Civil War', *Critical Asian Studies*, 33 (2001), 509–26.

62. Song Du Yol, 'Hana-dwen mirae' kwanyong-uro yolja' ('Let's Adopt the Tolerance of a "Unified Future" '), *Donga Ilbo*, 14.7.2000, p. 10. (Accessed October 2001 at: http://www.kinds.or.kr/); and 'Song Du Yol-shi, Nam-kwa Buk-un chaki sok-ae taja kwankae' ('Song Du Yol: North and South's "Other within oneself" relationship'), *Yonhap News*, 8 August 1999. (Accessed October 2001 at: http://www.hani.co.kr/POLITICS/data/9908/day13/00813734.htm.)

63. Moon Chung-in and Kim Tae-Hwan, 'Sustaining Inter-Korean Reconciliation: North-South Korea Cooperation', *The Journal of East Asian Affairs*, 15 (2001), 211.

64. William E. Connolly, *The Ethos of Pluralization* (Minneapolis, MN: University of Minnesota Press, 1995), pp. xxi–ii.

11 Remembering to Forget/Forgetting to Remember

1. I would like to thank Duncan S. A. Bell and Stuart Elden for their insightful comments on this chapter.
2. '8. Mai 1945 – Gegen das Vergessen', *Frankfurter Allgemeine Zeitung*, 28/04/95, p. 3 (All translations from German are mine).
3. '8. Mai 1945 – Gegen das Vergessen', *Frankfurter Allgemeine Zeitung*, 07/04/95, p. 3.
4. '8. Mai 1945 – Gegen das Vergessen', *Frankfurter Allgemeine Zeitung*, 07/04/95, p. 3.
5. Klaus Neumann, *Shifting Memories: The Nazi Past in the New Germany* (Ann Arbor, MI: The University of Michigan Press, 2000), p. 7f.
6. See *'Historikerstreit': Die Dokumentation der Kontroverse um die Einzigartigkeit der nationalsozialistischen Judenvernichtung* (Munich: Piper, 1987).
7. '8. Mai 1945 – Gegen das Vergessen', *Frankfurter Allgemeine Zeitung*, 05/05/95, p. 3.
8. Richard von Weizsäcker, 'Zum 40. Jahrestag der Beendigung des Krieges in Europa und der nationalsozialistischen Gewaltherrschaft', 08/05/85, www.dhm.de.
9. Helmut Dubiel, *Niemand ist frei von der Geschichte: die nationalsozialistische Herrschaft in den Debatten des Deutschen Bundestages* (Munich: Carl Hanser Verlag, 1999), p. 213. See also Ute Frevert, 'Geschichtsvergessenheit und Geschichtsversessenheit revisited', *Aus Politik und Zeitgeschichte* B40–41 (2003), p. 6.
10. Klaus Naumann, *Der Krieg als Text: das Jahr 1945 im kulturellen Gedächtnis der Presse* (Hamburg: Hamburger Edition, 1998), p. 232f.
11. Roman Herzog, 'Dresden – A Warning for the Future. Speech by the Federal President in Dresden on 13 February 1995' in *Remembrance and Perpetual Responsibility* (Bonn: Press and Information Office of the Federal Government, 1995), pp. 5–9.
12. Naumann, *Krieg als Text*, p. 54.
13. Deutscher Bundestag, *Plenarprotokoll*, 12/3, 17/01/91, p. 46.
14. Michael Schwab-Trapp, *Kriegsdiskurse: die politische Kultur des Krieges im Wandel 1991–1999* (Opladen: Leske + Budrich, 2002), p. 98.
15. For a more detailed analysis see Maja Zehfuss, *Constructivism in International Relations: The Politics of Reality* (Cambridge: Cambridge University Press, 2002), ch. 3.
16. Deutscher Bundestag, *Plenarprotokoll*, 13/48, 30/06/95, p. 3957.
17. Deutscher Bundestag, *Plenarprotokoll*, 13/48, 30/06/95, p. 3959.
18. Deutscher Bundestag, *Plenarprotokoll*, 13/48, 30/06/95, p. 3960.
19. Andreas Huyssen, 'Present Pasts: Media, Politics, Amnesia', *Public Culture*, 12 (2000), p. 21f.
20. Huyssen, 'Present Pasts', p. 23.
21. Huyssen, 'Present Pasts', p. 24f.
22. This is also evidenced in the ever-growing literature on memory, particularly in the context of war and atrocity. See, for example, Paul Antze and Michael Lambek (eds), *Tense Past: Cultural Essays in Trauma and Memory* (New York, NY: Routledge, 1996); Jenny Edkins, *Trauma and the Memory of Politics*

(Cambridge: Cambridge University Press, 2003); Jay Winter, *Sites of Memory, Sites of Mourning: The Great War in European Cultural History* (Cambridge: Cambridge University Press, 1995); and James E. Young, *The Texture of Memory: Holocaust Memorials and Meaning* (New Haven, CT: Yale University Press, 1993).

23. Jan-Werner Müller, 'Introduction: The Power of Memory, the Memory of Power and the Power over Memory', in Müller (ed.), *Memory and Power in Post-War Europe: Studies in the Presence of the Past* (Cambridge: Cambridge University Press, 2002), p. 13f.

24. Herzog, 'Dresden – A Warning for the Future', p. 6.

25. Avishai Margalit, *The Ethics of Memory* (Cambridge, MA: Harvard University Press, 2002), p. 5.

26. Margalit, *The Ethics of Memory*, p. 5.

27. Ilana R. Bet-El, 'Unimagined Communities: The Power of Memory and the Conflict in the Former Yugoslavia' in Müller (ed.), *Memory and Power in Post-War Europe*, p. 206.

28. Aleida Assmann, *Erinnerungsräume: Formen und Wandlungen des kulturellen Gedächtnisses* (Munich: Verlag C.H. Beck, 1999), p. 15.

29. For a powerful study that undermines both assumptions see Alistair Thomson, *Anzac Memories: Living with the Legend* (Melbourne: Oxford University Press, 1994).

30. Huyssen, 'Present Pasts', p. 25, though see also p. 37.

31. See, for example, Assmann, *Erinnerungsräume*, pp. 64f, 131 & 167f; Edith Wyschogrod, *An Ethics of Remembering: History, Heterology, and the Nameless Others* (Chicago, IL: The University of Chicago Press, 1998), p. xi.

32. Friedrich Nietzsche, *Unzeitgemäße Betrachtungen* (Stuttgart: Alfred Kröner Verlag, 1964), p. 104.

33. Nietzsche, *Unzeitgemäße Betrachtungen*, p. 124.

34. Nietzsche, *Unzeitgemäße Betrachtungen*, p. 103.

35. This is of course an oversimplification of Nietzsche's position which is in fact very close to Derrida's, discussed in a later section.

36. Michael Stürmer, 'Geschichte in geschichtslosem Land', in '*Historikerstreit*', p. 36.

37. See his second intervention in the *Bundestag* debate, reprinted in Heribert Prantl (ed.), *Wehrmachtsverbrechen: eine deutsche Kontroverse* (Hamburg: Hoffmann und Campe, 1997), p. 128.

38. Micha Brumlik, Hajo Funke and Lars Rensmann, *Umkämpftes Vergessen: Walser–Debatte, Holocaust-Mahnmal und neuere deutsche Geschichtspolitik* (Berlin: Verlag Das Arabische Buch, 1999), 'Einleitung', p. 7.

39. Martin Walser, 'Dankesrede zur Verleihung des Friedenspreis des Deutschen Buchhandels in der Frankfurter Paulskirche', 11 October 98, www.dhm.de.

40. Walser, 'Dankesrede'.

41. See Frank Schirrmacher (ed.), *Die Walser-Bubis-Debatte: eine Dokumentation* (Frankfurt am Main: Suhrkamp, 1999); and Brumlik/Funke/Rensmann, *Umkämpftes Vergessen*.

42. Walser, 'Dankesrede'.

43. This is noted in Michael Geyer, 'The Place of the Second World War in German Memory and History', trans. Michael Latham, *New German Critique*, 71 (1997), p. 37.

44. Assmann, *Erinnerungsräume*, p. 335.

45. Assmann, *Erinnerungsräume*, p. 333.
46. See, however, Edkins's fascinating study of memory practices that looks beyond the memorials at how people respond to them. Edkins, *Trauma and the Memory of Politics*.
47. See, however, Maja Zehfuss, 'Forget September 11', *Third World Quarterly*, 24 (2003), pp. 513–28. But note that this, too, is a conditional appeal to forget.
48. Andreas Huyssen, *Twilight Memories: Marking Time in a Culture of Amnesia* (New York and London: Routledge, 1995), p. 214.
49. Von Weizsäcker, 'Zum 40. Jahrestag'.
50. See, for example, M. Lane Bruner, *Strategies of Remembrance: The Rhetorical Dimensions of National Identity Construction* (Columbia, SC: University of South Carolina Press, 2002), ch. 2.
51. Von Weizsäcker, 'Zum 40. Jahrestag'.
52. Müller, 'Introduction', p. 1f.
53. See, for example, Antze and Lambek, *Tense Past*; Cathy Caruth, *Unclaimed Experience: Trauma, Narrative, and History* (Baltimore, MD: Johns Hopkins University Press, 1996); Edkins, *Trauma and the Memory of Politics*; and Young, *The Texture of Memory*.
54. Müller, 'Introduction', p. 2.
55. Müller, 'Introduction', p. 3.
56. Müller, 'Introduction', p. 22.
57. Snyder, 'The Memory of Sovereignty and Sovereignty over Memory: Poland, Lithuania and Ukraine, 1939–1999' in Müller (ed.), *Memory and Power in Post-War Europe*, p. 40.
58. Günter Grass, *Im Krebsgang: Eine Novelle* (Göttingen: Steidl, 2002), p. 7.
59. See John Hooper, 'Günter Grass Breaks Taboo on German War Refugees', *The Guardian*, 08/02/02, p. 16; Roman Bucheli, 'Die verspätete Erinnerung', *Neue Zürcher Zeitung*, 09–10/02/02, p. 63; and Volker Hage, 'Unter Generalverdacht', *DER SPIEGEL*, 15, 08/04/02, pp. 178–81.
60. Robert G. Moeller, *War Stories: The Search for a Usable Past in the Federal Republic of Germany* (Berkeley, CA: University of California Press, 2001).
61. Grass, *Im Krebsgang*, p. 7.
62. Grass, *Im Krebsgang*, p. 99.
63. Grass, *Im Krebsgang*, pp. 30, 88, 107, 176, & 216.
64. The *Gustloff* counted as a war ship because it was armed and had military personnel on board. It was 'fair game' in the context of the conduct of war by the Third Reich. Clemens Höges et al., 'Die verdrängte Tragödie', in Stefan Aust and Stephan Burgdorff (eds), *Die Flucht: Über die Vertreibung der Deutschen aus dem Osten*, 2nd ed. (Stuttgart and Munich: Deutsche Verlags-Anstalt, 2002), p. 60. See also Uwe Klußmann, 'Attacke des Jahrhunderts' in Aust and Burgdorff (eds), *Die Flucht*, pp. 69–70.
65. Grass, *Im Krebsgang*, p. 57.
66. Grass, *Im Krebsgang*, p. 19.
67. Grass, *Im Krebsgang*, p. 41.
68. Grass, *Im Krebsgang*, p. 94.
69. Grass, *Im Krebsgang*, p. 94.
70. Grass, *Im Krebsgang*, p. 73f.
71. Grass, *Im Krebsgang*, p. 192.

72. Grass, *Im Krebsgang*, p. 216.
73. Grass, *Im Krebsgang*, p. 63.
74. On this see however Heinrich Schwendemann, 'Tod zwischen den Fronten' in Aust and Burgdorff (eds), *Die Flucht*, esp. pp. 78–80.
75. Grass, *Im Krebsgang*, p. 105.
76. Grass, *Im Krebsgang*, p. 102.
77. Grass, *Im Krebsgang*, p. 136; but see also p. 132.
78. *Collins English Dictionary*, 3rd updated ed. (Glasgow: HarperCollins Publishers, 1994), p. 604.
79. Omer Bartov, *Germany's War and the Holocaust: Disputed Histories* (Ithaca, NY: Cornell University Press, 2003), p. 170.
80. Assmann, *Erinnerungsräume*, pp. 19 and 411.
81. Assmann, *Erinnerungsräume*, p. 408.
82. Jacques Derrida, *Dissemination*, trans. Barbara Johnson (London: The Athlone Press, 1981), p. 109.
83. Jacques Derrida and Bernard Stiegler, *Echographies of Television: Filmed Interviews*, trans. Jennifer Bajorek (Cambridge: Polity Press, 2002), p. 63.
84. Derrida and Stiegler, *Echographies of Television*, p. 64.
85. Deutscher Bundestag, *Plenarprotokoll*, 13/48, 30/06/95, p. 3957.
86. Deutscher Bundestag, *Plenarprotokoll*, 13/48, 30/06/95, p. 3959.
87. Deutscher Bundestag, *Plenarprotokoll*, 13/48, 30/06/95, p. 3962.
88. Deutscher Bundestag, *Plenarprotokoll*, 13/48, 30/06/95, p. 3963.
89. Deutscher Bundestag, *Plenarprotokoll*, 13/48, 30/06/95, p. 3982.
90. Deutscher Bundestag, *Plenarprotokoll*, 13/48, 30/06/95, p. 3974.
91. Deutscher Bundestag, *Plenarprotokoll*, 13/48, 30/06/95, p. 3980.
92. Prantl (ed.), *Wehrmachtsverbrechen*, and Bartov, *Germany's War*, pp. xi-xiii and 158.
93. Müller, 'Introduction', p. 23.
94. Cf. Jacques Derrida, *The Other Heading: Reflections on Today's Europe*, trans. Pascale-Anne Brault and Michael B. Naas (Bloomington, IN: Indiana University Press, 1992), p. 41.
95. As Grass's text reminds us events could easily have turned out differently. See, for example, *Im Krebsgang*, p. 174.
96. Volker Hage, 'Das tausendmalige Sterben', in Aust and Burgdorff (eds), *Die Flucht*, p. 45.

Index